W9-BOC-362

CLEVELAND BROWNS
FACTS & TRIVIA

by

Roger Gordon

Ravenstone Publishing Group, Inc.
Berlin, Wisconsin
Est. 1998

Ravenstone Publishing Group, Inc.
162 W. Huron
Berlin, WI 54923

ISBN: 0-9667300-2-X

First Printing: September 1999

Printed in USA

Table of Contents

Cleveland Browns Facts & Trivia

Cleveland Browns Facts & Trivia

Introduction

Having grown up in Canton, Ohio, located some 60 miles south of Cleveland and the home of the Pro Football Hall of Fame, I was a devoted Cleveland Browns fan for years (and still am). But the Browns weren't always my favorite team.

When I began to follow professional sports more than two decades ago at the age of 9, I became a fan of Major League Baseball's Cleveland Indians and the National Basketball Association's Cleveland Cavaliers, which seemed only natural, considering my proximity to the city of Cleveland. However, I chose a team some 2,500 miles away - the Oakland Raiders - as my preferred pro football team. My reasons? The name "Oakland Raiders" and the team's black-and-silver colors and skull-and-crossbones helmet. I loved the Raiders, and lived and died with them. The Browns were alright; I mean, I always rooted for them to beat Pittsburgh. But the Raiders, well ... Oakland was it.

My loyalty took a turn during the strike-shortened season of 1982. The Raiders had relocated south to Los Angeles prior to the '82 season, making the mausoleum-like Los Angeles Memorial Coliseum their home, half-filled with fans worried more about beach balls than football. Rooting for the Raiders just wasn't the same anymore.

If I could pinpoint exactly when my allegiance changed, I would have to say it was the afternoon of December 19, 1982, when I viewed on television a game between the Browns and the Pittsburgh Steelers. The game was played on a miserable day - rain and snow were ominous presences - on a muddy field in Cleveland Stadium. Although the Browns entered with just a 2-4 record, a victory would have kept alive their flickering playoff hopes. The game was not exactly one of the most memorable contests in terms of points or big plays. But for some inexplicable reason, the Browns' 10-9 victory over their hated rival from down the turnpike was the turning point, and the "birthday" if you will, of my true love for the Cleveland Browns, a love that will continue with the team's return from exile this coming season.

- Roger Gordon

Notes to the Reader

*Besides the Browns, there were three other teams - the Chicago Rockets, Los Angeles Dons, and San Francisco 49ers - that competed in the same city, with the same nickname, in all four years the All-America Football Conference (AAFC) existed - 1946-49. The 49ers joined the National Football League (NFL) in 1950.

*The Miami Seahawks folded after one season - 1946 - in the AAFC.

*The Buffalo Bisons of the AAFC changed their nickname to "Bills" (no relation to the current Buffalo Bills) in 1947.

*The Brooklyn Dodgers and New York Yankees of the AAFC merged to become the Brooklyn-New York Yankees in 1949, the last year the AAFC was in existence.

*The original Baltimore Colts of the AAFC folded after one year - 1950 - in the NFL; the city of Baltimore, though, welcomed a new NFL Colts franchise in 1953 with the holdings of the defunct Dallas Texans (no relation to the future American Football League [AFL] Dallas Texans), who existed in 1952, and had called New York their home in 1951 when they were known as the Yanks. The Colts relocated to Indianapolis in 1984.

*Besides the Browns, there were eight other teams - the 49ers, Chicago Bears, Detroit Lions, Green Bay Packers, New York Giants, Philadelphia Eagles, Pittsburgh Steelers, and Washington Redskins - that competed in the same city with the same nickname, from 1950-95.

*The Arizona Cardinals were located in Chicago prior to 1960, St. Louis from 1960-87, and were known as the Phoenix Cardinals from 1988-93.

*The Dallas Cowboys began play in 1960.

*The Minnesota Vikings began play in 1961.

*The Atlanta Falcons began play in 1966.

*The New Orleans Saints began play in 1967.

*Ten former AFL teams joined the NFL in 1970. Eight were the Buffalo Bills, Cincinnati Bengals, Denver Broncos, Houston Oilers, Kansas City

Cleveland Browns Facts & Trivia

Chiefs, Miami Dolphins, New York Jets, and San Diego Chargers.

*The New England Patriots, formerly of the AFL, joined the NFL in 1970 and were located in Boston that year.

*The Oakland Raiders, formerly of the AFL, joined the NFL in 1970 and were located in Los Angeles from 1982-94.

*The Seattle Seahawks and Tampa Bay Buccaneers began play in 1976.

*The St. Louis Rams were located in Los Angeles from 1950-95.

*The Carolina Panthers and Jacksonville Jaguars began play in 1995. The Panthers are not acknowledged because they never played the Browns.

*The Baltimore Ravens are not acknowledged because they began play in 1996 when there was no Browns team.

*The Tennessee Titans (re-named "Titans" for the 1999 season), who relocated from Houston in 1997, are referred to as the Houston Oilers since the team was still located in Houston in the last Browns' season of 1995.

*The Browns played 14 regular-season games from 1946-48; 12 from 1949-60; 14 from 1961-77; 16 from 1978-81; nine in 1982; 16 from 1983-86; 15 in 1987; and 16 from 1988-95.

*The Browns' home stadium was known as Cleveland Municipal Stadium from 1946-77 and as Cleveland Stadium from 1978-95.

*Although the Browns' three appearances in the NFL Playoff Bowl occurred following the regular season, the games are not acknowledged as part of the team's postseason history.

*Overtime (OT) in regular-season play began in 1974.

*The 1982 season was shortened to nine games and had no division champions due to a players' strike.

*Although the NFL did not begin recording sacks as an official statistic until 1982, the Browns began recording them in 1978.

*The 1987 season was shortened to 15 games - with Browns games from October 4-18 played mainly with replacement players - due to a players' strike.

*Unless indicated otherwise, players' career statistics include only regular-

Cleveland Browns Facts & Trivia

season play.

*The statistic "combined net yards" (also called all-purpose yards) includes the following yardage totals: rushing, receiving, punt return, kickoff return, interception return, and fumble return.

*The statistic "total net yards" includes rushing yards and net passing yards.

*In non-text parts and "The Answers," in years there were two teams in the same city and/or league/conference, the city is abbreviated and is followed by the team's nickname.

*When a touchdown (six points) is described and the resulting game score results in seven points for the team that scored, the point after touchdown (PAT) is assumed successful.

*When a team and/or league record being set is described, it is assumed the record still stands unless indicated otherwise.

*When an individual is described as having led the league/conference in an "average yards per" category, it is assumed that individuals with higher averages but a minute amount of attempts are not included.

*Preseason games are not included unless indicated.

*NCAA is an abbreviation for National Collegiate Athletic Association.

BROWNS THRU THE YEARS

1. The Birth of the Browns

Talk about a small world.

Not only was an "Arthur" responsible for the death (for three seasons, anyway) of the Cleveland Browns, but an "Arthur" was also responsible for the birth of the Browns. Whereas Arthur Modell pulled up stakes in 1996 after 35 years as majority owner of the Browns and moved the team to Maryland to become the Baltimore Ravens, Arthur McBride did almost the complete opposite some 50 years earlier.

McBride was the man responsible for bringing the Browns to Cleveland. It was quite ironic, too, because McBride never had time for football. He was never interested and never intended to be - that is, until he paid a visit to South Bend, Indiana, one day in early September 1940. A wealthy businessman in his 50s known to almost everyone in Cleveland as "Mickey," McBride journeyed to South Bend to watch the hometown Fighting Irish of Notre Dame University - where his son Arthur, Jr., had recently enrolled - defeat a helpless opponent.

McBride enjoyed the Notre Dame game so much, he began to follow the fortunes of the Fighting Irish religiously, and gained an interest in professional football, as well. Little did McBride know, however, that his presence at that Notre Dame game would be the impetus for a half century tradition of professional football in a town some 300 miles eastward. About two years after witnessing that Notre Dame game, McBride made a failed attempt at purchasing the fledgling Cleveland Rams franchise of the National Football League (NFL). However, on September 3, 1944, McBride was awarded a Cleveland franchise in the new All-America Football Conference (AAFC).

The rookie owner's first task was to find a head coach. He sought advice from John Dietrich, a respected veteran football writer for the *Plain Dealer* in Cleveland, on who the best man for the job was. Without hesitation, Dietrich told McBride the man he wanted was Paul Brown, who had compiled a prolific coaching record as head coach at Massillon (Ohio) Washington High School, Ohio State University, and the Great Lakes Naval Training Center, outside of Chicago. McBride then approached Arch Ward, sports editor of the *Chicago Tribune* and founder of the AAFC, for further approval of the living legend, who many regarded a football genius. After a second positive endorsement, McBride was convinced and hired Brown soon after.

The first player Brown signed was a young man from Northwestern University named Otto Graham, who would go on to become one of the finest quarterbacks ever. Brown built the team around a nucleus of veteran players, including four from the Los Angeles Rams, a team that despite poor attendance figures, won the 1945 NFL Championship when it still called Cleveland its home. Brown also filled the roster with men who had played for him at Ohio State and Great Lakes, such as bruising fullback Marion Motley, wide receiver Dante "Glue Fingers" Lavelli, and tackle-kicker Lou "The Toe" Groza (Groza never actually played directly under Brown but was a member of Ohio State's freshman team in 1942, a year in which Brown led the varsity Buckeyes to the national championship as voted by the Associated Press). All three men went on to Hall of Fame careers; Motley was inducted into the Pro Football Hall of Fame in Canton, Ohio, in 1968, Lavelli was enshrined in 1975, Groza in 1974.

The Browns were named after Paul Brown himself, the only man in NFL annals after whom a team has been named. In a public name-the-team contest, it was agreed the epithet most frequently appearing in the entries would be the choice. "Panthers" was the winner - until Brown learned that Cleveland had fielded a semi-pro team in the 1920s with the same name that folded. Brown wanted no part of a shoddy tradition and rejected the "Panthers" name. The second choice was "Browns," due most likely, it was said, to Brown's popularity throughout the state of Ohio. Although Brown was somewhat hesitant on his name being affixed to the team, he eventually gave in and agreed to it.

The Browns, who would call mammoth Cleveland Municipal Stadium - with a seating capacity of precisely 80,000 at the time - their home, were placed in the Western Division of the AAFC, along with the Chicago Rockets, Los Angeles Dons, and San Francisco 49ers.

2. In a League of Their Own

The Browns annihilated the Miami Seahawks, 44-0, in their regular-season debut in Cleveland Municipal Stadium on September 6, 1946, a game in which Otto Graham, incidentally, was not the starting quarterback (Cliff Lewis was). That victory - though no one knew at the time - was a foreshadow of things to come for the Browns. The word "domination" is an understatement in describing Cleveland's mastery of the All-America Football Conference. The Browns lost only four games the entire four years the conference existed, and won the championship each time. Including postseason, Cleveland's record from 1946-49 was an astounding 52-4-3 for a winning percentage of .903.

Dante Lavelli recalled Cleveland's first exhibition game, which occurred on August 30, **1946**, against the Brooklyn Dodgers in the Rubber Bowl in Akron, Ohio. "We were behind 19-7 (actually 13-7) at halftime," Lavelli wrote in the April 1997 edition of *Browns/News Illustrated*. "As we were heading to the locker room I remember a fan yelling at Paul Brown, 'You better go back to Massillon and coach high school football.'

"We won the game 35-19 (actually 35-20). You can imagine what Paul said at halftime. You can also imagine what that fan must have been thinking ten years later."

By the time a decade had indeed passed, the Browns were the dominant team in professional football. The team's success story began with seven straight victories - including three shutouts - to open that first regular season of 1946. The Browns closed the '46 season by scoring 193 points in their final four games - all wins, including a 66-14 blowout of Brooklyn in the finale on December 8. Led by an awesome running back tandem in Marion Motley and Edgar "Special Delivery" Jones, Cleveland won the Western Division title with a record of 12-2. The Browns fought back from two deficits to defeat the New York Yankees, 14-9, in the AAFC Championship game in Cleveland Municipal Stadium on December 22. The winning score came on a 16-yard pass from Graham to Lavelli late in the game.

Lavelli led the AAFC in receiving yards in 1946 with 843, and tied San Francisco's Alyn Beals for the conference lead in receptions with 40. Motley, meanwhile, ran wild, rushing the ball 73 times for 601 yards, an unbelievable average of 8.2 yards per carry. Jones wasn't bad himself, also with 73 carries, for 539 yards, a not-too-shabby 7.4 yards per carry average.

The Browns rolled through the 14-game schedule once again in **1947**, losing just once and tying another on the way to a second straight division championship. On November 2, wide receiver Mac Speedie took a screen pass from Graham and raced for a 99-yard touchdown - longest pass play in team history - in a 28-7 victory over the Buffalo Bills. The Browns clinched the division title two weeks later by blasting San Francisco, their biggest threat in the Western Division, 37-14. In a title-game rematch on December 14 in Yankee Stadium, Motley sprung the Browns with a 51-yard first-quarter gallop - on the way to a 109-yard rushing day - that set up Graham's one-yard scoring plunge. The lead held up and the Browns repeated as AAFC Champions, defeating the Yankees, 14-3.

Graham was named by the AAFC as its Most Valuable Player (MVP) in 1947. He led the conference in passing for the first of three straight seasons, throwing for 2,753 yards, 25 touchdowns, and just 11 interceptions, completing over 60 percent of his passes. Speedie led the AAFC in receptions with 67 and receiving yards with 1,146. Brown was voted AAFC Coach of the Year by *Pro Football Illustrated.*

Even with Lavelli out until mid-season with a broken leg, the Browns, who obtained speedy halfback William "Dub" Jones in an off-season trade with Brooklyn, rolled on again, finishing with a perfect 14-0 record. The **1948** Browns are one of only three teams in the history of pro football to go an entire season - regular season and postseason - undefeated and untied (the 1937 Los Angeles Bulldogs went 8-0 in winning an earlier AFL Championship [there was no postseason]; the 1972 Miami Dolphins went 17-0 in winning the NFL Championship that culminated with a victory in Super Bowl VII).

In the Browns' 31-28 division title-clinching win in San Francisco on November 28, Graham went the distance on a bad knee. Then, in the AAFC Championship game three weeks later in Cleveland, Motley rumbled for 133 yards and three touchdowns as the Browns buried Buffalo, 49-7, for their third straight title.

Graham was named the AAFC Most Valuable Player by the

United Press in 1948, and shared the conference's own MVP award with 49ers quarterback Frankie Albert. Motley led the conference - and his team for the third straight year - in rushing yards with 964. Speedie was the AAFC leader in receptions with 58. Brown won the conference Coach of the Year award again, this time by the *New York Daily News*.

In **1949**, the Browns got off to a fine start once again, winning four and tying one through five weeks. Then, a 56-28 whipping at the hands of the 49ers in San Francisco's Kezar Stadium caused Brown to explode in anger at his players afterwards. The coach's outburst must have helped because his team responded five days later by creaming Los Angeles, 61-14, on the West Coast, as Graham passed for a team-record six touchdowns, five to Lavelli.

With the AAFC down to seven teams (due to the Brooklyn-New York merger) and the two-division format scratched, the Browns wound up 9-1-2 and in first place in the conference under the new 12-game slate. They beat the fourth-place Bills, 31-21, in a playoff at home after tying them twice during the regular season. A week later, Cleveland wrapped up its fourth consecutive conference crown by defeating the visiting 49ers, 21-7. Graham copped the AAFC's own Most Valuable Player award, and Brown was named AAFC Coach of the Year by *The Sporting News* and the *New York Daily News* (the latter for the second straight time).

3. NFL? (No Sweat)

Due mainly to poor attendance and the fact the Browns so dominated the opposition that even their own fans lost interest, the All-America Football Conference folded following the 1949 season. That cleared the way for the Browns to bring their sophisticated passing attack to the NFL in 1950 (fellow ex-AAFCers Baltimore and San Francisco also joined the NFL that year). The Browns were placed in the NFL's American Conference (which in 1953 became the Eastern Conference) with the Chicago Cardinals, New York Giants, Philadelphia Eagles, Pittsburgh Steelers, and Washington Redskins. The Browns won the NFL Championship in their very first year in the league in 1950, and went on to claim the title again in 1954 and 1955. The Browns made six consecutive title-game appearances from 1950-55 (10 straight dating back to their AAFC days).

Because there were those who considered Cleveland's competition in the AAFC not exactly top notch, many believed the Browns - the "best" of the worst - had to prove they were worthy of competing in the more established NFL. The league decided to test the new kids on the block right off the bat, matching them against its two-time defending champions, the Philadelphia Eagles, in the NFL's **1950** season opener on Saturday night, September 16. Brosh Pritchard, a member of that Eagles team, remembered his squad as a confident bunch. "If you could feel cocky before a game, we felt cocky," Pritchard recalled in the NFL Films documentary *The Cleveland Browns - Fifty Years of Memories.* "This was a team from what we felt was maybe a bush league."

The Browns not only proved they belonged, they proved they were a powerhouse, no matter what competition was thrown their way, by destroying the heavily-favored Eagles, 35-10. In the process, they made believers out of more than 71,000 strong in Philadelphia's Municipal Stadium. "I don't believe any football team in the history of football was ever better prepared emotionally to play a game than we were then," said Otto Graham, the Browns' quarterback that night, in the documentary on the Browns. "Just to go out and prove that we had a good football team, and that we could play with anybody, was all we wanted to do."

After the thrashing of the Eagles, the Browns blanked Baltimore, 31-0, but then laid a goose egg themselves for the first time ever in a 6-0 loss to the visiting New York Giants. Three weeks later, the New Yorkers dealt the Browns their only other loss of the season, 17-13, and finished tied with Cleveland for first place in the American Conference at 10-2. The Browns avenged the two losses to the Giants on December 17 by beating their nemesis from New York, 8-3, in a conference playoff game in 10-degree weather in Cleveland. Middle guard Bill Willis saved the day by tackling Giants running back Eugene Roberts from behind at the Browns' four-yard line late in the game.

A week later on Christmas Eve in Cleveland, Lou Groza's 16-yard field goal with 28 seconds left capped a late rally and lifted the Browns to a wild 30-28 victory over the Los Angeles Rams in the NFL Championship game. Marion Motley led the league in 1950 with 810 rushing yards. The Browns' defense, led by future Hall of Famers Willis (enshrined in 1977) and right defensive end Len Ford (inducted in 1976), shined as well, as the team yielded just 144 points, second fewest in the league.

The Browns continued their winning ways in **1951**, rolling to 11 straight victories after a season-opening loss to the 49ers. They tied a team record by posting four shutouts in winning the American Conference for the second straight year. Dub Jones set a team record, and tied a league mark, for most touchdowns in one game by scoring six times in a 42-21 rout of the visiting Chicago Bears on November 25. Jones became the first running back other than Motley to lead the team in rushing yards for a season, compiling 492.

In a rematch of the 1950 title game on December 23 in Los Angeles, a 73-yard pass play from Norm Van Brocklin to Tom Fears broke a 17-17 fourth-quarter tie and lifted the Rams to a 24-17 victory over the Browns, and the NFL Championship. Paul Brown was named NFL Coach of the Year by the *New York Daily News*.

The Browns "slumped" to an 8-4 record in **1952**, but even with a three-point loss to the Giants on the final weekend, still managed to capture a third consecutive conference crown when Philadelphia was upset by Washington the same day, leaving the Eagles tied with the Giants at 7-5. Two weeks later in Cleveland Municipal Stadium, the Browns were beaten by a Detroit Lions team led by quarterback Bobby Layne and running back Doak Walker, 17-7, for the league title. Walker's third-quarter touchdown run of 67 yards was the crushing blow.

Mac Speedie led the NFL in receptions during the season with 62. Graham, meanwhile, set career highs in passing yardage (2,816), completions (181), and pass attempts (364), the latter which led the league. However, in addition to his 20 touchdown passes, Graham also set a career high in interceptions with 24.

After seven years of ownership, Mickey McBride sold the Browns in the off-season to a group headed by a gentleman named Dave Jones. New ownership did not affect the team one iota, though - at least in a negative fashion. In **1953**, Cleveland won its first 11 games and finished 11-1, capturing the Eastern Conference title. In a championship-game rematch on December 27 in Briggs Stadium (which eight years later became Tiger Stadium) in Detroit, however, Layne's 33-yard touchdown pass to wideout Jim Doran late in the game lifted the Lions to a 17-16 victory.

Graham, who led the league in passing for the first time and was voted NFL Most Valuable Player by the United Press, announced in the off-season he would compete one more year before calling it quits. Brown won league Coach of the Year honors from the *New York Daily News* for the second time in three seasons.

After a slow start in **1954**, including a 55-27 drubbing by the Steelers, the Browns rebounded to win eight straight games, finishing 9-3 and claiming the conference title once again. In a meaningless game on the final day of the NFL's regular season - both teams had already clinched their respective conference titles - Cleveland fell to Detroit, 14-10, at home. It was a different story seven days later, though. For the third straight year, the Browns opposed the Lions for all the marbles. In what was supposed to have been his last game, Graham not only passed for three touchdowns but scored three himself - and the defense intercepted Layne six times - as the Browns took out two years worth of frustration by hammering their Motor City menaces, 56-10, in the title game on December 26 in Cleveland.

Groza, who in addition to his left tackle duties connected on 37 of 38 extra point attempts and 16 of 24 field goal tries, was named the NFL's Most Valuable Player by *The Sporting News*. Brown was honored as NFL Coach of the Year once again, this time by the United Press.

Four games into the **1955** exhibition schedule, Paul Brown received an early Christmas present when Graham chose to return for one more season. Behind a balanced offensive attack featuring Graham's passing - he won league Most Valuable Player honors from the United Press and *The Sporting News* - and the running of Fred Morrison and Ed Modzelewski, the Browns scored 349 points, their most to date since entering the NFL, in rolling to a 9-2-1 record and yet another conference crown.

In front of nearly 88,000 fans in the Los Angeles Memorial Coliseum, Graham, who would be enshrined into the Pro Football Hall of Fame in 1965, went out in style. He threw for two touchdowns and ran for two in his swan song, leading the Browns to a 38-14 rout of the Rams in the NFL Championship game on December 26. It was Cleveland's second straight title and third since entering the league.

4. The Seven-Year Itch

After slumping to a losing record - a franchise first - in 1956, the Browns rebounded in 1957 to win the Eastern Conference title (they would not make another title-game appearance for seven years). The team's resurgence in 1957 was due in large part to the arrival of fullback Jim Brown, an All-American drafted in the first round out of Syracuse. Brown would go on to become one of the most feared, if not the most feared, backs in NFL history. Although Cleveland experienced somewhat mediocre seasons in the early part of his career, the back with his team's namesake enjoyed a level of success unparalleled by any other running back at the time, which later earned him induction into the Pro Football Hall of Fame (in 1971).

As the Browns' won-loss record plummeted, the players' faith in their head coach took a nosedive, too. On top of that, Art Modell, a former advertising executive from New York City who purchased majority ownership of the club on March 21, 1961, was experiencing philosophical differences, i.e., a power struggle, with Paul Brown, and did the unthinkable - he fired the living legend on January 9, 1963. Nine days later, Modell replaced Brown with offensive backfield coach Blanton Collier, who in turn opened up the offense on the way to a 10-win season in 1963, the Browns' highest victory total in a decade.

With Otto Graham and Dub Jones retired and Dante Lavelli at the tail end of his career, it showed in **1956**. A quarterback combination of George Ratterman, Vito "Babe" Parilli, and Tommy O'Connell just didn't cut it. The Browns were able to score more than 20 points just twice, and mustered just 167 all year long in suffering their first losing season ever. They finished in a fourth-place tie with Pittsburgh in the Eastern Conference at 5-7.

Center Frank Gatski, a member of the Browns from Day 1, was traded to the Detroit Lions two weeks prior to the start of the **1957** season for a third-round draft pick in 1958 (Gatski would be enshrined into the Pro Football Hall of Fame in 1985). With Brown in the backfield in 1957, Cleveland defeated defending league champion New York, 6-3, in the opener behind the rookie's 89 yards on the ground. In a 45-31 victory over Los Angeles on November 24, Brown carried the ball 31 times for 237 yards, at the time a single-game NFL record for rushing yardage, and a rookie record that would stand for 40 years (he would duplicate the feat four years later). Brown won his first of five consecutive NFL rushing titles in 1957 with 942 yards, sparking the Browns to a 9-2-1 record and the Eastern Conference title.

Brown not only was named NFL Rookie of the Year in 1957 by the Associated Press but also its Player of the Year (he won Rookie of the Year acclaim from the United Press, as well). Brown's presence, though, was not enough for Cleveland to claim a fourth NFL Championship. Injuries to quarterbacks O'Connell (the league passing leader) and rookie Milt Plum - the two rotated throughout the season - hampered both in a 59-14 bashing by the Lions in the NFL title game on December 29 in Detroit. Paul Brown was voted NFL Coach of the Year in 1957 for the final time, by both the United Press and the *New York Daily News*.

With O'Connell retired, Plum was firmly established as the starting quarterback when the **1958** season began. And with its seventh-round selection in that year's draft, Cleveland found itself a nice complement for Brown in the backfield in speedy halfback Bobby Mitchell from the University of Illinois. In fact, Brown and Mitchell combined for more than 1,200 yards on the ground in the team's season-opening five-game winning streak that was halted when the Browns blew a 10-point third-quarter lead in falling to the Giants, 21-17, on November 2 in Cleveland Municipal Stadium. Six weeks later, New York once again proved to be a thorn in Cleveland's side. The Browns entered a December 14 contest against the Giants with a 9-2 record, New York 8-3. All the Browns needed for a second straight Eastern Conference crown was a tie. But with time running out and the score 10-10 on the snow-covered field of Yankee Stadium, Pat Summerall booted a 49-yard field goal into the wind and through the driving snow to give the Giants a 13-10 victory and a share of the conference title. The two squared off a week later, again in New York, in a playoff to decide the conference champion. Brown, who had gained over 100 yards in each of the regular-season defeats to the Giants, and 1,527 overall, was held to just 18 this time - and the Browns themselves to 24 - as New York prevailed, 10-0.

Brown gained some solace by being honored as the NFL's Most

Cleveland Browns Facts & Trivia

Valuable Player by United Press International and the Newspaper Enterprise Association.

The Browns drafted two players in **1959** who would anchor an offensive line that would pave the way for Brown and Mitchell, among others, in the years to come. Dick Schafrath from Ohio State was chosen in the second round, guard John Wooten out of Colorado in the fifth. The team lost two of its first three games in 1959 but then reeled off five straight wins, including a 38-31 victory on November 1 at Baltimore, a game in which Brown rushed for all five of Cleveland's touchdowns (a team record for most rushing touchdowns in one game). The once-promising season came unraveled, though, as the Browns absorbed consecutive one-point defeats at home to Pittsburgh and San Francisco. Despite Brown's 1,329 rushing yards, the team finished in a second-place tie with Philadelphia at 7-5, three games behind the 10-2 Giants.

Lou Groza announced his retirement in the off-season; it was only temporary, however (he would return in 1961, but for kicking duties only [Sam Baker was the kicker in Groza's absence]). The **1960** Browns won their first, and last, three games. They floundered in between, though, due in large part to the lack of a long passing game (Plum, though, did lead the league in the throwing department, connecting for 21 touchdown passes and tossing just five interceptions, while completing more than 60 percent of his passes). The deteriorating relationship between Paul Brown and several players didn't help matters. Although the Browns finished with a solid record of 8-3-1, they wound up in second place, a game-and-a-half behind the Eagles in the Eastern Conference. The Browns' three losses came by just a combined 10 points. It marked the first time Cleveland failed to qualify for post-season play two straight years.

The Browns did play one more game, though, three weeks later, appearing in the first-ever Playoff Bowl, a contest that matched the second-place finishers in each conference in the Orange Bowl in Miami. The Browns lost to the Lions, 17-16.

Under the new ownership in Modell, Cleveland got off to a fast start in **1961**, which saw the second-year Dallas Cowboys join the Eastern Conference after one season in the Western. The Browns stood at 5-2 at the halfway point of the new 14-game schedule, the two defeats coming at the hands of the Eagles and Packers, the combatants in the previous year's NFL title game. The Browns were

Cleveland Browns Facts & Trivia

7-3 heading into a key November 26 clash with the Giants at home. The Browns' conference title hopes were given a crushing blow in a 37-21 defeat before 80,455 fans, the NFL's largest crowd of the year. Two weeks later, a 17-14 loss to the Bears left the Browns out of the post-season for the third straight year. Despite solid seasons from Jim Brown, who had 1,408 yards rushing on a back-breaking 305 carries, and Plum, who once again led the NFL in passing, Cleveland managed just an 8-5-1 record and third-place finish.

Paul Brown had his eyes on a new running mate for Jim Brown for the **1962** season, and got his man - 1961 Heisman Trophy winner Ernie Davis, whose speed and power helped him break most of Jim Brown's records at Syracuse. The Browns acquired Davis three days prior to the previous year's season finale by trading eventual 1983 Pro Football Hall of Fame inductee Mitchell and the rights to No. 2 draft choice Leroy Jackson, a defensive back, to Washington for the Redskins' first-round selection, which also happened to be the top pick in the draft. Unfortunately, tragedy struck as Davis contracted leukemia, and never played a game for the Browns. He would pass away on May 18, 1963, making for one of the more devastating tales in Browns history.

Also drafted in the first round in 1962 was wide receiver Gary Collins from Maryland. Plum was traded to Detroit in a deal that brought back Jim Ninowski, a fourth-round draft pick of the Browns four years earlier who had been Plum's backup in 1958 and 1959, and who had been shipped to the Lions in 1960. Ninowski shared the signal-calling duties with Frank Ryan, who joined the team by way of a trade with Los Angeles. The Browns started slowly in 1962 by dropping three of their first five, which set the tone for the season. In a year in which Brown failed to win the league rushing title for the first - and only - time in his career, the team finished 7-6-1 and in third place. Mike McCormack, Cleveland's stalwart right tackle the previous eight years, retired after the season. He would be inducted into the Hall of Fame in 1984.

Paul Brown was from the Old School, and several team members felt it showed. They believed the game was passing him by, that his play-calling had become too conservative for the changing times - quite simply, that a transformation was needed. Said Jim Brown in the NFL Films documentary *The Cleveland Browns - Fifty Years of Memories*, "At the end of Paul's career ... the players were united against him to have him open up the offense and do things that were more innovative."

The coach's military-like approach to dealing with his men - he had served in the Navy for two years - which had worked so well in the past, was losing its luster, too. The players got their wish with the firing of Brown and subsequent hiring of Collier, a natural-born teacher with a different style of coaching than his predecessor. "Blanton was more of a human being as far as dealing with the human feelings of players and their emotions, and what he did was, he gave us a free hand," Brown said in the documentary.

Added Bill Glass, a defensive end for the Browns from 1962-68, in the same documentary, "He (Collier) was just totally different than Paul Brown. Whereas Paul Brown would say, 'Do it because I say do it,' Blanton Collier treated you like a man, treated you with a respect."

Paul Brown would be inducted into the pro grid shrine four years later in 1967, some two months before he and his family made their return to the pro football scene. On September 27, 1967, the Brown family was awarded an AFL franchise that would turn out to be the Cincinnati Bengals, who would later become a bitter rival of the Browns in the NFL.

As if supplanting a legend wasn't hard enough, Collier had to mend the mental wounds created not only by Davis's passing in May but the deaths of two other players, as well. Two weeks after Davis passed on, standout safety Don Fleming was electrocuted on a construction project in Florida. Some five months before, No. 6 draft pick Tom Bloom, Purdue's Most Valuable Player as a running back in 1962, was killed in an automobile accident. Bloom, who had hoped to win a spot in Cleveland's defensive backfield, was driving the car he had purchased with the bonus money he had received for signing with the Browns.

Despite the sadness surrounding the club, with Ryan now firmly in control at quarterback of a revamped, more wide-open offense, the Browns reeled off six victories to begin the **1963** season. They were 9-3 heading into their own personal graveyard of Tiger Stadium for a December 8 matchup with Detroit. The Browns, who had lost all four games - two of them championship contests - they had played in the Motor City, were beaten handily, 38-10, all but ruining their conference title aspirations. A 27-20 victory in the finale at Washington the next week was meaningless since the Giants beat Pittsburgh the same day, clinching their third consecutive Eastern Conference title. New York finished one game ahead of the

10-4 Browns, who missed the postseason for the fifth straight year.

Cleveland did take the field one more time, three weeks later, falling to Green Bay, 40-23, in the Playoff Bowl.

Jim Brown reclaimed the league rushing title in 1963 with a career high 1,863 yards, plus a career best 6.4-yard average. He was voted the NFL's Most Valuable Player by United Press International and the Maxwell Club. He also shared the Newspaper Enterprise Association's MVP honor with Giants quarterback Y.A. Tittle. Ryan, meanwhile, threw for 25 touchdowns, more than any Cleveland quarterback had thrown since Graham's heyday.

5. Contenders Again

The Browns' players loved Blanton Collier's approach to the game; they showed their appreciation for their scholarly-looking coach when in 1964, led by the pinpoint passing of Frank Ryan and the superb running of Jim Brown, the team captured its first conference title in seven years and first league title in nine seasons. During the remainder of the decade, the Browns knocked on the door but played the role of bridesmaid, falling short in the NFL Championship game three times - in 1965, 1968, and 1969.

When the Browns selected spectacular wide receiver Paul Warfield from Ohio State with their top pick in the **1964** NFL Draft, it put the finishing touches on what had become an awesome offensive attack. Behind Brown, Ryan, Warfield, Gary Collins and Co., the Browns sprinted to an 8-1-1 start in 1964 but were underdogs for the first time all season long heading into a November 22 matchup with the Packers in Milwaukee. Although the Browns were defeated, 28-21, the feeling among many was that they had played one of their better games of the year.

The team was in position to clinch the Eastern Conference title two weeks later in St. Louis against the Cardinals, who trailed Cleveland by a game-and-a-half. The Browns lost, 28-19, reducing their lead to one-half game. But six days later in Yankee Stadium, they erupted for a 52-20 rout of the Giants, clinching the conference crown.

The Browns were heavy underdogs to Johnny Unitas and the

Cleveland Browns Facts & Trivia

Western Conference Champion Baltimore Colts in the NFL title game on December 27 in Cleveland. The team gained confidence by fighting the mighty Colts to a scoreless first half. Then, three scoring strikes from Ryan to Collins, for 18, 42, and 51 yards - the third an unbelievable one-handed catch in which No. 86 disappeared into a sea of fans in the bleachers - propelled the Browns to a stunning 27-0 victory. Pandemonium reigned as thousands in the throng 79,544 rushed the field to celebrate the team's fourth NFL title. Ryan repeated his 1963 total of 25 touchdown passes during the season. Brown rushed for 1,446 yards and Warfield led the team in receptions and receiving yards.

The injury bug hit the Browns in **1965** as a number of players went down at one time or another, most notably Ryan and Warfield. However, the team didn't miss a beat, due in large part to Brown, who led the league in rushing yards for the eighth time in nine seasons. Other than a humiliating 49-13 home loss to St. Louis in Week 2, a game in which Cardinals quarterback Charley Johnson passed for six touchdowns, the Browns waltzed their way to another Eastern Conference Championship. The title-clincher came by a 42-21 count on November 28 against the Steelers.

The Browns failed in their bid to repeat as champions as they were held to 64 yards rushing - Brown to 50 - in a 23-12 loss to the Green Bay Packers in the snow and mud of Lambeau Field in the NFL Championship game on January 2, 1966. The title-game defeat was not only memorable because of the manner in which the Packers stopped Brown, but also due to the fact that it was Brown's final game. After being honored as the Associated Press NFL Player of the Year and the league's Most Valuable Player by United Press International, the Newspaper Enterprise Association, and *The Sporting News* for 1965, the next summer the great fullback proclaimed he would continue performing - but not on the gridiron, rather on the movie set. The star runner found a calling in the acting profession. Brown finished his career with 12,312 yards rushing and 106 touchdowns on the ground (126 overall). He averaged 5.2 yards per carry and 104 yards rushing per game, both of which are NFL records.

The impact of Brown's departure was lessened when a halfback by the name of Leroy Kelly, an eighth-round draft pick two years before, stepped in and carried the torch quite well. "Leroy was the type of running back who had the speed and the agility to fake you out and make you look awful bad, but he also had the power to run you over," said Joe Scarpati, a safety with the Philadelphia Eagles from 1964-69, in an NFL Films documentary on Kelly.

"I think the thing that Leroy had as a player was his ability to hit a hole extremely quick, probably as quick as any running back that I can remember," recalled Fred Hoaglin, who played center for Cleveland in the late 1960s and early 1970s, in the same documentary. "He could get out of his stance real quick, hit the hole so fast that he was hitting the hole as it was opening. He might've only had a foot of daylight, but as he went into it, the hole opened wider, and he would pop through those things, and he had the quickness and the speed to run away from people once he got into the secondary."

Kelly had his first of three consecutive 1,000-yard seasons in **1966** with 1,141, finishing second by less than 100 yards to Chicago's Gale Sayers for the league rushing title. He helped keep the Browns in the thick of the race in the Eastern Conference, which fielded a new team in the first-year Atlanta Falcons. Cleveland was 7-3 when Dallas administered a 26-14 setback in Week 11. The Cowboys went on to win the conference title with a 10-3-1 record, a game-and-a-half ahead of the 9-5 Browns, who wound up in a second-place tie with Philadelphia.

The NFL had a new look in **1967**. Each conference was split into two divisions - the Capitol and Century in the Eastern Conference and the Coastal and Central in the Western. The Browns stayed put in the Eastern Conference and were placed in the Century Division with the Giants, Steelers, and Cardinals (the next year, New York would move to the Capitol and would be replaced in the Century by the New Orleans Saints; in 1969, the Giants would swap divisions once again with the Saints and were back in the Century).

For the first time in team history, Cleveland lost its first two games, beginning the 1967 season by falling to Dallas and Detroit. A 42-7 rout of the expansion Saints, though, ignited a four-game winning streak. But following a 55-7 trouncing by the Green Bay Packers on November 12, a game in which the reigning Super Bowl Champions rung up 35 points in the first quarter - a league record for most points yielded in the opening period - Cleveland stood at 5-4, one-half game behind St. Louis. The defeat to the Packers is a team record for worst loss ever (along with a 48-point beating by Minnesota two years later). The Browns rebounded and took over sole possession of first place the next week when with Minnesota trying to run out the clock, defensive tackle Jim Kanicki stripped the football from running back Dave Osborn, which led to a 14-10 victory over the Vikings. Cleveland clinched the Century Division title with a 20-16 win in St. Louis on December 10 and finished 9-5. Dallas laid waste to the Browns, though, 52-14, in the Eastern Conference Championship game on Christmas Eve in the Cotton Bowl. Cleveland got a shot at redemption two weeks later in the form of a Playoff Bowl battle with Los Angeles, but the Rams administered a 30-6 black eye on the Browns. Kelly's 1,205 yards on the ground was tops in the league in 1967, his first of two consecutive rushing titles.

Ryan had begun to experience arm trouble, prompting the Browns to obtain quarterback Bill Nelsen from Pittsburgh as part of a five-player deal in the off-season for backup insurance and possibly a quarterback of the future. Despite lingering knee problems, Nelsen was mentally tough, and with veterans such as Dick Schafrath and guard Gene Hickerson anchoring the offensive line, he now had protection, something he never enjoyed in Pittsburgh.

The Browns also had a new kicker in **1968**. Don Cockroft, drafted out of Adams State (Colorado) the year before and who spent a year on the taxi (practice) squad, beat out the veteran Lou Groza in preseason. "The Toe" retired after 21 years with the team.

After the Browns dropped two of their first three games in 1968, both defeats being awful offensive performances against Dallas and Los Angeles, Collier decided it was time for a change. The coach benched Ryan in favor of Nelsen, who promptly directed the team to a 31-24 victory over his former club, the Steelers, and a week later nearly engineered a comeback win in losing a close one to the Cardinals. Then, with such receiving stalwarts as Warfield, Collins, and 1966 draftee tight end Milt Morin to throw to, and the marvelous Kelly to hand off to, Nelsen led the team on an offensive binge Browns fans had never seen before. Beginning with a 30-20 upset of the Colts in Baltimore on October 20, the Browns won eight straight, scoring 30 or more in the first seven. In a three-week stretch from November 17 to December 1, the team tallied 45, 47, and 45 points, respectively.

The Browns clinched their second straight Century Division title with a 24-21 victory in Washington on December 8, finishing 10-4, and were rewarded with a rematch with the Cowboys for the

Cleveland Browns Facts & Trivia

Eastern Conference Championship - this time in Cleveland, though. Linebacker Dale Lindsey's 27-yard interception return early in the third quarter broke a 10-10 tie and helped avenge the previous year's playoff humiliation in Texas as the Browns dismantled the favored Cowboys, 31-20, on December 21. The jubilation from the Dallas victory was short-lived, though, as Baltimore, behind Tom Matte's three touchdown runs, flattened the Browns eight days later, 34-0, in the NFL Championship game in Cleveland Municipal Stadium. Kelly, voted the NFL's Most Valuable Player for 1968 by the Maxwell Club, was limited to just 28 yards rushing.

Nelsen had his most productive season in six years in the league, throwing for 2,366 yards, 19 touchdowns, and only 10 interceptions, while completing nearly 52 percent of his passes. Meanwhile, Warfield's 1,067 receiving yards were the most by a Browns player since Mac Speedie's 1,146 in 1947.

The Browns got off to a 5-1-1 start in **1969**, including a 42-10 demolition of Dallas on November 2. The team followed the ringing victory over the Cowboys with a dud up north, though, as they were trashed, 51-3, in Minnesota, a game in which the Browns were outgained more than 3-1 (454 yards to 151) and could manage just eight first downs to the home team's 31.

The embarrassing loss to the Vikings turned out to be just a brief interlude, however. The team pulled itself together and won five straight, chalking up its third straight Century Division title. In what was becoming a yearly ritual, the Browns faced the Cowboys for the Eastern Conference Championship for the third straight time. Behind Nelsen's 219 yards passing, Cleveland built a 17-0 lead by halftime and coasted to a 38-14 victory, and a chance at redemption against the Vikings in the NFL Championship game the following week. The rematch in Bloomington, played on January 4, 1970, was not exactly a marked improvement from the 48-point beating the Browns suffered some two months earlier in the same venue. On a cold, sunny day in Metropolitan Stadium, they trailed, 24-0, by halftime and lost, 27-7.

6. Phipps, Frustration, and Failure

Although Cleveland qualified for the postseason in two of the first three years of the 1970s, the aging Browns were on their last legs. Coaching changes began to occur on a frequent basis, beginning with longtime assistant Nick Skorich succeeding Blanton Collier, who stepped down following the 1970 season. Bill Nelsen was eventually replaced as the starting quarterback by former Purdue sensation Mike Phipps. The Browns acquired Phipps by trading the great Paul Warfield to Miami for the Dolphins' first-round draft choice - and third overall - on the evening of January 26, 1970, just hours prior to the next morning's NFL Draft, in a move that stunned the city of Cleveland. By the time Phipps left Cleveland seven years later, the Browns resembled their fine forerunners of the past not in the least.

The Browns experienced just their second losing season ever - and first in 18 years - in 1974. Forrest Gregg, the team's offensive line coach that year, replaced the fired Skorich in 1975. Gregg, a Hall of Fame offensive tackle for the Packers during Green Bay's heyday in the 1960s, got off to a rough start but did manage to improve the team's fortunes somewhat. Gregg eventually got the axe, too, though, albeit it was announced publicly as a resignation. Even former Browns defensive tackle Dick Modzelewski, the team's defensive coordinator, got into the act, coaching the final game of the 1977 season.

A rival professional football league had been competing with the NFL throughout the 1960s. The American Football League (AFL) was its name, vying for supposedly NFL-bound college players its game. The AFL began play in 1960 and aimed to appeal to the casual fan. To do this, the league accentuated the passing game. The AFL added even more excitement by implementing the two-point conversion rule; this allowed teams the opportunity to run or pass for two points following a touchdown rather than following in the NFL's footsteps by ruling that clubs must try for one point by place-kicking the ball through the uprights - unless, of course, a bad snap or something of the like occurred, and if so, the team could run or pass for the point (the NFL adopted the two-point rule in 1994). The AFL produced such offensive stars as George Blanda, Joe Namath, and Otis Taylor.

Cleveland Browns Facts & Trivia

Under an agreement reached four years before, the AFL merged with the NFL in **1970** to form one 26-team National Football League. With the new format, the Browns, along with Pittsburgh and Baltimore, agreed (with the help of a large sum of money waved their way) to join the former AFL teams in one of the NFL's two new conferences, the American Football Conference (AFC); the remaining NFL teams were placed in the National Football Conference (NFC). The switch by the Browns, Steelers, and Colts evened the number of teams in each conference at 13. Both the AFC and NFC were divided into three divisions - the Eastern, Central, and Western. The Browns were placed in the AFC's Central Division, along with old NFL buddy Pittsburgh and AFL brethren Cincinnati and Houston.

The Browns began the new decade with a bang, beginning with the move that sent Warfield to the Dolphins and brought Phipps to the shores of Lake Erie. The Browns drafted Phipps due mainly to Nelsen's bad knees, a situation not unlike two years before when due to Frank Ryan's arm troubles, they traded for Nelsen. The veteran Nelsen, though, remained the starter when the 1970 season began, with the rookie from Purdue waiting in the wings.

On September 21, 1970, the Browns helped inaugurate the ABC television network's *Monday Night Football* series by hosting its very first game. In front of a team-record (home or away) 85,703 fans, big plays led to a 31-21 victory over Joe Namath and the New York Jets. Homer Jones returned the second-half kickoff 94 yards for a touchdown. Linebacker Billy Andrews put the nail in New York's coffin when he made a diving interception of a Namath pass, got up, and returned it 25 yards for a score with 35 seconds left in the game.

The Browns were a model of inconsistency in 1970, but due to their division rivals' lackluster play, as well, remained in the Central Division title hunt. They lost out on the division championship on the final Sunday when the Cincinnati Bengals, after a 1-6 start, won their seventh straight game to finish 8-6, a game ahead of the 7-7 Browns, whose victory in Denver later that day, as a result, was deemed meaningless (although Collier was carried off the field following the game by team members, for it was his last game as head coach). Many blamed the Browns' mediocre year on the loss of Warfield, who went on to enjoy great success with the Dolphins in the form of two straight Super Bowl titles in 1972 and 1973.

Cleveland Browns Facts & Trivia

Under new head coach Skorich and with Nelsen still at the controls, Cleveland won four of its first five games in **1971**. The offense then took a month-long hiatus, however, as the team scored just 30 points in successive losses to the Broncos, Falcons, Steelers, and Chiefs. A 27-7 home win over New England, though, sparked a five-game winning streak to end the season, earning the Browns the Central Division title and a matchup with Baltimore in the AFC Divisional Playoffs. The visiting Colts, led by an aging but still savvy John Unitas, easily dismantled Cleveland, 20-3, one week after Hanukkah ended.

Skorich alternated between Nelsen and Phipps during the **1972** preseason, but after the Browns lost to Green Bay in the opener with Nelsen calling the signals, the coach inserted Phipps as the starter for game 2 in Philadelphia. Phipps passed for a touchdown and scored one himself in leading the Browns to a 27-17 victory over the Eagles, and in the process, received Skorich's stamp of approval to be his starter for the remainder of the season.

After an easy win over the Bengals, the Browns lost two in a row to drop to 2-3, but six straight wins ensued, including thrillers over the Chargers and Steelers. In San Diego on November 13, wide receiver Frank Pitts, acquired in a trade with Kansas City prior to the 1971 season, hauled in a 38-yard touchdown pass from Phipps with under a minute to play, giving the Browns a 21-17 Monday night victory. At home against Pittsburgh the next week, Don Cockroft's 26-yard field goal with 13 seconds left was the game-winner in a dramatic 26-24 win, forging a tie for the Central Division lead, evening both teams' records at 7-3. Two weeks later, the Browns and Steelers squared off once again - this time, though, in Pittsburgh - and with both teams 8-3, at stake was the outright Central Division lead. The Browns were limited to 27 yards through the air and were manhandled, 30-0. Pittsburgh won its final two games to nail down the division championship - its first title of any kind in 40 years of competition, finishing 11-3. The Browns, also winners of their last two, wound up 10-4, good enough for the AFC's wild card spot, and were rewarded with a trip down south to face the unbeaten Miami Dolphins in the divisional playoffs.

The Browns threw a huge scare into the heavily-favored Dolphins, and when Phipps tossed a 27-yard touchdown strike to Fair Hooker, had a one-point lead early in the fourth quarter. Miami bounced back, though, and sealed a 20-14 victory, when late in the game, linebacker Doug Swift intercepted a Phipps pass deep in Dolphins territory, the young quarterback's fifth pick of the day. Miami had taken one more step to what would become the only undefeated, untied season in NFL history, and the first overall in pro football since 1948, when the Browns themselves did it while a member of the All-America Football Conference.

With Nelsen retired and Phipps at the controls once and for all, Cleveland looked to be headed for the playoffs once again in **1973** when on November 25, rookie halfback Greg Pruitt dashed 19 yards for a touchdown late in the game to give the Browns a 21-16 triumph over the Steelers at home. The next week in Kansas City, the speedster from Oklahoma, Cleveland's third pick in the draft, scored on a 65-yard run as the Browns rallied from a 14-point fourth-quarter deficit to tie the Chiefs. That left the team with a 7-3-2 record and a virtual share of first place with Cincinnati and Pittsburgh, both 8-4. A 34-17 pounding at the hands of the Bengals, though, finished the Browns for all intents and purposes. They wound up 7-5-2 and in third place.

With Leroy Kelly, an eventual 1994 Pro Football Hall of Fame inductee, gone - the six-time Pro Bowler had been released before training camp began - the Browns were bombed by the Bengals, 33-7, in the **1974** season opener. The team never recovered, dropping five of its first six games, and wound up in last place at 4-10, by far the worst record in franchise history to date. Skorich was fired on December 12 but did finish out the season in a loss at Houston.

One bright spot for the Browns in 1974 was quarterback Brian Sipe, a 13th-round draft pick from San Diego State two years before, who had spent 1972 and 1973 on the taxi squad. Although Sipe, who filled in for the interception-prone Phipps on occasion, was picked off frequently himself, he was instrumental in three of Cleveland's wins. One was a foreshadow of things to come for Sipe, a stirring comeback at home against Denver in which the rookie scored twice - the second with 1:56 left in the game - after relieving Phipps in the fourth quarter.

Things did not exactly improve the next year with Gregg at the helm. The **1975** Browns lost their first nine games. Phipps finally passed the team to victory on November 23 in an upset of the red-hot Bengals. The Browns won three of their last five, but with another poor year from Phipps - he had four touchdown passes and 19 interceptions - looming large, still wound up 3-11, Central

Cleveland Browns Facts & Trivia

Division cellar dwellers for the second straight year. Nine defeats came by 11 points or more.

Despite the Browns' poor showing, there were bright spots individually in 1975. Pruitt became only the third Cleveland running back to rush for 1,000 yards in a season with 1,067, his first of three consecutive 1,000-yard seasons. The team found a future backfield mate for Pruitt in free agent Cleo Miller, picked up late that season. Meanwhile, Reggie Rucker, a wide receiver acquired in a draft-day deal with New England, led the team with 60 receptions and 770 receiving yards.

The Browns looked to further improve their offense with their first two selections in the **1976** NFL Draft - powerful fullback Mike (no relation to Greg) Pruitt from Purdue in the first round and sure-handed Colorado wide receiver Dave Logan in the third. In addition, Warfield was back after five seasons with the Dolphins and less than a year in the World Football League (WFL), which folded just over halfway through its 1975 season. The eventual 1983 Hall of Fame inductee played two more years before calling it quits.

Phipps held off a challenge from Sipe in training camp and remained the starter when the 1976 season began. After passing for three second-quarter touchdowns in leading the Browns to a 21-10 halftime lead against the New York Jets in the opener at home, Phipps suffered a separated shoulder early in the third quarter. Sipe came in and put the finishing touches on a 38-17 victory by tossing touchdown passes to Rucker and Steve Holden. Blowout losses to Pittsburgh, Denver, and Cincinnati followed, but Sipe was finally beginning to solidify himself as the starter.

Third-string quarterback Dave Mays, a WFL refugee, was the hero a week later as the Browns began a huge turnaround with a stunning upset (18-16) of the two-time defending Super Bowl Champion Steelers in Cleveland Municipal Stadium. Though not spectacular, Mays did what was needed in replacing Sipe, who was knocked out of the game in the second quarter. Defensive end Joe "Turkey" Jones put the stamp on Cleveland's fine defensive effort early in the fourth quarter by not only sacking Steelers quarterback Terry Bradshaw, but lifting him up and slamming him head first to the ground. Bradshaw would miss the next two games due to back and neck injuries suffered on the play.

With Sipe back the next week, the Browns beat the Falcons, and lost just one more game heading into the season's final week. Tied with the Steelers and Bengals at 9-4 but in the precarious position where they would lose out in tie-breakers to both teams, the Browns knew the only way they could advance to the postseason was by winning the AFC Central outright (they had no shot at the AFC's wild card berth). Before the Browns even took the field for their finale in Kansas City, however, their title dreams, as faint as they were, had been shattered by Pittsburgh's 20-0 victory over Houston the day before. They played like it, too, in an embarrassing 39-14 loss to the lowly Chiefs. The Browns still finished 9-5, though, in third place, a game behind the division champion Steelers, and Bengals, who like Pittsburgh, finished 10-4 (but lost out on the division crown due to their two defeats to the Steelers during the season).

Despite the disaster in Arrowhead Stadium, Gregg was still voted AFC Coach of the Year by the Associated Press for his team's six-game improvement from the year before. Defensive tackle Jerry Sherk, who led the Browns with 12 sacks (unofficially) in 1976, was named NFL Defensive Player of the Year by the Newspaper Enterprise Association. Sipe enjoyed a fine season, too, completing more than 57 percent of his passes, the highest completion percentage by a Cleveland quarterback since Frank Ryan back in 1962. Sipe also became the first Browns' signal caller to throw for more touchdowns than interceptions - 17 to 14 - since Bill Nelsen in 1969.

With Phipps gone - the Browns had traded the much-maligned quarterback and his 81 career interceptions to the Bears in the off-season - Sipe led the team to a fine start in **1977**. Cleveland won five of its first seven, including a 30-27 sudden death thriller against the Patriots on a Monday night and a 44-7 rout of the Chiefs on October 30, and found themselves in an unfamiliar position at the season's halfway mark - in first place looking *down* at Pittsburgh and Cincinnati in the standings. A 10-7 home loss to the Bengals ignited a horrendous second half of the season in which Sipe was lost for the year to a separated left shoulder in a loss to the Steelers. In addition to saying "So long" to Gregg, the Browns also bid farewell to a playoff berth for the fifth straight year by dropping six of their last seven games. They finished in the division basement at 6-8. Turmoil prevailed as Art Modell set out to search for a new head coach who would give the team a new direction.

7. A Kardiac Revival

The hiring of the personable Sam Rutigliano, who had worked his way through the NFL assistant coaching ranks, as head coach for the 1978 season, coincided with the continued development of Brian Sipe into one of the NFL's premier quarterbacks. The two helped bring excitement - via the passing attack - back to the Browns. Rutigliano's offensive philosophy was simple - air it out and go for it. His carefree mindset allowed Sipe and his arsenal of receivers and backs to cause havoc on opposing defenses.

The Browns not only put up big numbers offensively but also left their fans gasping for air. Their penchant for late-game heroics earned them the moniker "Kardiac Kids" as 12 games in both the 1979 and 1980 seasons were in doubt until the final moments. Cleveland's fantastic-finish frenzy was capped off by a Central Division title in 1980, the team's first in nine years.

The Browns had a whale of a draft in **1978**, using their two first-round selections (they had a pair due to a previous trade) on linebacker Clay Matthews out of Southern California and Ozzie Newsome, a wide receiver from Alabama who would go on to become one of the finest tight ends of all time.

With Rutigliano now strolling the sidelines, the '78 Browns got off to their first 3-0 start since 1963, including an overtime win at home against the Bengals and a heart stopper against the Falcons in Atlanta. The Browns easily could have been 5-0 if not for two highly-disputed officiating calls that led to stinging defeats to Pittsburgh and Houston. The team rebounded, though, by beating the Saints in the Superdome to improve to 4-2. Four losses in the next five games pretty much finished the Browns before victories over Baltimore and Los Angeles renewed slim playoff hopes. Against the Colts, Sipe connected on 15 of 22 passes for 309 yards. A 47-24 pasting in Seattle on December 3, though, quickly ended any realistic postseason aspirations. The Browns wound up 8-8, in third place in the Central Division. Sipe enjoyed his finest year to date, throwing for nearly 3,000 yards and 15 touchdowns.

After having flirted with late-game heroics in 1978, the Browns made a habit of it in **1979**. After three nailbiting victories to open the season, they routed the defending NFC Champion Dallas Cowboys

Cleveland Browns Facts & Trivia

- "America's Team" - 26-7, under the bright lights of *Monday Night Football* on September 24 in a rocking Cleveland Stadium, to improve to 4-0. The Browns split their next eight games, two of which were pulse-pounding victories over contenders Philadelphia and Miami. Against the Eagles, linebacker Charlie Hall intercepted a Ron Jaworski pass on the Cleveland one-yard line as time expired to preserve a 24-19 win in Veterans Stadium. Two weeks later at home against the Dolphins, Sipe fired a 35-yard touchdown pass to Newsome to tie the score at 24 with 1:21 left in the game. Sipe drilled a 39-yarder to Reggie Rucker 1:59 into sudden death to win it, upping the Browns' record to 8-4, leaving them a game behind Pittsburgh and Houston, with a trip down the turnpike set for seven days later.

The Browns invaded Three Rivers Stadium on November 25 and led almost the entire game when leads of 20-6 and 27-13 evaporated. The defending Super Bowl Champion Steelers hung a 33-30 heartbreaker of a humdinger on the visitors when future Brown Matt Bahr nailed a 37-yard field goal with nine seconds left in sudden death. The next week in the home finale, Mike Pruitt outgained the awesome Earl Campbell as the Browns beat the Oilers in the snow to improve to 9-5. The Browns' postseason dreams were given a crushing blow the next week, however, with a 19-14 loss to wild-card rival Oakland on the West Coast.

The Browns entered the final weekend of the season with a 9-6 record. They needed a win in Cincinnati on the final Sunday and losses by the Raiders, 9-6, later that day to Seattle, and Denver, 10-5, the following night in San Diego, in order to overtake the two AFC West rivals for the second and final AFC Wild Card Playoff position (a Raiders' tie would have been alright, as well).

The scenario with Oakland was simple - the Raiders, due to their victory over the Browns the previous week, owned the head-to-head tiebreaker advantage over Cleveland, meaning the Browns had to finish with a better record than Oakland. Matters were a touch more confusing, though, when it came to the situation with the Broncos. Due to the complicated NFL tiebreaking formula, the total points differential in the Browns' win over the Bengals and the Broncos' loss to the Chargers would have had to total 43 points, which would have put the Browns in a tie with Denver in net points in conference games. In that scenario, the Browns would have won the next tiebreaker - net points in all games.

Although Oakland did its part by losing to the Seahawks, and the Broncos their part (somewhat) by falling to the Chargers (by just 10 points, though), the tiebreaking scenario went for naught as the Browns had already dropped a 16-12 heartbreaker to the lowly Bengals when Browns receiver Ricky Feacher had a fourth-down pass from Brian Sipe ricochet off his fingertips in the end zone in the final minute (in retrospect, though, the Browns would have had to defeat the Bengals by at least 33 points to qualify for the playoffs). The Browns finished 9-7 and in third place in the AFC Central, behind division champion Pittsburgh and wild card Houston.

Mike Pruitt had his first of four 1,000-yard seasons in 1979, rushing for a career-high 1,294 yards, which ranked second in the AFC, behind Campbell's 1,697. Sipe passed for 3,793 yards and an NFL-high 28 touchdowns, but his 26 interceptions and a porous Cleveland defense - despite the presence of defensive end Lyle Alzado, acquired in an off-season trade with Denver - kept the Browns out of the playoffs for the seventh straight year. Despite the team's season-ending letdown, Rutigliano was named AFC Coach of the Year by United Press International.

If the Browns had made a habit of late-game heroics in 1979, they turned it into an art form in **1980**. After starting the season 0-2, the team won 10 of 12, including consecutive close calls over Green Bay (26-21), Pittsburgh (27-26), Chicago (27-21), and Baltimore (28-27). Included also was a 17-14 upset of Houston on November 30 in the Astrodome in a battle for first place (both teams entered the game at 8-4). Clarence Scott's late interception of Kenny Stabler iced the 17-14 victory that not only gave the Browns sole possession of first place for the first time in three years, but also caused an estimated crowd of 15,000 fans - and thousands of dollars worth of damage - at Cleveland Hopkins International Airport upon the team's near midnight arrival that evening.

The Browns had a chance to nail down a playoff berth with a win in Minnesota in Week 15. The Vikings, though, gave the Kardiac Kids a dose of their own medicine. The Browns blew a 14-point fourth-quarter lead but were still in good shape, leading by one with four seconds to go and Minnesota 46 yards from the Cleveland end zone. Vikings quarterback Tommy Kramer heaved one down the right sideline into a sea of purple and orange. The ball was batted by cornerback Thom Darden, and as fate would have it, fell into the left hand of Ahmad Rashad as the Vikings' receiver backpedaled - cradling the ball against his body - into the end zone. Rashad's miracle catch not only gave the Vikings a stunning 28-23 victory but also the NFC Central Division title, and turned the Browns' finale a week later in Cincinnati into a must win (or tie), unless wild card rival New England (9-6), which owned the head-to-head tiebreaker advantage over Cleveland due to a victory over the Browns in the season opener, could manage to lose to the 1-14 Saints (they wouldn't).

The Browns held off a late charge by the Bengals in a wild 27-24 victory that not only clinched the AFC Central Division title but also caused another overflow crowd at Hopkins Airport that night. Both the Browns and Oilers finished 11-5, but Cleveland won the division based on a better conference record (8-4) than their rivals from the south (7-5). The Browns were in the postseason for the first time in eight years.

Sipe led the NFL in passing in 1980 with a 91.4 rating, completing 337 of 554 pass attempts for a team-record 4,132 yards. He had 30 touchdown passes, tops in the AFC, and just 14 interceptions. He was voted the NFL Player of the Year by the Associated Press, Most Valuable Player by the Pro Football Writers Association of America and *The Sporting News*, Offensive Player of the Year by *Pro Football Weekly*, and AFC Most Valuable Player by United Press International. Sipe spread the wealth well, too, as five Browns - Mike Pruitt, Rucker, Dave Logan, Newsome, and Greg Pruitt - had at least 50 receptions apiece. Rutigliano was voted by UPI as AFC Coach of the Year for the second straight season.

The Browns' opponent in the AFC Divisional Playoffs was the Oakland Raiders, who had disposed of the Oilers a week earlier in the conference wild card game. The contest was played in Cleveland on January 4, 1981, a day when the wind chill made the 1 degree temperature feel like 37 below zero at game time. The frigid air, frozen field, and swirling winds caused havoc on both offenses all day.

With 2:22 remaining in the game, Cleveland's much-maligned defense stopped the Raiders on a key fourth down deep in Browns territory. Trailing, 14-12, the Browns took over possession of the ball on their own 15-yard line, hoping to warm the hearts of their frozen fans once again with yet another Kardiac finish. Sipe was masterful, and with the help of a successful draw play to Mike Pruitt late in the drive, directed his team down to the Raiders' 13-yard line with 49 seconds left. Following a Browns' timeout, Rutigliano, even with his "Riverboat Sam" reputation, stunned 77,655 fans expecting a run

Cleveland Browns Facts & Trivia

or two up the middle to set up a field goal attempt by Don Cockroft when Sipe dropped back to pass on second-and-nine. This was risky business, but rather than Tom Cruise choosing between right and wrong, it was Sipe deciding between Logan, Newsome, and Rucker.

" ... At that point, I would rather put my money on Sipe's arm to win. Our kicker had a lot of things happen all day (Cockroft had missed two field goals and an extra point) ... " Rutigliano reasoned following the game, as taken from *The Beacon Journal* in Akron, Ohio, on January 5, 1981. "It was our plan to throw on second down and if we don't score run on third down, run the clock down, kick the field goal and kick off with almost no timeouts left for Oakland."

The coach's blueprint for victory never came to fruition. On a play - known as "Red Right 88" - in which Logan was the primary target, Sipe tried to get the ball to No. 85 but changed his mind when he saw the Raiders were coming after him (Sipe). Sipe admitted he was a victim of his own programming. "... When a team blitzes ... it means (tight end) Ozzie (Newsome) should be open behind him (Logan)," he explained after the game, as taken from the same article in *The Beacon Journal*. "I saw the free safety (Burgess Owens) come up behind Dave and my key tells me when that happens go to Ozzie. That's an automatic reaction."

So Sipe threw for Newsome. He failed to notice, though, that strong safety Mike Davis was hot on Newsome's trail (Owens was now in the vicinity, too, helping Davis cover Newsome) as the "Wizard" was "ice-skating" toward the left corner of the end zone. With Logan open at the eight and Rucker all alone in the middle of the end zone - with not a Raider in sight - Sipe spotted Newsome and released the ball under heavy pressure from linebacker Ted Hendricks. Sipe's floater wobbled through the wicked winds, giving Davis time to gain a step on the Browns' tight end. The ball fell into the hands of Davis, who tumbled to the frozen gridiron, leaving a frustrated, flailing Newsome behind.

The exhilarating ride was suddenly, shockingly over.

8. Dull Days, Losing Ways

The Kardiac Kids had reached their zenith in 1980 as the playoff loss to Oakland ignited a rapid reversal in fortunes for the Browns. The team fell on hard times, seeing little success over the next four years, with only one winning season (and a playoff team with a losing record). Sam Rutigliano was given his walking papers at the midpoint of the 1984 season when the Browns' record stood at 1-7 following a 12-9 last-second loss to the lowly Bengals in Cincinnati. Rutigliano was replaced by defensive coordinator Marty Schottenheimer, a former linebacker who instilled into the team a new sense of pride, toughness, and discipline.

The Browns opened the **1981** season with an embarrassing 44-14 drubbing by Dan Fouts and the San Diego Chargers - a.k.a., "Air Coryell" - in the much-hyped *Monday Night Football* season-opener September 7 in Cleveland Stadium. They followed that with a miserable offensive performance in a 9-3 loss to Houston at the Stadium on a day in which they were outscored by even the Indians, Cleveland's bumbling baseball team, who lost, 8-6, to Detroit some 200 miles to the northwest in the Motor City.

The Browns were able to turn it around somewhat but were a model of inconsistency all season, and stood at 5-6 following a shocking victory over the Super Bowl-bound 49ers on November 15 in Candlestick Park. With their division title hopes all but dead, what little hope the Browns did have for a second straight playoff berth went out the window with convincing losses - at home, no less - to Pittsburgh (32-10) and Cincinnati (41-21). Cleveland failed to win another game and finished the season with a 10-turnover performance in a 42-21 loss to Seattle in the Kingdome. The Browns finished 5-11, in the Central cellar, a complete reversal from 1980.

Although Sipe threw for nearly 4,000 yards in 1981, his touchdown passes dropped from 30 the year before to 17, while his interceptions total jumped from 14 to 25. Newsome, on a more positive note, caught 69 passes - a team record at the time - for 1,002 yards, becoming the first Brown to attain 1,000 yards receiving in 13 years.

The Browns acquired two solid linebackers in **1982** - Chip Banks and Tom Cousineau. Banks, from Southern California, was Cleveland's top selection in the NFL Draft that year. The Browns picked up Cousineau, the No. 1 pick in the 1979 draft (by Buffalo) who had spent three years in the Canadian Football League, in a trade with the Bills. The team also selected center Mike Baab from Texas with their fourth pick in the 1982 draft.

The Browns opened the 1982 slate the same place the 1981 season ended so sourly - Seattle. But this time, the visitors weren't "sleeping." They were much improved, and defeated the Seahawks, 21-7. Clay Matthews suffered a broken left ankle, though, and would not return until late in the season. The next week, the Browns played well despite losing in the last minute to Philadelphia. A players' strike wiped out the next seven weeks of the season (each team, however, made up one of the seven games the first weekend of January, pushing back the first three rounds of the expanded playoff format). Upon returning from the walkout, the Browns edged New England, 10-7, on a last-second field goal by former Steeler Matt Bahr, obtained in a deal with the 49ers the year before. Next, though, came an embarrassing 31-14 loss on Thanksgiving Day in Dallas, a game in which Paul McDonald, a third-year southpaw from Southern California, came off the bench to replace Sipe, and led two late touchdown drives.

With the team 2-4 following defeats to San Diego and Cincinnati, Rutigliano benched Sipe once and for all in 1982 and gave McDonald the starting nod for the December 19 home game against Pittsburgh. McDonald directed the Browns to a 10-9 victory over the Steelers in a mudfest and then a 20-14 conquest of the Oilers, giving Cleveland four wins. Although beaten by the Steelers on the final Sunday (in the makeup game), the Browns knew the only way they would miss the playoffs was if Buffalo and New England, both 4-4, played to a tie the same day in Foxboro, Massachusetts. The Patriots won, 30-19, giving Cleveland, 4-5, the eighth and final AFC Playoff position in the postseason tournament. The Browns were awarded the playoff spot over the Bills and Seattle, the AFC's two other 4-5 teams, based on a better conference record (4-3) than the Bills (3-3) and Seahawks (3-5). The Browns, along with the Detroit Lions (eighth in the NFC at 4-5), became the first - and only - two teams in NFL history to qualify for postseason play with losing records.

With McDonald still at the controls, the Browns stayed right with the top-seeded Los Angeles Raiders in a first-round playoff game in the Los Angeles Memorial Coliseum - but only for 30 minutes. They trailed by three at the intermission but folded in the second half, and lost, 27-10.

Banks was named 1982 NFL Defensive Rookie of the Year by the Associated Press and *Pro Football Weekly*.

It looked as if the Kardiac in Cleveland was beginning to resurface as the **1983** season got underway. Sipe, who had outdueled McDonald in training camp to win his job back, led the Browns to four victories in their first six games, including tight ones over San Diego and the Jets. Against the Chargers in Southern California, Sipe hit rookie tight end Harry Holt on a 48-yard touchdown catch-and-run to give the Browns a 30-24 victory in sudden death. Against the Jets, Bahr connected on a 43-yard field goal as time expired for a 10-7 home win.

As the team went into a tailspin - including a six-interception performance by Sipe in a 44-17 defeat at Pittsburgh - Rutigliano went to McDonald, giving him the starting nod for the October 30 home game against Houston. McDonald performed admirably in a 25-19 overtime win, but Sipe was back as the starter the next week against Green Bay. After falling to the Packers, Cleveland won three straight, including successive shutouts of the Buccaneers and Patriots - the Browns' first back-to-back bagels in 32 years - and stood at 8-5, just a game behind the Steelers with three to go.

Aware that a win in Denver on December 4 would create a first-place tie (Pittsburgh had been upset at home by Cincinnati earlier in the day), the Browns ran into a buzz saw - a rookie quarterback by the name of John Elway - who gave Cleveland a Mile High migraine. The former Stanford star completed 16 of 24 passes for 284 yards in a 27-6 Browns' loss, the first of several Cleveland defeats to Elway-led Denver teams in the years to come. About the only bright spot in the Broncos game was Steve Cox's 58-yard field goal in the second quarter (a team record for longest field goal until Cox would break his own mark a year later with a 60-yarder in Cincinnati).

If the defeat in Denver wasn't bad enough, what followed was. The next week in the Astrodome, the Browns were upset by a Houston Oilers team that had won just a single game all year long. The 34-27 defeat, a game in which the Browns fought back from a 24-6 deficit to take a late lead, only to lose it, ended any division title hopes and even put Cleveland's wild card aspirations in jeapordy.

Cleveland Browns Facts & Trivia

A 30-17 triumph over Pittsburgh in the season finale on December 18 at home salvaged a 9-7 record and second-place finish for the Browns; they wound up a game behind the Steelers. Seattle's win over New England later that day, however, left Cleveland as the only one of five 9-7 teams to miss the NFL Playoffs. The Browns lost out to the Seahawks and Broncos, the AFC's two other 9-7 clubs, for the two conference wild card spots, due to their defeats to Denver, and also Seattle, during the season.

The victory over Pittsburgh was Sipe's final game in a Cleveland - and NFL - uniform. He proved recent rumors correct by signing with the New Jersey Generals of the rival United States Football League (USFL) after the season. Despite lingering arm problems, Sipe enjoyed a fine year, throwing for 3,566 yards and an AFC-high 26 touchdowns, completing nearly 59 percent of his passes. He also had 23 interceptions, though. Sipe left Cleveland as the club's all-time leader in several categories, most notably passing yards, with 23,713, which remains tops in team history. Meanwhile, Newsome broke his own team mark by snagging 89 receptions in 1983.

With Sipe gone, the Browns embarked on a new era in **1984** as McDonald had the starting quarterback job all to himself. New additions included safeties Don Rogers and Chris Rockins, the team's top two picks in the NFL Draft, respectively. Other draftees included Rickey Bolden, who switched from tight end to offensive tackle early in his career, wide receiver Brian Brennan, and fullback Earnest Byner.

McDonald found the going rough in 1984 - he was sacked a team-record 55 times (right tackle Cody Risien's season-ending knee injury in the final preseason game didn't help) - as Cleveland dropped eight of its first nine games and finished 5-11, in third place in the now weak Central Division. The team's problems stemmed from its inability to perform in the clutch. Other than routs by Seattle and San Francisco, the Browns were competitive in every game. In fact, eight of their defeats came by seven points or less. Schottenheimer's no-nonsense approach made an immediate impact as the team split its last eight games after he succeeded Rutigliano. Newsome, a 1999 Hall of Fame inductee, duplicated his 1983 receptions total of 89, for 1,001 yards. Another bright spot was Byner, an 11th-round pick from East Carolina, who rushed for 188 yards in the team's season-ending triumph in Houston.

Cleveland Browns Facts & Trivia

Browns Blues I

The following is a recap of the Cleveland Browns' frustrating failures during the 1984 season:

(In games in which the Browns were leading, their largest [also sometimes only] lead is given; if they were leading by that margin more than once, their latest lead [by quarter] is given)

*Browns lead L.A. Rams, 17-10 (4th) ... lose, 20-17 (Sept. 9 at L.A.)

KILLER - Duriel Harris's unsportsmanlike penalty on a late drive that destroys Cleveland's chances for at least a game-tying field goal.

*Browns lead Denver, 14-0 (2nd) ... lose, 24-14 (Sept. 16 at Cle.)
KILLER - Defensive back Randy Robbins's 62-yard interception return for a touchdown with 37 seconds left.

*Browns lead Kansas City, 6-3 (4th) ... lose, 10-6 (Sept. 30 at K.C.)
KILLER - Eleven sacks by the Chiefs' defense.

*Browns lead New England, 16-3 (3rd) ... lose, 17-16 (Oct. 7 at Cle.)
KILLER - Sam Rutigliano's decision to throw the ball rather than try for the winning field goal with the ball on the Patriots' 21-yard line and 23 seconds remaining; McDonald is intercepted.

*Browns lead N.Y. Jets, 20-17 (4th) ... lose, 24-20 (Oct. 14 at Cle.)
KILLER - Three straight sacks - two by defensive end Mark Gastineau - that stall the Browns' final drive.

*Browns lose to Cincinnati, 12-9 (Oct. 21 at Cin.)
KILLER - Eight - count 'em, eight - dropped passes. Jim Breech's last-second field goal from 33 yards out wins it.

*Browns lead New Orleans, 14-10 (4th) ... lose, 16-14 (Oct. 28 at Cle.)
KILLER - A holding call on offensive tackle Bill Contz that negates a 40-yard pass completion from McDonald to Brian Brennan at the

Saints' five-yard line with less than two minutes left and the Browns leading by one. Morten Andersen's 53-yard field goal wins it with 0:00 showing on the clock (Mike Hudak, pro sportswriter for the former *Painesville* (Ohio) *Telegraph* from 1983-85, recalled a bleak aftermath for everyone involved with the team, from players all the way up to management. "I'll never forget seeing [Browns Director of Public Relations] Kevin Byrne leaning up against a wall in tears," said Hudak, now co-managing editor of *The Free Press* in Canton, Ohio).

*Browns lead Cincinnati, 17-7 (4th) ... lose, 20-17 (OT) (Dec. 2 at Cle.)
KILLER - A blocked punt by Rodney Holman deep in Browns territory with 1:08 left in regulation and the Bengals trailing by seven; that leads to Anthony Munoz's tackle-eligible touchdown catch from Boomer Esiason, forcing overtime.

*Browns lead Pittsburgh, 3-0 (1st) ... lose, 23-20 (Dec. 9 at Pit.)
KILLER - Two crucial third-quarter interceptions by McDonald. Gary Anderson's 34-yard trey with five seconds left wins it.

9. The Denver Dilemma

After having lifted the team's spirits in the second half of the 1984 season, Marty Schottenheimer led Cleveland to a division title in 1985, albeit with a .500 record. A bitter loss to the Miami Dolphins in the divisional playoffs, frustrating as it was, seemed to give the team a resolve, though, as the Browns responded by winning 41 regular-season games - the most in the AFC - over the next four seasons.

Behind local-boy-turned-star-quarterback Bernie Kosar, the Browns appeared in three AFC Championship games during that period, losing to the Denver Broncos each time - the first two in gut-wrenching fashion, the third under the direction of a new head coach. Philosophical differences between Art Modell and Schottenheimer led to the latter's resignation following the 1988 season. That, in turn, led to the hiring of longtime defensive guru Bud Carson, the architect of Pittsburgh's vaunted "Steel Curtain" defense of the 1970s (Carson was the Steelers' defensive coordinator from 1973-77), as head coach on January 27, 1989. Also notable during the late 1980s was the popularization of the "Dawg Pound" - i.e., the Cleveland Stadium bleachers section. Cornerbacks Hanford Dixon and Frank Minnifield (with some help from linebacker Eddie Johnson) were the ones responsible for starting the crazy canine antics of the fans in the bleachers by barking - yes, barking - to the people there, actually late in the 1984 season. Those in the Dawg Pound more than took the corners' cues when they began woofing, wearing dog masks, painting their faces brown, orange, and white, and - yes - even eating dog biscuits. The Dawg Pound, although a bit too boisterous (i.e, fans hurling biscuits, batteries, and eggs, among other inanimate objects at opposing players) at times, was a definite boost to the Browns and their new winning ways.

With the arrival of Kosar in **1985** through the supplemental draft that year (and via some slick maneuvering by Executive Vice President of Football Operations Ernie Accorsi) came an air of hometown pride throughout the city of Cleveland. Raised in Boardman, Ohio, just outside nearby Youngstown, Kosar made it clear he desired to play in Cleveland, an uncommon trait among many professional athletes at the time. Other new faces on offense included wide receiver Reggie Langhorne, whom the Browns selected in the seventh round of the NFL Draft that year, and running back Kevin Mack, taken in the supplemental draft the year before, after a brief stint in the United States Football League (USFL).

Kosar, the former University of Miami star who had led the Hurricanes to the 1983 NCAA championship at age nineteen, didn't see action his rookie year until Week 6. That's when veteran Gary Danielson, acquired in a trade with the Detroit Lions before the season to stand in for Kosar until the rookie was ready to take over, went down with a severe right shoulder injury in the second quarter against New England. Although Kosar fumbled his first snap, he completed his first seven passes as the Browns used a late goal-line stand to defeat the Patriots, 24-20, in front of the hometown fans, leaving the team alone atop the Central Division for the first time in two years.

Kosar's first start was a winning one as he connected with Clarence Weathers for a 68-yard touchdown pass in a 21-6 triumph over the Oilers the next week in the Astrodome, upping Cleveland's record to 4-2. With Danielson still out and Kosar the starter, the Browns lost their next four games, though, to drop to 4-6 and a tie with Houston for last place. But with the AFC Central experiencing another down year overall, the Browns were far from out of the race. The rookie got the team back on track by leading the Browns to a victory over Buffalo - albeit one of the weaker teams in the league. Schottenheimer opted for the veteran Danielson to start the next Sunday at home against Cincinnati. In his first action since the Patriots game, Danielson directed the Browns to a key win over the Bengals when he beat a blitz and hooked up with Weathers on a perfect 72-yard pass play for a touchdown early in the third quarter - the Browns' only pass of the entire second half - that virtually sealed a 24-6 victory.

A week later in the Meadowlands, Danielson - aching arm and all - came off the bench to engineer two late touchdown drives in a stirring 35-33 comeback win over the New York Giants, Cleveland's highest point total in two seasons. The Browns dodged a bullet when Giants kicker Eric Schubert misfired on a 34-yard field goal try as time expired. The team was 7-6 and alone atop the AFC Central once again. Despite Danielson's gutsy performance in Giants Stadium, the veteran was done for the year. Late in the New York game, he had re-aggravated his shoulder on a harmless swing pass to Mack that fell incomplete as the Browns were driving toward the winning score.

As a result, it was up to the rookie Kosar to lead the Browns to their first postseason berth in three years. Kosar produced just one victory - a 28-21 triumph over Houston - in the final three games, but it was enough for the team to sneak into the playoffs, its modest 8-8 record good enough for the championship of the aforementioned weak Central Division ("Eight Is Enough" would have been a fitting title for the team's 1985 NFL Films highlights video, huh?). The Browns became the first, and remain the only, team in NFL history to win a division (conference, league prior to the formation of divisions) title with a .500 record.

The young Browns were heavy underdogs in their divisional playoff matchup with the Dan Marino-led Dolphins in the Orange Bowl on January 4, 1986. Earnest Byner's relentless effort sparked Cleveland, though, and when he scored his second touchdown on a 66-yard run early in the third quarter, the Browns found themselves ahead, 21-3. In addition, cornerbacks Hanford Dixon and Frank Minnifield, Cleveland's "Corner Brothers," were stifling Miami's vaunted "Marks Brothers," receivers Mark Duper and Mark Clayton, holding the pair to one reception between the two. One of the most stunning upsets in NFL Playoff history turned to ashes as the Dolphins rebounded to pull out a 24-21 victory. Despite the tough defeat, Byner set a Browns record for most rushing yards in a postseason game with 161. The team's 251 yards on the ground is also a club record.

Mack (1,104), United Press International AFC Rookie of the Year in 1985, teamed with Byner (1,002) to become just the third pair of backs to attain 1,000 yards rushing in one season for the same team.

Whereas the focus in 1985 was the running game, Byner's early-season ankle injury in **1986** led to the unfolding of one of the league's premier passing attacks, under the direction of new offensive coordinator Lindy Infante. The addition of wide receiver Webster Slaughter from San Diego State, Cleveland's top pick in the draft that year, was a big boost to the offense.

Despite the tragic death of Don Rogers to a drug overdose some three-and-a-half weeks before training camp began, the Browns rallied to an unbeaten preseason and hung tough in a season-opening 41-31 loss to the defending champion Bears in Soldier Field. The Browns won four of their first six, including a rather satisfying 27-24 triumph over Pittsburgh October 5 in Three Rivers Stadium, highlighted by Gerald "The Ice Cube" McNeil's 100-yard kickoff return for a touchdown just before halftime. The victory was the Browns' first ever in Three Rivers after 16 defeats, finally ending the Three Rivers Jinx.

Next came an embarrassing home loss to the previously winless Packers, but two dome wins - a come-from-behind job in Minnesota and a 24-9 victory in Indianapolis - got the Browns back on track. A week later on *Monday Night Football*, Kosar officially "came of age," had his coming-out party. Although he didn't throw for a single touchdown, the young quarterback passed for more than 400 yards in outdueling Marino and the Dolphins, as the Browns avenged the bitter playoff loss from 10 months earlier; they defeated Miami, 26-16, at home in a game that wasn't nearly as close as the final score indicated. After a sound beating by the Raiders in Los Angeles, a game in which Kosar was sacked six times, the Browns rebounded to improve to 8-4 with a 37-31 sudden death win at home against the Steelers when Kosar connected with Slaughter for a 36-yard touchdown pass 6:37 into the extra period. The Browns won out and finished 12-4, clinching the division title on December 14 by blowing out the supposedly superior Bengals, 34-3, in Cincinnati. Cleveland's record, tops in the AFC, earned it home field advantage throughout the AFC Playoffs.

Schottenheimer, voted AFC Coach of the Year by United Press International and the Pro Football Writers Association of America, led the Browns into the postseason with a divisional playoff matchup at home against the New York Jets on January 3, 1987. Assisted by a costly roughing-the-passer penalty on Jets defensive end Mark Gastineau, Kosar led his team back from a 10-point - yes, 10-point - deficit with just 4:14 to go in the game, to an incredible 23-20 double-overtime victory. It was the Browns' first postseason win in 17 years. Kosar, who passed for 3,854 yards during the season, completed 33 of 64 attempts against the Jets for an NFL Playoff record 489 yards. The AFC Championship was next.

Eight days later in the title contest against the Denver Broncos at home on January 11, Kosar found Brian Brennan on a spectacular 48-yard touchdown catch-and-run late in the game; Brennan caught Kosar's underthrown aerial at the 16-yard line, completely faked out Broncos strong safety Dennis Smith, and waltzed into the end zone. Brennan's heroics gave the Browns a 20-13 lead - and an apparent berth in Super Bowl XXI - with just 5:43 left in the game. That's when John Elway took control, however. With the Broncos pinned back on their own two-yard line following the kickoff, the fourth-year "Browns Killer" led his team on a remarkable 98-yard touchdown drive - including a 20-yard completion to receiver Mark Jackson on a third-and-18 play - to tie the game with 38 seconds left. The final salvo of the 15-play march was a five-yard scoring strike to Jackson with but 37 seconds left. Elway's masterpiece, known simply as "The Drive," was the impetus for Denver's stunning 23-20 overtime win.

Just like five years before, the Browns split their first two games in **1987** when a players' strike surfaced. But this time, the walkout canceled only one week of games (three weeks were played, though, with replacement players, for the most part, while the majority of regular NFL players negotiated with management). The "replacement" Browns - with help from a few selected regular team members in the final "replacement" game against the Bengals - won two of three to give the team a 3-2 record heading into an October

Cleveland Browns Facts & Trivia

26 Monday night meeting with the Los Angeles Rams in Cleveland Stadium. Free safety Felix Wright stole the show as his two first-half interception returns - of 68 and 40 yards, the latter for a touchdown - lifted Cleveland to a 30-17 victory.

On November 22, the Browns carried a 6-3 record into the Astrodome for a showdown with Houston, also 6-3, in a battle for the AFC Central lead. The Browns destroyed the Oilers, 40-7, but successive losses to the 49ers and Colts dropped Cleveland into a three-way tie for first with Houston and Pittsburgh on December 6, all three teams 7-5. The Browns, though, showed their grit by beating the Bengals, Raiders, and Steelers - the last two on the road - to finish 10-5 and Central Division Champions for the third straight year.

After ousting Indianapolis, 38-21, in the divisional playoffs at home - avenging the regular-season loss to the Colts - the Browns packed their bags for Denver and a rematch with the Broncos for the AFC title. Denver dominated early and led, 21-3, by halftime. The score was 28-10 early in the third quarter when Kosar and Byner went to work and led a brilliant comeback that fell just short, when with Cleveland down by seven late in the game and the ball on the Broncos' eight-yard line, Byner, bursting off left tackle and smelling the end zone, was stripped of the football by cornerback Jeremiah Castille at the three-yard line; Castille then fell on the ball at the three. Byner's blunder (or Castille's great defensive play) became aptly known as "The Fumble," and Denver eked out a second straight trip to the Super Bowl, 38-33.

Kosar, the thinking man's quarterback, led the AFC in passing in 1987 with a 95.4 quarterback rating, tossing 22 touchdown passes and just nine interceptions in 12 games. He drew accolades galore, despite his awkward throwing style. "He doesn't look like a fleet of foot, nimble athlete, but he's an athlete because he's a quick-minded guy," said Sam Wyche, head coach of the Cincinnati Bengals from 1984-91 and the Tampa Bay Buccaneers from 1992-95, in the NFL Films documentary *No Apologies Necessary.* "He's able to have instant recall as to where the ball should be. He throws the ball to the man that's supposed to get it, on time, and therefore cuts down the chances of a knockdown or an interception."

Fred Smerlas, a nose tackle for 14 seasons from 1979-92, mainly with the Buffalo Bills, likened Kosar to a walking football computer in the same documentary. "He reads things so well," Smerlas said. "He can get himself out of danger by thinking real quick."

Danger, though, was one thing Kosar was unable to escape in the opening game the following season. The **1988** Browns were many prognosticators' preseason picks to represent the AFC in the Super Bowl when an avalanche of quarterback injuries that began when Kosar was blindsided by Chiefs safety Lloyd Burruss in an opening-day win in Kansas City stacked the deck against the team from the start. But with Kosar, Danielson, Mike Pagel, and Don Strock (signed for emergency purposes) calling the signals at one time or another, the Browns were still able to sneak into the playoffs as a wild card, finishing in second place in the Central Division with a 10-6 record, two games behind the Bengals.

The Browns qualified for the postseason, when in the finale, the veteran Strock engineered a memorable 28-23 comeback victory over Houston in the snow after his team trailed, 23-7. That earned the Browns a matchup with none other than the 10-6 Oilers in the AFC Wild Card game six days later on Christmas Eve, again in Cleveland (the Browns finished ahead of Houston based on a better division record [4-2] than the Oilers [3-3]). In the playoff game, Slaughter's two-yard touchdown grab from Pagel pulled the Browns to within one point with 31 seconds left. It was too little, too late, though. Houston won the penalty-marred contest, 24-23.

Soon after stepping down, Schottenheimer went on to become head coach of the Kansas City Chiefs.

Under new head coach Carson, the Browns opened the **1989** season with two convincing wins. First, they benefited from (and forced) nine Pittsburgh turnovers in a 51-0 destruction of the Steelers in Three Rivers Stadium. Next came a 38-24 victory over the Jets, a team for which Carson had been defensive coordinator the preceding four years. Wright, who would go on to lead the NFL with nine interceptions during the season, picked off two Ken O'Brien passes in the win. The Browns scored just 47 points over the next four games. The lone triumph in the horrific stretch was a rather satisfying one, though - a 16-13 home win over Denver on Matt Bahr's last-second 48-yard field goal, the Browns' first win over the Broncos in 15 years. The Cleveland defense limited Elway to six completions in 19 attempts, albeit for 198 yards. The Broncos' quarterback was intercepted once and sacked four times, once by right defensive tackle Michael Dean Perry, who was second on the team in the sack category with seven for the season, and was voted

Cleveland Browns Facts & Trivia

1989 AFC Defensive Most Valuable Player by United Press International.

The offense rose from the dead on October 23 against the Bears on *Monday Night Football* as Kosar hooked up with Slaughter for a 97-yard pass play that - surprise! - went for a touchdown. The 27-7 victory sparked a four-game winning streak that landed the Browns in first place in the AFC Central and gave them a 7-3 record. A 10-10 tie with Kansas City in Schottenheimer's imminent return to Northeast Ohio, and three straight losses, however, dropped Cleveland to 7-6-1 and the brink of playoff elimination. An overtime win at home against the Vikings - on a Pagel-to-Van Waiters pass on a fake field goal - put the Browns right back in contention, though, and set up a season-ending Saturday night showdown in Houston for the AFC Central Division Championship. The Browns jumped out to a big lead against the Oilers, fell behind (with the help of a curious botched lateral attempt by the usually cool-headed Clay Matthews), then rode the shoulders of Mack on a late drive to his own winning score - a four-yard run with 39 seconds left - and their fourth division title in five years, ending 9-6-1.

After pulling a Houdini by barely beating Buffalo, 34-30, in a divisional playoff shootout at home - finalized when Matthews, redeeming himself for his blunder in the Astrodome two weeks earlier, picked off Jim Kelly at the Cleveland one with three seconds to go - the Browns headed for Denver and yet another conference title tilt with the Broncos, their third in four years. Once again, the Browns fell behind in the madness of Mile High Stadium, cut the margin to three, then watched helplessly as Elway took control in the late going. Denver denied the Browns a trip to the Super Bowl once again, this time, 37-21.

10. Bummed Out in Brownstown

The 1990s brought several changes to the Cleveland organization, beginning with a dismal 1990 season that saw yet another coaching change when Bud Carson was replaced by former Browns defensive back Jim Shofner, a longtime Browns assistant, on an interim basis after nine games. When the season ended, Art Modell went searching for who at the time he said would be his final head coach.

On February 5, 1991, Modell announced the hiring of 38-year-old Bill Belichick, who nine days earlier was in Tampa Stadium as the New York Giants' defensive coordinator, directing his unit in the Giants' victory over Buffalo in Super Bowl XXV. Modell handed Belichick a high degree of authority - he allowed him to hire his own staff and to have a say come draft day, among other things. Belichick utilized this power to gut the club of many veteran players who had contributed to Cleveland's recent success. That, in addition to his ho hum play-calling and lack of communication skills, didn't exactly endear him to the fans, and when he talked Modell into releasing Bernie Kosar midway through the 1993 season, that was the final straw. Belichick officially joined the ranks of Frank Lane and Ted Stepien as one of the most hated leaders in the history of Cleveland professional sports.

Despite his shortcomings, Belichick - who did have a fine defensive mind - managed to improve the Browns from the depths of despair to competitiveness with three respectable yet losing seasons; in his fourth year, 1994, the Browns actually qualified for the postseason, and even came within a victory of the AFC Championship game. But even through the successful 1994 campaign, the bond between the team and the town that was so strong for years was missing. Then, in 1995, not only was the bond gone but the Browns themselves were bidding farewell, too. With the team still in contention (albeit with a 4-5 record), Modell did something no one ever dreamed would happen - he made it official on November 6 that he would relocate the team to Baltimore after the 1995 season, himself joining (actually overtaking) the ranks of the aforementioned Lane and Stepien. Modell's announcement was not unexpected; rumors had been swirling for months. With sadness in the air, the Browns finished the year 5-11 in what many believed at the time to be the final season in the history of the Cleveland Browns.

The **1990** season got off to a sour start before it even began as a number of veterans held out during training camp, and an already questionable offensive line lost longtime stalwart Cody Risien and the always-tough Rickey Bolden to retirement. The Browns dropped three of their first four games, including a 34-0 rout in Kansas City on September 30. Next, though, came a spectacular 30-29 Monday night miracle in Denver on newcomer Jerry Kauric's last-second field goal, Cleveland's first win in Mile High Stadium in 18 years, and the one shining moment in an otherwise "Season From Hell."

The Browns not only lost their next eight games - the team's longest losing skein in 15 years - but lost their head coach, too, as Carson's firing occurred the day after a 42-0 rout at home by Buffalo on November 4, a game in which Mike Pagel started in place of the struggling Kosar. The embarrassing loss to the Bills was the worst shutout loss - and worst home defeat - ever for the Browns. Kosar returned to the starting lineup in the next game against Houston until he injured his right thumb during a 13-10 victory over the Falcons on December 16, and was done for the year. Kosar wound up completing 230 of 423 passes for 2,562 yards, with 10 touchdown passes and 15 interceptions. His quarterback ranking was only 65.7.

Under Shofner, the team lost seven of eight, finishing a franchise-worst 3-13, in the far reaches of the Central Division basement. The Browns didn't just lose in 1990, they lost big. They lost seven games by 15 points or more and yielded 462 points, by far the most in team history. In addition, they were shut out a club-record three times.

Belichick's first Browns team was improved but had a penchant for poor play in the clutch. In fact, the **1991** Browns stood at 4-4 and in solid playoff contention when they experienced a nightmarish November, suffering three consecutive crushing defeats by a total of eight points, squandering late-game leads in each. Victories over the Chiefs and Colts renewed slim playoff hopes, but three losses to end the season gave the Browns a 6-10 record and third-place finish.

Despite the team's sub par performance, Kosar rebounded nicely from the disaster the year before, passing for 3,487 yards, 18 touchdowns, and just nine interceptions, completing more than 62 percent of his passes. He broke Bart Starr's 26-year-old NFL record for most consecutive passes without an interception (308 dating back to - shockingly - the horrific 1990 season, to Starr's 294). Meanwhile, Leroy Hoard, a second-year fullback out of Michigan, scored 11 touchdowns - nine receiving, two rushing - many in spectacular fashion. In addition, the Browns, last in the league the year before with a minus-24 in the giveaway/takeaway category, led the AFC with a plus-15.

After starting the **1992** season 0-2 and losing Kosar to a broken ankle, backup Todd Philcox stepped in and hooked up with Eric Metcalf for three touchdown passes (Metcalf also scored on a six-yard run) as the Browns beat the Raiders on the road, 28-16, for win No. 1. However, Philcox suffered a broken thumb on his throwing hand in the second quarter of the Raiders game and was placed on the injured reserve list until mid-November. Thus Mike Tomczak, acquired as a free agent the week before the Raiders game, took over as the starter and led the Browns to a split in their next eight games. With Kosar back, the Browns routed the Bears and Bengals to improve to 7-6 and renew slim playoff hopes. However, a lethargic loss to the Lions and a crushing defeat to Houston ended those hopes quickly. The Browns finished in third place with a record of 7-9, losing their last three games for the second year in a row.

The Browns began the **1993** season 3-0 - including upsets of the 49ers and Raiders - for the first time since 1979, when they opened with four wins. In the midst of a quarterback controversy between Kosar and Vinny Testaverde, obtained in an off-season trade with Tampa Bay, the team lost two straight. Belichick decided to stop playing musical quarterbacks, benched the struggling Kosar, and named Testaverde, a former teammate of Kosar's at the University of Miami, his starter for the October 17 game against the Bengals in Riverfront Stadium. Testaverde passed for three touchdowns in leading the Browns to a 28-17 victory, upping Cleveland's record to 4-2 and setting up a showdown with Pittsburgh, also 4-2, seven days later in Cleveland Stadium for the Central Division lead.

Although Testaverde was now the main man, Eric Metcalf was the hero against the Steelers, returning punts 91 and 75 yards - both for touchdowns, the second the game-winner with 2:05 left - that stunned the Steelers in a memorable 28-23 victory. Metcalf

Cleveland Browns Facts & Trivia

became the first - and only - player in NFL annals to return two punts for touchdowns 75 yards or more in the same game. Testaverde was sandwiched between hits from linebackers Kevin Greene and Reggie Barnes in the fourth quarter against the Steelers, and was out of action for the next four games with a separated shoulder. So despite the early-season quarterback controversy, the Browns - with Kosar back as the starter - found themselves in first place at 5-2, but with old tormentor John Elway and the Denver Broncos coming to town.

Although things may have seemed somewhat promising on the surface, there was turmoil brewing behind the scenes between coach and quarterback. What many believed to be a personality conflict between the two - Belichick called it Kosar's " ... lack of production and loss of physical skills," as taken from the *Plain Dealer* in Cleveland on November 9, 1993 - led to the veteran quarterback's release from the team on November 8, a move that warranted local front page newspaper headlines and dominated area radio waves. The day before, the Broncos had routed the Browns, 29-14, in a beating much worse than the final score showed. Kosar had drawn his coach's wrath for the final time when he evidently drew up a play in the dirt toward the end of the loss to the Broncos. The play turned out to be a 38-yard touchdown pass to wide receiver Michael Jackson, Kosar's final pass in a Cleveland uniform. Belichick had apparently called for a running play.

With Kosar gone and Testaverde injured, all the team had left was Philcox, who had attempted all of 37 passes in his brief career, and Brad Goebel, signed as the emergency third quarterback two weeks before when Testaverde went down (Goebel had been on and off the roster several times since being acquired in a trade with Philadelphia in August 1992).

Belichick believed - at least he said he did - that Philcox gave the Browns a better chance to win than the floundering yet battle-tested Kosar. Thus the starting quarterback job fell into the feeble hands of Philcox, who subsequently fumbled his first snap that was a foreshadow of things to come in an embarrassing 22-5 loss to Seattle on November 14 in the Kingdome. After two more defeats ensued, Testaverde returned to action midway through the second quarter of a home game against New Orleans on December 5, and helped finish off the Saints in a 17-13 victory, evening Cleveland's record at 6-6.

So despite the four straight losses prior to the Saints game, the

Cleveland Browns Facts & Trivia

Browns were fortunate in that their fast start had them in position to actually make a run at the playoffs. They traveled to first-place Houston with a chance - remarkably - to realistically move right back in the thick of the Central Division title hunt. In a crazy contest that had a little bit of everything, a Cris Dishman interception - Testaverde's second of the day - resulted in Al Del Greco's winning field goal from 25 yards out early in the fourth quarter. The Oilers' 19-17 victory put to rest the Browns' division title dreams and all but ended their hopes for a wild card berth.

The Browns finished their tumultuous season at 7-9 and in third place for the second straight year, out of the playoffs once again. Testaverde performed admirably under trying circumstances, completing 130 of 230 passes for 1,797 yards, with 14 touchdown passes and only nine interceptions. Included was a 21-for-23 performance - an NFL completion percentage (91.3) record for quarterbacks with at least 20 pass attempts in a game - against the Rams in Los Angeles on December 26 (incredibly, both of Testaverde's incompletions were *intentional*).

The Browns enjoyed a soft early-season schedule in **1994**, starting 6-1 while feasting on the likes of the Bengals (twice), Cardinals, and Colts. Denver brought the Browns back to earth with a 26-14 victory on October 30 in Mile High Stadium. The Browns rebounded, though, by beating Drew Bledsoe and the Patriots at home and surprising Philadelphia in Veterans Stadium, leaving the team 8-2 and in first place, one game ahead of Pittsburgh. The Browns' record was their finest in the first 10 games of a season in nearly 30 years. The Browns split their next four games - including a stunning upset of two-time defending champion Dallas in Texas Stadium - leaving them at 10-4, a game behind the red-hot Steelers heading into a showdown in Three Rivers Stadium on December 18. Pittsburgh, which had beaten the Browns earlier in the season, did it again, winning handily, 17-7, to clinch the Central Division title. Cleveland went on to finish 11-5, one game behind the Steelers, and did qualify for the playoffs as a wild card team.

The Browns defeated New England again, 20-13, in an AFC Wild Card affair in Cleveland on New Year's Day 1995. A week later in the divisional playoffs, the Browns made a return trip to Pittsburgh for their third meeting of the season - and first-ever postseason matchup - with the Steelers. The third time, though, was undoubtedly not the charm for the Browns, with mistakes plaguing them throughout. They were completely outclassed, falling, 29-9, in a game that was actually much worse for Cleveland than the final score indicated.

Despite the dreadful performance in the playoff loss to Pittsburgh, the Cleveland defense had been solid during the regular season as the team yielded just 204 points, fewest in the NFL. Free safety Eric Turner tied Cardinals cornerback Aeneas Williams for the league lead in interceptions with nine. Testaverde, relieved by backup Mark Rypien for a few games during the season due to a recurring concussion, had a decent year, too, completing more than 55 percent of his passes for 2,575 yards and 16 touchdowns. As had been his trademark throughout his career, though, he also had a knack for the untimely interception (he was picked off on 18 occasions). Hoard, meanwhile, rushed for 890 yards, the most by a Cleveland running back since Kevin Mack and Earnest Byner both eclipsed the 1,000-yard barrier nine years earlier.

The Browns began the **1995** season 3-1 and stood atop the Central Division following a 35-17 rout of the undefeated Chiefs on September 24 in Cleveland. But beginning with a mistake-plagued Monday night loss to Buffalo, followed by a 38-20 spanking by the Lions in the Silverdome, the team's glossy record disintegrated. An upset loss to the new division rival expansion Jacksonville Jaguars - at home, no less - prompted Belichick to make a change. He did so by naming rookie Eric Zeier the starting quarterback - to give the team a spark, the coach said - in place of Testaverde, who was actually leading the AFC in passing at the time! Zeier, who had set numerous records while at the University of Georgia, raised some eyebrows by passing the Browns to a dramatic 29-26 overtime win in Cincinnati on October 29 - a game in which Cleveland amassed 480 total yards, the team's highest amount in nearly 10 years - evening the Browns' record at 4-4.

The season, though, turned sour after that - into a nightmare, in fact; Modell's official declaration of the Browns' impending move to Maryland cast a dark cloud over not only the Cleveland metropolitan area and its surrounding regions, but Browns fans everywhere. The day before the ominous announcement, the uninspired Browns - with Zeier launching 54 passes - were zapped, 37-10, by Houston at ... well ... the commencement of calling hours at the Stadium, before a sparse gathering (for Cleveland, at least) of 57,881 (the no-shows numbered nearly 8,000).

The remainder of the 1995 schedule, in which Zeier started two more games before Testaverde returned midway through a 31-20 loss to the Packers on November 19, was basically a moot point, with many fans wondering what it would be like with no professional football in Cleveland, Ohio. The team finished in fourth place (ahead of only the Jaguars) at 5-11, winning just one more game - a 26-10 decision over the Bengals on December 17 - in what many believed at the time to be the final home game in the history of the Cleveland Browns.

BROWNS BIOS

1. Otto Graham: He Was the Man

Ten title games in 10 years.

That's what Otto Graham achieved in his decade as quarterback of the Cleveland Browns from 1946-55. Graham led Cleveland to 10 championship games - four in the All-America Football Conference and six in the NFL. No quarterback in the history of the NFL has come close to duplicating Graham's feat. Not Bart Starr, not Terry Bradshaw, not even Joe Montana. Starr led the Green Bay Packers to six NFL Championship games in 16 years. Bradshaw directed the Pittsburgh Steelers to four Super Bowls in 14 seasons. Montana did the same with the San Francisco 49ers (he also played two seasons with the Kansas City Chiefs). Graham, even minus his four years in the AAFC, led his team to six NFL Championship games in six years.

When it came down to actually winning championships, Graham's numbers were still remarkable. Whereas Starr led his team to five titles in 16 years, Bradshaw his team to four championships in 14 seasons, and Montana his teams to four titles in 16 years, Graham led Cleveland to seven titles in his 10 years overall, three championships in six years in the NFL.

Gridiron greatness, though, did not exactly come on a silver platter for Graham. He wasn't even invited out for the football team his freshman year in college at Northwestern University. Recruited out of high school in 1939 for his basketball talents, Graham was eventually discovered by some Wildcats football coaches in an intramural football league, and was asked to try out for the team. Needless to say, he made it.

After a year as a running back, Graham was switched to quarterback and helped lift the Wildcats from the depths of the Big Ten to a 6-2 overall record and 5-1 Big Ten mark by his senior year, good enough for third place in the conference. He was drafted by the Detroit Lions in 1944 but later became the first player the Browns ever signed. He joined the team in time for its first season in 1946 after spending two years with the University of North Carolina Navy V-12 Pre-Flight team.

Although Graham didn't start Cleveland's very first game (Cliff Lewis did), his first four seasons with the Browns were almost too easy. He threw 86 touchdown passes and just 41 interceptions from 1946-49, and won the AAFC passing title three times. He was named by the AAFC as its Most Valuable Player in 1947. He was voted MVP once again in 1948, this time by the United Press, and shared the conference's own MVP award with 49ers quarterback Frankie Albert. He won the AAFC's own MVP honor once again in 1949.

It wasn't quite as easy, but Graham continued his prowess upon Cleveland entering the NFL in 1950. In the league championship game that year, he tossed four touchdown passes in leading his team past the visiting Los Angeles Rams, 30-28, a contest in which the Browns battled back from an eight-point deficit late in the fourth quarter.

"Otto Graham was one of the greatest throwers of all time," said Tom Fears, a member of that 1950 Rams team, in the NFL Films documentary *The NFL's Greatest Games - Volume II*.

Graham continued to pass the Browns to victory after victory the next three seasons, but Cleveland fell short in the championship game each year, the Detroit Lions the culprits in the final two. After leading the league in passing and winning the NFL's Most Valuable Player award by the United Press in 1953, Graham led the team to its second NFL title in 1954, passing for three touchdowns and scoring three himself as the revenge-minded Browns buried the Lions, 56-10, in the championship game in Cleveland Municipal

Stadium.

Graham retired for a short time but four games into the 1955 exhibition schedule decided to return for one more season. In winning both the league passing title and Most Valuable Player award, once again by the United Press, and also *The Sporting News*, Graham led the Browns to a second straight championship in 1955. In the title game that year, he brilliantly engineered a 38-14 destruction of the Rams in the Los Angeles Memorial Coliseum in what was his final game. When Cleveland head coach Paul Brown removed his star quarterback from the field toward the end of the title contest, the Coliseum crowd responded with a standing ovation, which dumbfounded Graham, who in 1994 was voted to the NFL's 75th Anniversary All-Time team.

"You don't find that happening too often in professional sports, where the opposition - the fans - who hate your guts, to put it mildly, will stand up and give you a standing ovation," Graham fondly recalled in the NFL Films documentary *The Cleveland Browns - Fifty Years of Memories*.

Summoned an emotional Brown in the same documentary, "When he (Graham) got to the sideline, he walked over to me and said, 'Thanks, coach.' And I said, 'Thank you, too, Otto.' That's all that was said."

And other than the fact that 10 years later Graham was inducted into the Pro Football Hall of Fame, nothing more needs to be said.

2. Jim Brown: the One and Only

Imagine Earl Campbell, O.J. Simpson, and Barry Sanders all rolled into one and what do you get? Probably the greatest running back to ever live.

That extraordinary being, many would argue, was not a fictitious character but indeed a reality, and a mainstay in the Cleveland Browns' backfield for nine years, from 1957-65, in the name of Jim Brown. Brown was a fullback who might not have had the brute power of Campbell, the sizzling speed of Simpson, nor the amazing moves of Sanders, but he combined the three skills quite possibly better than any running back ever. "Jimmy Brown, to me, was the best runner that I ever played against," said Ray Nitschke, a Hall of Fame linebacker for the Green Bay Packers from 1958-72, in an NFL Films documentary on Brown. "He had it all. He had great size, he had power, he had speed. But I think his biggest asset was that he was smart. He knew exactly where the defense was, he knew where his offensive players were, and he utilized all the talents that he had. He was just unreal."

Former Dallas Cowboys quarterback Don Meredith recalled the time in 1965 when during a game in the Cotton Bowl in Dallas, he was so enthralled by a run Brown made, he found himself literally applauding for his opponent on the sideline. "It was the greatest run I ever saw," Meredith said in the NFL Films documentary *75 Seasons*. "He went left, and he came back right, and he came back left, and our guys kept hitting him, and they kept falling off. He bounced back and he scored. And I'm on the sideline, and I just have never seen anything like this and I'm saying, 'Wow! God!' And then I realized that I was on the wrong side of this deal."

The accolades just keep coming.

"Jimmy Brown did things humanly impossible," recalled Frank Gifford, a Hall of Famer who played 12 years for the New York Giants in the late 1950s and early 1960s, in the documentary on Brown. "And I watched him do it over and over and over. You watch a film of Jimmy Brown running the football and he's moving away from things that there's no way that he could see. They're instincts that other football players have never even thought of, I'm sure. He had all of that, plus he had the great determination to be the very best."

A major reason Brown just might have been the best running back ever is that tackling him was nearly impossible at times. And even when he did absorb a punishing blow from a defender, his psychological ploys afterwards kept players on opposing defenses thinking. "Once the hitting began, every time I was tackled I'd get up slowly, deliberately," Brown recalled in his autobiography *Out of Bounds*. "Like most things I did as an athlete, this was calculated ... Whenever I would hurt, I'd never let the defense know."

If Brown was still in pain by the time he returned to the huddle, he would hide behind his much larger offensive linemen. That way, the defense couldn't see him suffer. "You let the defense know you're hurt, next play they'll be twice as motivated to finish the job," he wrote in the book. "By getting up with leisure every play, every game, every season, they never knew if I was hurt or if I wasn't. I was screwing with their heads, trying to save my own."

Recalled Chuck Bednarik, a notoriously tough linebacker for the Philadelphia Eagles from 1949-61, in *75 Seasons*, "You gang-tackled him, gave him extracurriculars. He'd get up slow, look at you, and walk back to that huddle and wouldn't say a word ... just come at you again, and again. You'd just say, 'What the hell, what's wrong with this guy? For heaven's sake, when is he going to stop carrying the ball? How much more can he take?'"

Before making his presence known in the NFL, Brown was taking hits from opposing defenders in college as a running back at Syracuse University. After finishing runner-up in the Heisman Trophy voting in 1956, he was Cleveland's top pick in the 1957 NFL Draft. Paul Brown, the star fullback's head coach his first six seasons with the team, knew Brown was a great talent, but didn't realize just how great. "It turns out that for my money he's the greatest running back of all time," the former coach said in the NFL Films documentary *The Cleveland Browns - Fifty Years of Memories*.

Brown not only was voted the 1957 NFL Rookie of the Year by the Associated Press and the United Press, but also the league's Player of the Year by the AP. That year, Brown won the league rushing title with 942 yards, leading Cleveland to the Eastern Conference Championship, and would go on to win the rushing crown in eight of his nine seasons. His rookie year included a 237-yard rushing performance against the Los Angeles Rams, an NFL record that stood for 14 seasons until, ironically, the Rams' Willie Ellison broke it in 1971 by gaining 247 yards against the New Orleans Saints. Brown's feat was a rookie record for 40 years until Cincinnati's Corey Dillon rung up a 246-yard game against the Tennessee (formerly Houston) Oilers in 1997.

In 1958, Brown rushed for 1,527 yards, topping the 100-yard mark nine times, and in the process, was named the Most Valuable Player of the NFL by United Press International and the Newspaper Enterprise Association. Despite the team's rather mediocre records the next three years, Brown's ground yardage totals were still exceptional - 1,329, 1,257, and 1,403, respectively. In 1959, Brown set a team record for most rushing touchdowns in one game when he totaled five on November 1 against the Baltimore Colts, and in 1961 repeated his feat of four years before by totaling 237 yards in a home game against the Philadelphia Eagles.

After a "fall-off" year in 1962 when he gained "just" 996 yards - only the second and final time he didn't reach the 1,000-yard mark - and failed to win the league rushing title, Brown rebounded big time in 1963. He rushed for a career-high 1,863 yards that season, nearly doubling his output from the year before, basking in new head coach Blanton Collier's wide-open offensive attack that saw the team win 10 games for the first time in a decade (Collier had replaced the fired Paul Brown following the 1962 season).

Brown was named the NFL's Most Valuable Player in 1963 by United Press International, the Newspaper Enterprise Association, and the Maxwell Club, sharing the latter with Giants quarterback Y.A. Tittle. Brown powered his way to 1,446 yards in 1964, a year in which his 46-yard third-quarter dash in the NFL Championship game ignited Cleveland's 27-0 upset of Baltimore. He racked up 1,544 yards in 1965 as the Browns returned to the title game, but were defeated by the Green Bay Packers in a frozen Lambeau Field. Brown was voted the Associated Press NFL Player of the Year for 1965 and the league's Most Valuable Player by United Press International, the Newspaper Enterprise Association, and *The Sporting News*. The loss to Green Bay, it turned out, was Brown's final performance - at least on the gridiron. The great running back announced his retirement the following summer, opting for an acting career in the movies.

Brown gained a team-record 12,312 yards rushing in his career, averaging an astounding 104 yards per game and 5.2 yards per carry, both NFL records. He rushed for 106 touchdowns - and scored 126 overall - and was inducted into the Pro Football Hall of Fame in 1971. In 1994, he was named to the NFL's 75th Anniversary All-Time team.

Brown not only was indescribable as a running back but indestructible. He never missed a game, an incredible feat considering he was the main target of opposing defenses most of the time. "Jimmy Brown obviously took more shots than any of these running backs today because he carried the ball more," said Steve Stonebreaker, a two-way player for a handful of teams in the 1960s, in the documentary on Brown. "Everybody wanted to knock him down. He never wore hip pads, he never wore thigh pads. He only wore shoulder pads and a helmet, and everybody took their shots at Jimmy. He asked no quarters, he gave no quarters. He got up after every play."

In addition to being the primary target of opposing defenses, Brown was also the object of heavy scrutiny by many for his not-exactly-Puritan ways off the field, and his penchant for poignant remarks. Recalled Bobby Mitchell, Brown's running mate from 1958-61, in the documentary on the great running back, "Jim Brown was a very intelligent individual. He was his own man. He was coming along at a time in professional football where you didn't speak out too much, white or black. And I guess being a black ballplayer and being as strong as he was, mentally and away from the field, caused him some problems. But Jim Brown was not a bad individual. He was just a man who spoke out a little early."

Added Stonebreaker in the same documentary, "I personally don't like Jimmy Brown ... But I certainly had to respect him as a football player. To play nine years and only miss one half of one game with a broken wrist is remarkable."

Mitchell, in *75 Seasons*: "Until you lined up next to this guy and watched him time after time make it come out alright for the Cleveland Browns, you can't fully respect how good he was. If we had the capabilities today to show him from 15 different angles, people would have said that was not a human."

Jim Brown ... Superman.

3. Paul Warfield: Nureyev in Cleats

When the Cleveland Browns traded wide receiver Paul Warfield to the Miami Dolphins on January 26, 1970, in exchange for the third pick in the following day's NFL Draft, it was Ron Harper for Danny Ferry two decades early.

The Browns coveted sensational quarterback Mike Phipps from Purdue - and got him. Phipps had led the Boilermakers to 24 victories in 30 games - including a pair of Associated Press top 10 finishes - the three previous autumns. The move sent shock waves throughout the city of Cleveland reminiscent of when the National Basketball Association's Cleveland Cavaliers would ship Harper, the spectacular shooting guard, along with three draft picks, to the Los

Angeles Clippers for forward Danny (I ain't quite Larry) Ferry and guard Reggie Williams in November 1989.

The Warfield trade caused confusion and heartache among several players. One was Jim Houston, a Browns linebacker from 1960-72. "It didn't make sense to me. I don't know what went on in the background or up in the offices," Houston said in the NFL Films documentary *The Cleveland Browns - Fifty Years of Memories.*

Billy Andrews, a linebacker mate of Houston's who played for Cleveland from 1967-74, believed the move likely cost the Browns a chance to be in the Super Bowl that year. "The 1970 team, I thought, was one of the better teams that I had played on," Andrews said in the same documentary.

A sensational six-year veteran at the time of the trade, Warfield had given Browns fans innumerable thrills with his artistry on the field. Warfield in action was Picasso with a paintbrush, Spielberg with a script. He was fast, fearless, and agile, with great hands, and moves that left defenders in a trance. "He had those subtle moves that you really don't see where he can get a defensive back off balance and make the break," said veteran talent evaluator Bobby Beathard, now general manager of the San Diego Chargers, in an NFL Films documentary on Warfield. "A lot of those great receivers have that. They don't just come down and break. They've done something in that move to get that guy off balance, and he was a master at that."

Recalled Raymond Berry, a Hall of Fame wide receiver for the Baltimore Colts from 1955-67, of Warfield in the same documentary, "He just popped my eyes open watching him with his fluid movement. ... Trying to cover the guy was a man-sized job because he had the great speed, but he could cut on a dime."

Warfield had an awareness that seemed superhuman at times; his concentration was unbreakable. " ... When the football basically was coming in flight, I could block out everything else that was occurring in that environment," the great receiver explained in the documentary. "I was not aware of the defender. I was not aware of the stadium crowd. ... It was just that football, and I had an obsession with catching it, and I was catching it at its highest point. ... I never wanted to be in a ball game where I'd be so totally surprised that I could not react, and I would be ineffective. So it took a lot of study off the field."

On the field, while the 1970 Warfield-less Browns failed to qualify for postseason play for the first time in four years, Warfield led the Dolphins to their first playoff berth ever that season. The years that followed saw Cleveland plummet to the depths of despair and Miami ascend to greatness, topped off by two straight Super Bowl titles in 1972 and 1973. While Phipps turned out to be a first-rate flop whose best year came in 1972 when he had 13 touchdown passes and 16 interceptions, Warfield continued in the Sunshine State where he left off on the shores of Lake Erie, leading the Dolphins in receiving yards every year from 1970-73.

A first-round draft pick out of Ohio State University in 1964, Warfield made an immediate impact as the burner the Browns were looking for to complement sure-handed receiver Gary Collins. Warfield had team highs of 52 receptions for 920 yards his rookie year, and helped Cleveland win its first NFL Championship in nine seasons. His yardage total in 1964 was the highest for any Browns player since the team joined the NFL in 1950.

Warfield would go on to lead the Browns in receptions just once more - in 1968. It wasn't the quantity of his catches, though, that likely earned him induction into the Pro Football Hall of Fame in 1983. Rather, it was, in all probability, the quality of his receptions that landed him in Canton, Ohio. Warfield may not have caught the most balls of anyone, but when he was on the receiving end, he was usually either going deep or turning a screen pass into a long gainer. Other than the 1965 season in which he missed 10 games due to a preseason shoulder injury, Warfield averaged an incredible 20.7 yards per catch for Cleveland from 1964-69, a period in which the Browns appeared in four NFL title games. He led the team in receiving yardage in four of those years, and in 1967 became the first Cleveland player to achieve 1,000 yards receiving (1,067) since Mac Speedie in 1949.

In addition to his god given talents, Warfield also had a knack for being in the right place at the right time, in terms of winning. Cleveland's poorest won-loss record in Warfield's stint with the team from 1964-69 was 9-5. In his five seasons in Miami, the Dolphins' worst record was 10-4. Even when Warfield left the NFL in 1975 to play for the Memphis Southmen of the World Football League, which folded just more than halfway through its 1975 season, that team, too, had a winning record, while the Warfield-less Dolphins missed the playoffs for the first time in six seasons. Warfield returned to Cleveland in 1976, and the Browns, 3-11 the year before, improved to 9-5. And when the Browns began the 1977 season 5-2, it looked as if Warfield would play for his 14th consecutive winning team as a pro. But the Browns stumbled in the second half of the season - Warfield's last - dropping six of their last seven games, and finished 6-8.

Paul Warfield, though, will be remembered not for his last few seasons but his glory years. Don Shula, Miami's head coach during Warfield's days with the Dolphins, in the documentary on his former star, described the fleet-footed receiver best in recalling a dazzling play he made against the Oakland Raiders on a Saturday night in 1970.

" ... He caught a ball, broke away from some defenders, and did a pirouette, and got away and got into the end zone. ... Poetry in motion," Shula said.

4. Brian Sipe: Kardiac Kingpin

Quarterbacks chosen in the late stages of the NFL Draft usually do not experience much success, let alone go on to a distinguished career.

Brian Sipe is an exception.

Sipe was a 13th-round draft choice of the Cleveland Browns in 1972 out of San Diego State University. Although he set 11 Aztecs passing records and was the NCAA passing champ in 1971, scouts worried about his small frame (6-foot-1, 195 pounds). By the end of his career, though, Sipe not only surprised the Doubting Thomases, but also threw for a team-record 23,713 yards, in a playing career that lasted from 1974-83.

Sipe was as cool as they come. Though he struggled his first few years and stumbled a bit toward the end, the prime of his career produced some thrilling moments. During that period, Sipe was at his best when the chips were down, when his team needed a lift late in the game. "He's a winner, and I think that just says it all in a whole," said Cleveland's all-time receptions leader Ozzie Newsome, a tight end for the Browns from 1978-90, following the 1980 season in the NFL Films documentary *Kardiac Kids ... Again.* "He does whatever he thinks it takes for us to win the game."

Remarked Reggie Rucker, a Browns receiver from 1975-81, also after the 1980 season in the same documentary, "Brian gets the football to the person that's open, and he probably reads defenses as well as anybody that I've ever played with, and I've played with Roger Staubach."

Sipe's talents, though, were questioned early in his career - due mainly to his size, and arm that was seen as too weak to compete at the professional level - and spent his first two years on the Browns' taxi squad. His attitude didn't help matters. He admitted his head was not totally in the game. "The first year I was in Cleveland I think I was more interested in having a good time than I was in impressing the coaches. ... I was not 100 percent committed to making a career out of professional football," he revealed in the book *Sam, Sipe, & Company - The Story of the Cleveland Browns.* "I more or less figured it was an opportunity, that if somebody wanted to pay me to stick around ... "

"We didn't really know whether Brian wanted to play professional football or not," recalled Art Modell, majority owner of the team from 1961-95, in the book.

Sipe eventually got his act together, and decided to seriously pursue the opportunity with the Browns. He finally made the regular squad in 1974, and two years later became the full-time starter when Mike Phipps went down with a separated shoulder in the opening game. After two decent years in 1976 and 1977 in which he began to blossom into a solid quarterback, Sipe really hit his stride upon the arrival of Sam Rutigliano as head coach in 1978. Utilizing Rutigliano's pass-oriented offense, Sipe threw for 2,906 yards and 21 touchdowns that year, and followed that up with 3,793 yards and an NFL-high 28 touchdowns in 1979.

In the process, the Browns were becoming one of the NFL's most exciting teams, and were aptly nicknamed "Kardiac Kids" due to numerous victories (and some losses, too) in the late going. However, Cleveland still missed the NFL Playoffs for the seventh straight year in 1979, finishing behind the always powerful Pittsburgh Steelers, and Houston Oilers, respectively, in the AFC Central Division.

Sipe's knack for pulling victories out of the bag continued into what became a magical 1980 season. In leading Cleveland to an 11-5 record and the AFC Central Division title, Sipe was the NFL passing leader with a 91.4 rating, and broke his own team record from the year before by passing for 4,132 yards. His 30 touchdown passes, tops in the AFC, broke Frank Ryan's team record of 29, set in 1966. Sipe also completed 60.8 percent of his passes (337 of 554). A major factor in the Browns getting over the Pittsburgh-

Cleveland Browns Facts & Trivia

Houston hump in 1980 was the fact that Sipe was intercepted only 14 times, after having tossed 26 the year before.

The awards that were bestowed upon Sipe made up a seemingly never-ending list. Sipe was named the league's Player of the Year by the Associated Press, Most Valuable Player by the Pro Football Writers Association of America and *The Sporting News*, Offensive Player of the Year by *Pro Football Weekly*, and AFC Most Valuable Player by United Press International.

Ironically, it was a miscue by Sipe that ended Cleveland's season that year. In an AFC Divisional Playoff game played in arctic-like conditions in Cleveland Stadium, the Browns were defeated by the Oakland Raiders, 14-12, in heartbreaking fashion. Defeat was assured when a pass from Sipe was intercepted by Raiders strong safety Mike Davis in the Oakland end zone - the play was called "Red Right 88" - with under a minute to go in the game.

In 1981, Sipe passed for nearly 4,000 yards, but his touchdown passes total dropped to 17, while his interceptions sum skyrocketed to 25, as the Browns plummeted to a last-place finish. Sipe was benched after six games the next year in favor of second-year lefty Paul McDonald, who directed the team to two straight wins, enough to qualify the Browns for the expanded playoffs (and a quick exit) in the strike-shortened season, despite a 4-5 record.

As the 1983 season approached, Sipe was determined to win his starting job back, and due to a strong preseason performance, did. "Paul McDonald is a very good quarterback," Sipe said, half smiling, toward the end of the '83 exhibition schedule in the NFL Films documentary *A Step Away*. "He's a very talented guy and I respect him more than I'm around him. Someday, he'll be a very good quarterback in this league, but right now he still has a few things to learn from me."

The veteran backed up his words by passing for 3,566 yards in 1983, completing 58.7 percent of his passes, the second-highest completion percentage of his career. He threw an AFC-best 26 touchdown passes, but his 23 interceptions - and rumors of his exodus to the rival United States Football League (USFL) - were contributing factors in the Browns being the NFL's only 9-7 team (out of five) that year to miss the playoffs. Sipe did opt for the USFL, signing with Donald Trump's New Jersey Generals after the season. He left behind a legacy, though, that will linger in the minds of Browns fans forever.

5. Eric Metcalf: Returnmaster

The calendar said Halloween was just around the corner, but it felt like the Fourth of July, and Eric Metcalf provided the fireworks. The date was October 24, 1993, the setting Cleveland Stadium, early evening. Darkness having set in, the lights were bright. Metcalf, the fifth-year Cleveland Browns' speedster, had just scored on a spectacular 75-yard punt return with 2:05 left in a game against the Pittsburgh Steelers, in a battle for first place in the AFC Central Division. Metcalf's masterpiece gave the Browns the lead and eventually an electrifying 28-23 victory. "I get to be the Joe Carter of this game ... " Metcalf said afterwards, in the NFL Films documentary *A Season of Change.* Metcalf's reference to the Toronto Blue Jays' left fielder was in light of what had transpired the night before in the SkyDome in Toronto. That's when Carter slammed a three-run home run in the bottom of the ninth inning of Game 6 of the World Series to lift the Blue Jays to an 8-6 win over the Philadelphia Phillies, and their second straight world championship.

No, Metcalf didn't score the winning touchdown in the Super Bowl, but his unbelievable, unforgettable return in front of 78,118 frenzied fans - and a near national television audience - made it seem so. What made Metcalf's touchdown return even more amazing - as if there wasn't already enough drama - was the fact that it was his second of the game. Earlier, he had given the Browns a 14-0 lead on a masterful 91-yard Houdini-like scamper in the second quarter. Metcalf became the first player in NFL history to return two punts for touchdowns 75 yards or more in the same game.

Although Metcalf's claim to fame came as a return man, he was used out of the backfield, as well. He inherited many of the skills his father Terry possessed as a superb running back, and return man, himself in the 1970s and early 1980s. The younger Metcalf was Cleveland's first selection - and 13th overall - in the 1989 NFL Draft. The number "13," though, did not turn out to be unlucky for the former Texas Longhorn, who accumulated 1,748 combined net yards his rookie year, a season that included several spectacular plays.

One occurred in an early-season contest in Cincinnati on a Monday night in which Metcalf took a screen pass from Bernie

Kosar and jitterbugged his way into the end zone, completely faking out two Bengals defenders along the way. Metcalf's finest performance of the year may have come on November 5 in Tampa. Late in the first quarter, he turned a simple swing pass into a 24-yard touchdown reception in which he sidestepped cornerback Rod Jones before cutting into the end zone, tying the score at seven. Metcalf put the finishing touches on an explosive day all-around for the Browns early in the fourth period with a picturesque 43-yard touchdown run off a fake reverse that gave the Browns a 42-24 lead, on the way to a 42-31 victory over the Bucs.

On Saturday night, December 23, in a season-ending, nationally-televised showdown for the AFC Central Division title in the Astrodome, Metcalf took a short pass from Kosar once again and raced down the right sideline for a 68-yard score, a key play in Cleveland's memorable 24-20 come-from-behind triumph over Houston.

Metcalf's forte, though, came on special teams, and two weeks after the Oilers game he became the first (and remains the only) Brown to score on a kickoff return in postseason play. He sprinted 90 yards for a third-quarter touchdown in the Browns' 34-30 triumph over the Buffalo Bills in an AFC Divisional Playoff.

Metcalf continued to show his brilliance on the special teams in the years to come. He returned two kickoffs for touchdowns in 1990 - one for 101 yards against the Oilers - and scored on a 75-yard punt return against the Bears two years later before his double whammy against the Steelers in 1993, a year in which he led the NFL in all-purpose yards with 1,932. The next year, Metcalf burned the Bengals twice on punt returns, scoring on a 92-yarder in a season-opening victory and a 73-yarder that helped seal a 37-13 win October 23.

Metcalf was traded to the Atlanta Falcons following the 1994 season but left behind an indelible mark in his six years with the Browns. His abilities were summed up best by the great Jim Brown, the former Cleveland star considered by many to be the finest running back of all time, in *A Season of Change*.

"He's a tremendous talent," Brown said.

DAWG BYTES

1. Dub's Half Dozen

There have been many fine running backs to don the Cleveland Browns' uniform over the years, but none of them - nor any Cleveland player - ever experienced a day like William "Dub" Jones did one afternoon in 1951. Not Jim Brown, not Leroy Kelly, not Marion Motley.

Jones scored six touchdowns in one game. That's correct. Half a dozen. He did it on November 25 against the Chicago Bears (he scored seven the entire *season*). With Motley, a bruising fullback who had led the Browns in rushing yards every year since the team's inception in 1946, slowed down by knee problems, Jones stepped in - or for that matter, took over - at least on that Sunday afternoon in Cleveland Municipal Stadium.

The fourth-year halfback's remarkable feat set a team record, and tied an NFL mark, as the Browns rolled to a 42-21 victory over the Bears, improving to 8-1 on their way to a second straight American Conference title. Jones's six touchdowns broke the team record of four, set by receiver Dante Lavelli on October 14, 1949, when each of Lavelli's scores came on receptions in a 61-14 rout of the Los Angeles Dons. Jones matched the feat of Ernie Nevers, who totaled six touchdown catches on November 28, 1929, when he led the Chicago Cardinals to a 40-6 thumping of the crosstown Bears on Thanksgiving Day.

Whereas Lavelli and Nevers scored their touchdowns on receptions alone, Jones tallied his by way of both the air and the ground, scoring four on runs and two on catches. Even more remarkably, all six touchdowns came in the final three quarters (running back Gale Sayers of the Bears equaled Jones's and Nevers's feat on December 12, 1965, when he scored six touchdowns - four rushing, one receiving, and one on a punt return - in a 61-20 rout of the 49ers in Wrigley Field).

After a scoreless first period in the Browns' victory over the Bears, Jones dove in from two yards out in the second quarter for his first touchdown, capping off a 34-yard drive, and soon after scored on a 34-yard pass from quarterback Otto Graham.

Jones had just scratched the surface, though. In the third quarter, he scored on runs of 11 and 27 yards, the second of which he started left but made a dazzling cut to the right that completely crossed up the Bears' defense. The fourth quarter saw more of the same as Jones broke free on a 43-yard run down the right sideline for his fifth touchdown of the day.

With equaling Nevers's record now a distinct possibility and the game well in hand - the Browns led, 35-7 - Paul Brown, Cleveland's no-nonsense head coach from the Old School, did the unthinkable. Recalled Jones in the NFL Films documentary *The Cleveland Browns - Fifty Years of Memories*, " ... (Assistant coach) Blanton Collier was in the press box and he relayed down and said, 'Listen, Dub Jones is just one touchdown within tying Ernie Nevers's record.' Well, this was unheard of for Paul Brown, but he walked over to me and he said, 'If we get the ball again, what do you want to do?' And I said, 'Well, I want to do this.'"

"This" turned out to be a perfect 43-yard scoring strike from Graham to Jones for touchdown No. 6. What made Jones's feat even more remarkable was the fact that the last five times he touched the ball, he scored. He had nine rushes for 116 yards and three receptions for 80 more. Jones, who led Cleveland with 492 yards on the ground in 1951, admitted he was nowhere to be found in the game plan against the Bears.

"There was no design to put the ball in my hands," he said in the documentary on the Browns. "It just happened to be one of those days where I touched the ball and things happened."

Jones, whose son Bert later quarterbacked the Baltimore Colts to three straight AFC Eastern Division titles in the 1970s, might have had a chance to break the record, but to avoid any sort of senseless injury, Brown removed his sudden star from the game, which featured an abundance of rough play on both sides. Things got so dirty, in fact, that the Browns and Bears set single-game records for most penalties against both teams (37) and most yards penalized against both teams (374). In addition, the Browns set the single-game record for most yards penalized against one team (209). Several players had to be helped off the field; Graham suffered a broken nose.

The fact that Jones was able to accomplish what he did in a game so intense only further indicates what kind of day it was for one Dub Jones.

2. A Legend's Revenge

It was a classic case of clashing egos - Paul Brown vs. Art Modell. From Day 1, when Modell purchased majority ownership of the Cleveland Browns on March 21, 1961, it was the Hatfields and McCoys, Ewings and Barneses, Iraq and Iran.

Modell had been a young advertising executive from New York City with an avid interest in professional football who had always dreamed of owning a professional team; Brown was Cleveland's legendary head coach who had re-built tradition-steeped programs at places like Massillon (Ohio) Washington High School and Ohio State University, before doing the same with the Cleveland franchise beginning in 1946. He even had the team named after him.

Unlike the previous ownership, Modell desired to be involved in the day-to-day operation of the club, including player personnel decisions. This didn't exactly endear him to Brown, who was accustomed to making player moves himself. As the Browns were sinking to mediocrity - an 8-5-1 record in 1961 and 7-6-1 in 1962 - after years of success, Modell's relationship with his head coach was deteriorating, as well, and at a rapid pace.

The fact that several players' faith in Brown was crumbling, too, only worsened matters. Many of the Browns felt their coach's play-calling had become too conservative for the changing times, that the game was passing him by. "Everybody was catching up with him (Brown). In his waning years, he may have gotten into a little bit of a rut," recalled former Browns defensive tackle Bob Gain in the NFL Films documentary *The Cleveland Browns - Fifty Years of Memories*.

Many players were also growing tired of Brown's boot camp-like mentality, which had worked so well in the past (Brown had served in the military for two years as head football coach and athletic officer at the Great Lakes Naval Training Center, outside of Chicago).

D-Day - Dismissal Day - came January 9, 1963, when Modell shocked the city of Cleveland, not to mention the football world, by announcing Brown's firing. As the news spread, many had difficulty fathoming what had transpired. Here was a former advertising executive whose football know-how was not exactly George Halas-like letting go a man whose knowledge of the game was at such a high level that he was the one who invented the face mask.

A bitter - and devastated - Brown spent the following year in Cleveland, free of grumbling players and interfering owners, then took up the quiet life, at his home in La Jolla, California. Meanwhile, new coach Blanton Collier, Brown's offensive backs coach, injected a much-needed drive into the stagnant franchise, and subsequently led the team back to the upper echelon of the league. With Collier implementing a more wide-open offensive attack, the Browns won the NFL Championship in his second year at the helm, 1964, and made three more title-game appearances in his tenure, which lasted through 1970.

With his former team busy playing in championship games, Brown decided to return to the game he loved. He and his family sold the city of Cincinnati on a professional football team, and the Brown family was awarded an American Football League (AFL) franchise on September 27, 1967, some two months after Brown had been enshrined into the Pro Football Hall of Fame. Brown named his new team "Bengals" after two previous Cincinnati Bengals franchises that competed in two different AFLs in the late 1930s and early 1940s.

A rivalry with his old team, not to mention a revenge factor, surely stirring in his mind, Brown outfitted the Bengals in similar attire to that of the Browns. Brown would be part-owner and general manager, and head coach until he retired from the sidelines after the 1975 season.

After two years in the AFL, the Bengals joined the NFL in 1970, and were placed in the AFC Central Division with Pittsburgh, Houston and, yes, Cleveland. Brown finally got the revenge he longed for when on November 15 of that year, the Bengals defeated the Browns, 14-10, in Riverfront Stadium in Cincinnati. Following the game, Brown was overflowing with emotion. "Satisfied, that's the way I feel," he was quoted as saying following the victory in the book *Sam, Sipe, & Company - the Story of the Cleveland Browns*. The Bengals went on to finish 8-6 that year - after a 1-6 start - and capture the Central Division crown by a game over their new rivals to the north.

The Bengals and Browns, evenly matched for the most part over the next quarter century plus, had begun a bitter, hard-hitting, tempers-flaring rivalry whose signature was the team owners' mutual distaste for one another. Although the Bengals failed to win a league championship in Brown's lifetime (he passed away on

August 5, 1991), and still haven't, Cincinnati's two Super Bowl appearances, in 1981 and 1988 - and Cleveland's absence from the title game - gave Paul Brown all the more satisfaction he needed.

3. Jinxed?!

Jinx, as defined by *The American Heritage Dictionary* (third edition): "A person or thing believed to bring bad luck."

Jinx, as could have been defined by the Cleveland Browns of the 1970s and early- to mid-1980s: "A thing, namely Three Rivers Stadium, believed to bring bad luck."

Beginning with a 28-9 defeat on November 29, 1970, the Browns lost 16 consecutive games in Three Rivers, the home of their arch-rivals, the Pittsburgh Steelers, who had moved into the brand new stadium that very same year of 1970. The Steelers had spent seven seasons in Pitt Stadium on the University of Pittsburgh campus and 30 prior to that in Forbes Field (for the most part).

Not coincidentally, the start of the losing streak coincided with the arrival of one Terry Bradshaw in Steeltown. The young quarterback was Pittsburgh's top pick - and the No. 1 selection overall - in the 1970 NFL Draft, held earlier that year. Although Three Rivers Stadium itself was believed by many Browns followers (and the Browns themselves) to be "haunted," Bradshaw, the ex-Louisiana Tech star with the machine gun for a right arm, had much to do with the Steelers' domination of the Browns in Pittsburgh, which came to be known as the "Three Rivers Jinx."

The fact that Pittsburgh was one of the NFL's top teams during much of the streak's duration should make its success against Cleveland at home come as no surprise. However, at the same time they found the going rough in southwestern Pennsylvania, the Browns were able to muster road wins over other top teams, including Miami in 1970, Oakland in 1973, and Cincinnati and San Francisco in 1981 (the Browns failed to make the playoffs in each of those three seasons). One would think that once - just once - Cleveland would have pulled one out in Pittsburgh, stolen one, somewhere along the way. But not only were the Browns unable to steal one, the Steelers themselves were thieves at times, and the Browns were "ripped off" on occasion, too (with a little help from the officials).

Cleveland Browns Facts & Trivia

Pittsburgh's mastery of the Browns in this period came during a time when Cleveland was on the downswing and Pittsburgh the upswing. Heading into the 1970 season, the Browns had built a rich tradition, having won four NFL Championships - appearing in 11 title games - in their 20 years in the league; they had won eight championships in all, including four in the All-America Football Conference. They had treated Pittsburgh like a whipping bag for years, having won 31 of 40 games, including 15 of 20 in Pittsburgh. The Steelers, on the other hand, had never won a title of any kind in their nearly 40-year history, except for maybe that of ... well ... loser.

After an easy home win over the Browns in 1971, Pittsburgh's victory in 1972 was notable not for its competitiveness, but for another reason - the marking of the changing of the guard. The Browns, an aging team attempting to make one last stand, had several veterans at or near the end of their career. The Steelers, meanwhile, were in the midst of building a dynasty. Chuck Noll was in his fourth year as head coach, and through excellent drafts, had improved the team from 1-13 his first season to 8-3 entering this December 3 contest against the Browns, also 8-3. In this battle for AFC Central supremacy, the battle turned into a Three Rivers thrashing as Pittsburgh routed the Browns, 30-0. The Steelers went on to win the division title with an 11-3 record. The Browns, who finished 10-4, qualified for the playoffs as the AFC Wild Card team, which would turn out to be the franchise's last postseason appearance until the dawning of the next decade. Both teams were ousted by eventual Super Bowl Champion Miami in the playoffs, the Browns in the divisional round and the Steelers in the conference championship game. With the tide now turned, the Steelers won the next four contests, three of them with ease.

Beginning in 1977, the heart of the Jinx took its course, as the next five games between the "turnpike rivals" hinged on thrilling finishes, suspect (officiating) calls and hard hits, as usual. In the five games from 1977-81, Pittsburgh won by just an average of 4.4 points per game. The following is a recap of the five Browns-Steelers games in Three Rivers Stadium from 1977-81:

*Pittsburgh 35, Cleveland 31 (Nov. 13, 1977)
- Quarterback Brian Sipe fractures his left shoulder blade and is out for the year.

Cleveland Browns Facts & Trivia

*Pittsburgh 15, Cleveland 9 (OT) (Sept. 24, 1978)
- In an early-season showdown for first place, Ricky Feacher recovers a fumble on the overtime kickoff deep in Steelers territory. Although television replays confirm the play was indeed a fumble, officials rule the play had been blown dead prior to the miscue, and the ball is awarded to Pittsburgh. Minutes later, Terry Bradshaw hits tight end Bennie Cunningham for a 37-yard touchdown pass on a flea-flicker.

*Pittsburgh 33, Cleveland 30 (OT) (Nov. 25, 1979)
- Cleveland enters 8-4, a game behind Pittsburgh and Houston. The Browns squander leads of 20-6, 27-13, and 30-20. They trail one time - when Matt Bahr connects on a 37-yard field goal with nine seconds left in sudden death.

*Pittsburgh 16, Cleveland 13 (Nov. 16, 1980)
- Bradshaw's three-yard touchdown pass to Lynn Swann with 11 seconds to go - a play in which Steelers receiver Theo Bell admits after the game he'd illegally picked Cleveland cornerback Ron Bolton - gives Pittsburgh the victory and costs the Browns a share of first place.

*Pittsburgh 13, Cleveland 7 (Oct. 11, 1981)
- Paul McDonald replaces a dazed Sipe, who suffers a concussion on a ferocious hit by linebacker Jack Lambert in the third quarter. McDonald leads the Browns on two late drives, but his interception on a tipped pass in the Steelers' end zone kills one; time expires on the second when officials rule that Reggie Rucker fails to get out of bounds - Rucker claims he did - after his 17-yard reception moves Cleveland to the Steelers' 32.

The Browns' frustration at their failings in Three Rivers led them to the depths of superstition. Chuck Heaton, the team's beat writer for the *Plain Dealer* in Cleveland from 1954-77, recalled the club resorting to extreme measures in trying to halt the Jinx. "They (the Browns) tried flying to Pittsburgh, they took a bus for awhile. ... I think one time they even drove over in cars," Heaton said. "They also changed hotels several times."

"Sometimes I wondered if we were going to have to ask for volunteers to go to Pittsburgh," joked Sam Rutigliano, Cleveland's head coach from 1978 until midway through the 1984 season, in his autobiography *Pressure.*

After lopsided losses in 1982 and 1983, the Browns were defeated on last-second field goals the next two years, but the tide was slowly turning back in favor of Cleveland. By the time the 1986 season began, the Browns' talent level was far superior to the Steelers' for the first time since the streak began, and the Three Rivers Jinx finally came to an end on October 5 of that year. Cleveland defeated Pittsburgh, 27-24, that day - highlighted by Gerald "The Ice Cube" McNeil's 100-yard kickoff return for a touchdown - the first of four straight wins for the Browns in what will forever be known as their own personal "House of Horrors."

4. A Canine Commotion

With the Cleveland Browns at the tail end of a rather disheartening 1984 season that produced several close defeats and a 5-11 finish, there wasn't much for fans of the team to cheer about. Hanford Dixon and Frank Minnifield decided to ham it up a bit and began barking - yes, barking - to fans in the bleachers section during a home game in order to give the Cleveland Stadium crowd a lift, some sort of spark, to liven things up a bit. Little did the Browns' starting cornerbacks know that their woofing would be the start of quite possibly the largest, loudest, longest-running canine commotion this side of the motion picture *101 Dalmations.*

During the next 10-plus seasons, legions of Browns fans in the bleachers section not only barked their lungs out but also attired themselves in dog masks, and painted their faces brown, orange, and white. Some even feasted on dog biscuits! If someone completely oblivious to Cleveland Browns football had walked into Cleveland Stadium during a home game at this time and saw the goings-on in the bleachers, they probably would have thought to themselves, What's a dog pound doing in a football stadium? Well, that's exactly what the bleachers section had turned into - a "Dawg Pound," which is what it came to be known not only in Cleveland but nationwide. The creation of the Dawg Pound coincided with the team's new winning ways after recent less-than-mediocre seasons, which increased the excitement level even more. "Our relationship with our fans really made our team special, and it created a bond with the fans and with each other," recalled Minnifield in the NFL Films documentary *The Cleveland Browns - Fifty Years of Memories.*

Said Mike Johnson, a Browns linebacker from 1986-93, following the 1987 season in the NFL Films documentary *No Apologies Necessary*,"Their (the fans) excitement is contagious, and it rubs off on us. When you're in the middle of a game, and you hear the crowd start to rev up and roar and start barking, it really gets the adrenaline flowing, and it makes it that much easier to be successful on the next play."

The rapport between the Browns and the city of Cleveland was almost on a par with a college atmosphere, even B.D.P. (Before Dawg Pound). Ron Bolton, a Browns cornerback from 1976-82, remembered it well. "It was like family. ... You could look up in the stands, you'd see people that you've seen in the street," Bolton said in the documentary on the team.

Although self-proclaimed "Top Dawg" Dixon and "Mighty Minnie" Minnifield were the first to fire up the bleacher-goers, it was linebacker Eddie Johnson who got the whole "Dawg" thing going during the 1984 training camp. "Eddie's the original Dawg," former Browns nose tackle Dave Puzzuoli said in the *Official Cleveland Browns Countdown to '99 Yearbook.* "When a guy really showed he could get after someone, make a big hit or play aggressively on defense, Eddie would start barking at him."

"We felt all of the best defenses in NFL history had names, like the Steelers' Steel Curtain or the Vikings' Purple People Eaters," Johnson was quoted as saying in the same publication. "We had the makings of a great defense, and we needed a name to go along with it. So we created the Dawg Defense."

Dawg Pound-goers became a little too enthusiastic at times, though, as several "Canine Quarterbacks" would hurl biscuits, batteries and eggs, among other inanimate objects, at opposing players. Their rowdiness made life so miserable for the opposition that at one point during a victory over the Denver Broncos in 1989, officials were forced to move play to the closed end of the stadium. But all in all, the positives outweighed the negatives, and the Cleveland Stadium bleachers section will forever be known as the pound that knew how to party.

5. Bill 'n' Bernie

Diminishing skills.

Those two words will be etched in the minds of Cleveland Browns fans forever. They were saddled on one Bernie Kosar at a news conference on November 8, 1993; the popular quarterback's release from the Browns was announced that day. The communicator was Browns majority owner Art Modell, who in addition to describing Kosar's skills as diminishing, spoke of the quarterback's physical limitations. The culprit was Browns head coach Bill Belichick, who wanted Kosar out, and attributed his release to, as taken from the *Plain Dealer* in Cleveland on November 9, 1993, " ... his lack of production and loss of physical skills."

The impact of those words were only further heightened due to the fact they came from Belichick, not exactly the most popular head coach in Browns history, due in large part to his play-calling from the Dark Ages and personality of a wet blanket. The fact that he had been slowly gutting the team of several popular veteran players since his hiring in 1991 didn't help matters.

Kosar received his pink slip the day after tossing a 38-yard touchdown pass to wide receiver Michael Jackson at the tail end of a 29-14 loss to the Denver Broncos on a play he had drawn up in the dirt of Cleveland Stadium. The pass, which turned out to be Kosar's last as a Brown, presumably infuriated Belichick, who had apparently called a running play. It was not the first time during the Broncos game that Kosar audibled, a strategic tool quarterbacks often turn to. This was evidently the last straw for Belichick, who had apparently experienced a rocky relationship with the star quarterback, to say the least, from the start. Reports there was a physical confrontation between the two in the tunnel leading to the locker room after the game swirl about to this day.

Jackson, a member of the Browns from 1991-95, believed an abundance of mind games were going on at the time. "The whole thing's a power play between Bernie and Belichick. Bill has brought a lot of commotion between the players, and actually every day we expect it," Jackson was quoted as saying in the October 18, 1993, edition of *Browns News/Illustrated*.

Some observers felt Belichick was threatened by Kosar's god like status in the minds of many Cleveland fans, for he was a hometown hero raised in nearby Boardman, Ohio, just outside of Youngstown, and had led the Browns to three AFC Championship games. Others believed Belichick wanted to field a team consisting mainly of his own players - for whom he himself drafted or traded - as receivers Brian Brennan, Reggie Langhorne, and Webster Slaughter (among others) were already gone. Then there were those who thought Belichick simply didn't think Kosar was a quality quarterback anymore, that he wanted to stick with the more mobile, stronger-armed Vinny Testaverde, acquired in an off-season trade with Tampa Bay.

A slight predicament existed, however. Testaverde couldn't play. The ex-teammate of Kosar's at the University of Miami was out o action with a separated shoulder suffered two weeks before in a victory over Pittsburgh. This made the news of Kosar's release - in itself a bombshell, a tough pill to swallow for many Cleveland fans - sting even more. Why? Because with the team tied for first place, the starting quarterback position was inherited by one Todd Philcox, who had attempted all of 37 passes in his brief career (Brad Goebel, who had been on and off the roster since being acquired in a trade with Philadelphia in August 1992, was re-signed as the emergency third quarterback two weeks before when Testaverde went down). Belichick said he believed Philcox gave the team a better chance to win than Kosar. In effect, the coach was saying that Todd Philcox was a better quarterback than Bernie Kosar. Philcox showed just how *much* better by fumbling twice - including on the first play from scrimmage in which the ball was returned for a touchdown - and tossing two interceptions in a horrific 22-5 loss in Seattle. By the time Testaverde returned to action, the Browns were 5-6 and sinking fast. They wound up 7-9 and in third place in the AFC Central Division.

Rick Telander, a reporter for *Sports Illustrated* at the time, supported the move. He offered his opinion on the situation in the NFL Films documentary *A Season of Change*: "Belichick saw, under Kosar's guidance, that the team was just not that good. It may win a few games, it may sneak up on some people, but sooner or later it was all going to cave in. It was best to clean house at the time that he did so that they could start to build for the future, even if it may look ridiculous and like cutting your own throat at the time that you do it."

Two days after the Browns cut him, Kosar signed with the Dallas

Cleveland Browns Facts & Trivia

Cowboys, filling in for the injured Troy Aikman for a couple of weeks until the Cowboys' superstar returned to action. While Belichick and the Browns were relegated to viewing the postseason on television, Kosar was helping the Cowboys advance in the playoffs with a key touchdown pass in the NFC Championship game that foiled the 49ers. A week later, Dallas beat Buffalo in Super Bowl XXVIII. Thus Kosar got his championship ring - albeit in a backup role - then went on to caddy for Dan Marino in Miami for three years before calling it quits. Belichick, meanwhile, continued his part in severing what had been a special relationship between a town and its team.

BROWNS BY THE NUMBERS

1. Individual Top Tens

-Career-
Scoring (Points)

1. Lou Groza   1,608
2. Don Cockroft   1,080
3. Jim Brown   756
4. Matt Bahr   677
5. Leroy Kelly   540
6. Matt Stover   480
7. Gary Collins   420
8. Dante Lavelli   372
9. Ray Renfro   330
10. Kevin Mack   324

Rushing Yards

1. Jim Brown   12,312
2. Leroy Kelly   7,274
3. Mike Pruitt   6,540
4. Greg Pruitt   5,496
5. Kevin Mack   5,123
6. Marion Motley   4,712
7. Earnest Byner   3,364
8. Ernie Green   3,204
9. Bobby Mitchell   2,297
10. Cleo Miller   2,286

Passing Yards

1. Brian Sipe   23,713
2. Otto Graham   23,584
3. Bernie Kosar   21,904
4. Frank Ryan   13,361
5. Bill Nelsen   9,725
6. Milt Plum   8,914
7. Mike Phipps   7,700
8. Vinny Testaverde   7,255

9. Paul McDonald   5,269
10. Jim Ninowski   2,630

Pass Completions

1. Brian Sipe   1,944
2. Bernie Kosar   1,853
3. Otto Graham   1,464
4. Frank Ryan   907
5. Bill Nelsen   689
6. Mike Phipps   633
7. Milt Plum   627
8. Vinny Testaverde   578
9. Paul McDonald   411
10. Jim Ninowski   184

Receiving Yards

1. Ozzie Newsome   7,980
2. Dante Lavelli   6,488
3. Mac Speedie   5,602
4. Ray Renfro   5,508
5. Gary Collins   5,299
6. Paul Warfield   5,210
7. Reggie Rucker   4,953
8. Webster Slaughter   4,834
9. Dave Logan   4,247
10. Milt Morin   4,208

Receptions

1. Ozzie Newsome   662
2. Dante Lavelli   386
3. Mac Speedie   349
4. Gary Collins   331
5. Greg Pruitt   323

Cleveland Browns Facts & Trivia

6. Brian Brennan	315	7. Bobby Mitchell	607
7. Reggie Rucker	310	8. Ken Konz	556
8. Webster Slaughter	305	9. Keith Wright	467
9. Eric Metcalf	297	10. Brian Brennan	435
10. Ray Renfro	281		

Interceptions

Kickoff Return Yards

1. Dino Hall	3,185
2. Eric Metcalf	2,806
3. Glen Young	2,079
4. Randy Baldwin	1,872
5. Leroy Kelly	1,784
6. Keith Wright	1,767
7. Walter Roberts	1,608
8. Bobby Mitchell	1,550
9. Greg Pruitt	1,523
10. Billy Lefear	1,461

Interceptions:

1. Thom Darden	45
2. Warren Lahr	44
3. Clarence Scott	39
4. Tommy James	34
5. Ken Konz	30
6. Bernie Parrish	29
7. Ross Fichtner	27
Mike Howell	27
9. Hanford Dixon	26
Felix Wright	26

Combined Net Yards

1. Jim Brown	15,459
2. Leroy Kelly	12,329
3. Greg Pruitt	10,700
4. Eric Metcalf	9,108
5. Mike Pruitt	8,538
6. Ozzie Newsome	8,147
7. Marion Motley	7,019
8. Kevin Mack	6,725
9. Ray Renfro	6,569
10. Earnest Byner	6,564

Punting Yards

1. Don Cockroft	26,362
2. Horace Gillom	21,207
3. Gary Collins	13,764
4. Jeff Gossett	10,307
5. Brian Hansen	10,112
6. Johnny Evans	8,463
7. Steve Cox	7,974
8. Bryan Wagner	6,696
9. Tom Tupa	6,042
10. Sam Baker	4,605

-Season-

Scoring (Points)

1. Jim Brown	126 (1965)
2. Leroy Kelly	120 (1968)
3. Lou Groza	115 (1964)
4. Matt Stover	113 (1995)
5. Matt Stover	110 (1994)

Punt Return Yards

1. Gerald McNeil	1,545
2. Eric Metcalf	1,341
3. Leroy Kelly	990
4. Dino Hall	901
5. Cliff Lewis	710
6. Greg Pruitt	659

Cleveland Browns Facts & Trivia

6. Lou Groza   108 (1953)
   Jim Brown   108 (1958)
   Jim Brown   108 (1962)
9. Matt Bahr   104 (1988)
10. Matt Bahr   101 (1983)

Rushing Yards

1. Jim Brown   1,863 (1963)
2. Jim Brown   1,544 (1965)
3. Jim Brown   1,527 (1958)
4. Jim Brown   1,446 (1964)
5. Jim Brown   1,408 (1961)
6. Jim Brown   1,329 (1959)
7. Mike Pruitt 1,294 (1979)
8. Jim Brown   1,257 (1960)
9. Leroy Kelly 1,239 (1968)
10. Leroy Kelly 1,205 (1967)

Passing Yards

1. Brian Sipe   4,132 (1980)
2. Brian Sipe   3,876 (1981)
3. Bernie Kosar   3,854 (1986)
4. Brian Sipe   3,793 (1979)
5. Brian Sipe   3,566 (1983)
6. Bernie Kosar   3,533 (1989)
7. Bernie Kosar   3,487 (1991)
8. Paul McDonald 3,472 (1984)
9. Bernie Kosar   3,033 (1987)
10. Frank Ryan   2,974 (1966)

Pass Completions

1. Brian Sipe   337 (1980)
2. Brian Sipe   313 (1981)
3. Bernie Kosar   310 (1986)
4. Bernie Kosar   307 (1991)
5. Bernie Kosar   303 (1989)
6. Brian Sipe   291 (1983)

7. Brian Sipe   286 (1979)
8. Paul McDonald 271 (1984)
9. Bernie Kosar   241 (1987)
   Vinny Testaverde 241 (1995)

Receiving Yards

1. Webster Slaughter 1,236
                              (1989)
2. Mac Speedie   1,146 (1947)
3. Paul Warfield   1,067 (1968)
4. Mac Speedie   1,028 (1949)
5. Ozzie Newsome1,002 (1981)
6. Ozzie Newsome1,001 (1984)
7. Dave Logan   982 (1979)
8. Ozzie Newsome 970 (1983)
9. Gary Collins   946 (1966)
10. Paul Warfield   920 (1964)

Receptions

1. Ozzie Newsome   89 (1983)
   Ozzie Newsome   89 (1984)
3. Ozzie Newsome   69 (1981)
4. Mac Speedie   67 (1947)
5. Greg Pruitt   65 (1981)
   Webster Slaughter   65 (1989)
7. Webster Slaughter 64 (1991)
8. Mike Pruitt   63 (1980)
   Mike Pruitt   63 (1981)
   Eric Metcalf   63 (1993)

Interceptions

1. Tom Colella   10 (1946)
   Thom Darden   10 (1978)
3. Cliff Lewis   9   (1948)
   Tommy James   9   (1950)
   Felix Wright   9   (1989)
   Eric Turner   9   (1994)

Cleveland Browns Facts & Trivia

7. Warren Lahr   8   (1950)
Bobby Franklin   8   (1960)
Jim Shofner   8   (1960)
Ross Fichtner   8   (1966)
Mike Howell   8   (1966)
Ben Davis   8   (1968)
Thom Darden   8   (1974)

Punting Yards

1. Bryan Wagner   3,817 (1989)
2. Don Cockroft   3,643 (1974)
3. Brian Hansen   3,632 (1993)
4. Don Cockroft   3,498 (1972)
5. Jeff Gossett   3,423 (1986)
6. Brian Hansen   3,397 (1991)
7. Horace Gillom   3,321 (1951)
    Don Cockroft   3,321 (1973)
9. Don Cockroft   3,317 (1975)
10. Jeff Gossett   3,261 (1985)

Punt Return Yards

1. Gerald McNeil   496 (1989)
2. Eric Metcalf   464 (1993)
3. Eric Metcalf   429 (1992)
4. Gerald McNeil   386 (1987)
5. Greg Pruitt   349 (1974)
6. Gerald McNeil   348 (1986)
    Eric Metcalf   348 (1994)
8. Gerald McNeil   315 (1988)
9. Dino Hall   295 (1979)
10. Leroy Kelly   292 (1971)

Kickoff Return Yards

1. Eric Metcalf   1,052 (1990)
2. Dino Hall   1,014 (1979)
3. Gerald McNeil   997 (1986)
4. Glen Young   898 (1985)

5. Herman Fontenot 879 (1988)
6. Dino Hall   813 (1981)
7. Keith Wright   789 (1978)
8. Randy Baldwin   753 (1994)
9. Homer Jones   739 (1970)
10. Bo Scott   722 (1969)

Combined Net Yards

1. Jim Brown   2,131   (1963)
2. Leroy Kelly   2,014   (1966)
3. Eric Metcalf   1,932   (1993)
4. Jim Brown   1,917   (1961)
5. Jim Brown   1,872   (1965)
6. Greg Pruitt   1,798   (1975)
7. Jim Brown   1,786   (1964)
8. Greg Pruitt   1,769   (1974)
9. Jim Brown   1,761   (1960)
10. Eric Metcalf 1,752   (1990)

-Game- vs. - Denotes home

Rushing Yards

1. Jim Brown   237
   (Nov. 24, 1957, vs.. L.A.)
   Jim Brown   237
   (Nov. 19, 1961, vs. Phi.)
3. Bobby Mitchell   232
   (Nov. 15, 1959, at Was.)
   Jim Brown   232
   (Sept. 22, 1963, at Dal.)
5. Jim Brown   223
   (Nov.3, 1963, at Phi.)
6. Greg Pruitt   214
   (Dec. 14, 1975, vs. K.C.)
7. Greg Pruitt   191
   (Oct. 17, 1976, at Atl.)
8. Marion Motley   188

(Oct. 29, 1950, vs. Pit.)
Jim Brown   188
(Oct. 18, 1964, at Dal.)
Earnest Byner   188
(Dec. 16, 1984, at Hou.)

Passing Yards

1. Brian Sipe   444
   (Oct. 25, 1981, vs. Bal.)
2. Bernie Kosar   414
   (Nov. 23, 1986, vs. Pit.)
3. Otto Graham   401
   (Oct. 4, 1952, at Pit.)
   Bernie Kosar   401
   (Nov. 10, 1986, vs. Mia.)
5. Brian Sipe   391
   (Oct. 19, 1980, vs. G.B.)
6. Otto Graham   382
   (Nov. 20, 1949, Bro.-N.Y.)
7. Brian Sipe   375
   (Sept. 7, 1981, vs. S.D.)
8. Otto Graham   369
   (Oct.15,1950,vs.Chi. Cardinals)
9. Frank Ryan   367
   (Dec. 17, 1966, at St.L.)
10. Otto Graham   362
    (Oct. 14, 1949, at L.A.)

Receiving Yards

(Does not include games against
Brooklyn on Dec. 8. 1946, and
Baltimore on Dec. 7, 1947)

1. Mac Speedie   228
   (Nov. 20, 1949, Bro.-N.Y.)
2. Dante Lavelli   209
   (Oct. 14, 1949, at L.A.)
3. Ozzie Newsome   191
   (Oct.14, 1984, vs. N.Y. Jets)
4. Webster Slaughter   186

(Oct. 23, 1989, vs. Chi.)
5. Webster Slaughter   184
   (Oct. 29, 1989, vs. Hou.)
6. Dante Lavelli   183
   (Oct. 27, 1946, vs. S.F.)
7. Pete Brewster   182
   (Dec. 6, 1953, vs. N.Y.)
8. Gern Nagler   177
   (Nov. 20, 1960, at Pit.)
   Reggie Rucker   177
   (Nov. 18, 1979, vs. Mia.)
   Eric Metcalf   177
   (Sept. 20, 1992, at L.A.
Raiders)

2. Individual Top Fives
(Postseason)

-Career-
Scoring (Points)

1. Lou Groza   83
2. Matt Bahr   46
3. Otto Graham   36
   Earnest Byner   36
5. Edgar Jones   30
   Dante Lavelli   30
   Marion Motley   30
   Gary Collins   30
   Webster Slaughter   30

Rushing Yards

(Does not include games against
Buffalo on Dec. 4, 1949, and Los
Angeles on Dec. 24, 1950, for Otto
Graham and Marion Motley, and
game against New York Giants on
Dec. 17, 1950, for Motley)

1. Marion Motley   512
2. Earnest Byner   480

Cleveland Browns Facts & Trivia

3. Leroy Kelly   427
4. Kevin Mack   424
5. Otto Graham   247

Passing Yards

1. Otto Graham   2,001
2. Bernie Kosar   1,860
3. Bill Nelsen   839
4. Frank Ryan   534
5. Vinny Testaverde   412

Pass Completions

1. Otto Graham   159
2. Bernie Kosar   146
3. Bill Nelsen   68
4. Frank Ryan   35
5. Vinny Testaverde   33

Receiving Yards
(Does not include games against New York Giants on Dec. 17, 1950, and Los Angeles on Dec. 24, 1950, and portion of game against Buffalo on Dec. 4, 1949)

1. Dante Lavelli   526
2. Paul Warfield   404
3. Webster Slaughter   381
4. Ozzie Newsome   373
5. Reggie Langhorne   370

Receptions

(Does not include game against New York Giants on Dec. 17, 1950, and portion of games against Buffalo on Dec. 4, 1949, and Los

Angeles on Dec. 24, 1950)

1. Dante Lavelli   30
2. Mac Speedie   27
   Ozzie Newsome   27
4. Reggie Langhorne   26
5. Paul Warfield   24

Punting Yards

1. Horace Gillom   1,943
2. Don Cockroft   965
3. Jeff Gossett   792
4. Gary Collins   595
5. Bryan Wagner   451

-**Game**- vs. - Denotes home

Scoring (Points)

1. Marion Motley   18
   (Dec. 19, 1948, vs. Buf.)
   Otto Graham   18
   (Dec. 26, 1954, vs. Det.)
   Gary Collins   18
   (Dec. 27, 1964, vs. Bal.)
4. Edgar Jones   12
   (Dec. 19, 1948, vs. Buf.)
   Dante Lavelli   12
   (Dec. 24, 1950, vs. L.A.)
   Ray Renfro   12
   (Dec. 26, 1954, vs. Det.)
   Otto Graham   12
   (Dec. 26, 1955, at L.A.)
   Leroy Kelly   12
   (Dec. 21, 1968, vs. Dal.)
   Bo Scott   12
   (Dec. 28, 1969, at Dal.)
   Earnest Byner   12
   (Jan. 4, 1986, at Mia.)

Cleveland Browns Facts & Trivia

Earnest Byner 12
(Jan. 9, 1988, vs. Ind.)
Earnest Byner 12
(Jan. 17, 1988, at Den.)
Webster Slaughter 12
(Dec. 24, 1988, vs. Hou.)
Webster Slaughter 12
(Jan. 6, 1990, vs. Buf.)
Brian Brennan 12
(Jan. 14, 1990, at Den.)

Rushing Yards

1. Earnest Byner 161
   (Jan. 4, 1986, at Mia.)
2. Marion Motley 133
   (Dec. 19, 1948, vs. Buf.)
3. Earnest Byner 122
   (Jan. 9, 1988, vs. Ind.)
4. Jim Brown 114
   (Dec. 27, 1964, vs. Bal.)
5. Marion Motley 109
   (Dec. 14, 1947, at N.Y.)

Passing Yards

1. Bernie Kosar 489
   (Jan.3, 1987, vs. N.Y. Jets)
2. Bernie Kosar 356
   (Jan. 17, 1988, at Den.)
3. Otto Graham 326
   (Dec. 4, 1949, vs. Buf.)
4. Otto Graham 298
   (Dec. 24, 1950, vs. L.A.)
5. Paul McDonald 281
   (Jan.8,1983, at L.A. Raiders)

Pass Completions

1. Bernie Kosar 33

(Jan. 3, 1987, vs. N.Y. Jets)
2. Bernie Kosar 26
   (Jan. 17, 1988, at Den.)
3. Otto Graham 22
   (Dec. 4, 1949, vs. Buf.)
   Otto Graham 22
   (Dec. 24, 1950, vs. L.A.)
5. Otto Graham 20
   (Dec. 28, 1952, vs. Det.)
   Bernie Kosar 20
   (Jan. 9, 1988, vs. Ind.)
   Bernie Kosar 20
   (Jan. 6, 1990, vs. Buf.)
   Vinny Testaverde 20
   (Jan. 1, 1995, vs. N.E.)

Receiving Yards

(Does not include portion of games against Buffalo on Dec. 4, 1949, and Los Angeles on Dec. 24, 1950)

1. Gary Collins 130
   (Dec. 27, 1964, vs. Bal.)
2. Ricky Feacher 124
   (Jan.8,1983,at L.A. Raiders)
3. Michael Jackson 122
   (Jan. 1, 1995, vs. N.E.)
4. Earnest Byner 120
   (Jan. 17, 1988, at Den.)
5. Ozzie Newsome 114
   (Jan.3,1987, vs. N.Y. Jets)
   Webster Slaughter 114
   (Jan. 6, 1990, vs. Buf.)

Receptions
(Does not include game against Los Angeles on Dec. 24, 1950, and portion of game against Buffalo on

Cleveland Browns Facts & Trivia

Dec. 4, 1949)

1. Paul Warfield   8
  (Dec. 28, 1969, at Dal.)
2. Mac Speedie   7
  (Dec. 4, 1949, vs. Buf.)
  Mac Speedie   7
  (Dec. 23, 1951, at L.A.)
  Herman Fontenot   7
  (Jan. 11, 1987, vs. Den.)
  Earnest Byner   7
  (Jan. 17, 1988, at Den.)
  Michael Jackson   7
  (Jan. 1, 1995, vs. N.E.)

Punting Yards

1. Horace Gillom   363
  (Dec. 17, 1950, vs. N.Y.)
2. Bryan Wagner   338
  (Jan. 14, 1990, at Den.)
3. Jeff Gossett   310
  (Jan. 3, 1987, vs. N.Y. Jets)
4. Dick Deschaine   304
  (Dec. 21, 1958, at N.Y.)
5. Steve Cox   291
  (Jan.8,1983, at L.A. Raiders)

3. Team Top Fives, Season

Scoring (Points)

1. 415 (1964)
2. 403 (1966)
3. 394 (1968)
4. 391 (1986)
5. 390 (1987)

Rushing Yards

1. 2,639 (1963)
2. 2,557 (1947)
  2,557 (1948)
4. 2,526 (1958)
5. 2,488 (1978)

Passing Yards

1. 4,339 (1981)
2. 4,132 (1980)
3. 4,018 (1986)
4. 3,932 (1983)
5. 3,838 (1979)

Pass Completions

1. 348 (1981)
2. 337 (1980)
3. 324 (1983)
  324 (1995)
5. 315 (1986)

Interceptions

1. 41 (1946)
2. 32 (1947)
  32 (1968)
4. 31 (1950)
  31 (1960)

Punting Yards

1. 3,822 (1989)
2. 3,645 (1974)
3. 3,629 (1993)
4. 3,499 (1972)
5. 3,420 (1986)

Cleveland Browns Facts & Trivia

Punt Return Yards

1. 563 (1993)
2. 537 (1946)
3. 523 (1974)
4. 503 (1947)
5. 496 (1989)

Kickoff Return Yards

1. 1,697 (1978)
2. 1,537 (1981)
3. 1,531 (1979)
4. 1,526 (1975)
5. 1,455 (1995)

Total Net Yards

1. 5,915 (1981)
2. 5,772 (1979)
3. 5,588 (1980)
4. 5,583 (1983)
5. 5,394 (1986)

4. Team Top Fives, Game (Postseason)

Rushing Yards

1. 251 (Jan. 4, 1986, at Mia.)
2. 227 (Dec.28,1952, vs. Det.)
3. 218 (Dec.29,1957, at Det.)
4. 217 (Dec.11,1949, vs. S.F.)
5. 215 (Dec.19, 1948, vs. Buf.)

Passing Yards

1. 494 (Jan.3,1987,vs.N.Y.Jets)
2. 356 (Jan.17,1988, at Den.)
3. 326 (Dec. 4, 1949, vs. Buf.)
4. 298 (Dec.24, 1950, vs. L.A.)
5. 281 (Jan. 8, 1983, at L.A. Raiders)

Pass Completions

1. 34 (Jan.3,1987, vs. N.Y. Jets)
2. 26 (Jan. 17, 1988, at Den.)
3. 22 (Dec. 4, 1949, vs. Buf.)
   22 (Dec. 24, 1950, vs. L.A.)
5. 20 (Dec. 28, 1952, vs. Det.)
   20 (Dec. 28, 1969, at Dal.)
   20 (Jan. 9, 1988, vs. Ind.)
   20 (Jan. 6, 1990, vs. Buf.)
   20 (Jan. 1, 1995, vs. N.E.)

Interceptions

1. 7 (Dec. 26, 1955, at L.A.)
2. 6 (Dec. 26, 1954, vs. Det.)
3. 5 (Dec. 19, 1948, vs. Buf.)
   5 (Dec. 24, 1950, vs. L.A.)
5. 4 (Dec. 21, 1968, vs. Dal.)

Punting Yards

1. 363 (Dec.17,1950,vs.N.Y. Giants)
2. 338 (Jan.14, 1990, at Den.)
3. 310 (Jan. 3, 1987, vs. N.Y. Jets)
4. 304 (Dec.21, 1958, at N.Y.)
5. 291 (Jan.8, 1983, at L.A. Raiders)

Cleveland Browns Facts & Trivia

Punt Return Yards
(Does not include game against Buffalo on Dec. 4, 1949)

1. 81 (Jan. 4, 1981, vs. Oak.)
2. 74 (Dec. 26, 1971, vs. Bal.)
3. 65 (Jan.3,1987, vs. N.Y. Jets)
4. 61 (Dec. 11, 1949, vs. S.F.)
5. 46 (Dec. 24, 1972, at Mia.)

Kickoff Return Yards

1. 180 (Jan. 6, 1990, vs. Buf.)
2. 163 (Dec. 29, 1957, at Det.)
3. 155 (Jan. 2, 1966, at G.B.)
4. 132 (Dec. 23, 1951, at L.A.)
5. 130 (Jan. 14, 1990, at Den.)

Total Net Yards

1. 558 (Jan.3,1987,vs.N.Y. Jets)
2. 464 (Jan. 17, 1988, at Den.)
3. 404 (Jan. 9, 1988, vs. Ind.)
4. 398 (Dec. 4, 1949, vs. Buf.)
5. 384 (Dec. 28, 1952, vs. Det.)

5. Highest-Scoring, Lowest-Scoring, Most One-Sided Games

Ten Highest-Scoring Games
1. 66 - Cleveland 66, Brooklyn 14 (Dec. 8, 1946, at Bro.)
2. 62 - Cleveland 62, New York 14 (Dec. 6, 1953, at Cle.)
   Cleveland 62, Washington 3 (Nov. 7, 1954, at Cle.)
4. 61 - Cleveland 61, Los Angeles 14 (Oct. 14, 1949, at L.A.)
5. 55 - Cleveland 55, Brooklyn 7 (Sept. 12, 1947, at Bro.)
6. 52 - Cleveland 52, New York 20 (Dec. 12, 1964, at N.Y.)
7. 51 - Cleveland 51, Chicago 14 (Nov. 17, 1946, at Cle.)
   Cleveland 51, Pittsburgh 0 (Sept. 10, 1989, at Pit.)
9. 49 - Cleveland 49, Chi. Cardinals 28 (Dec. 2, 1951, at Cle.)
   Cleveland 49, Philadelphia 7 (Oct. 19, 1952, at Phi.)
   Cleveland 49, Atlanta 17 (Oct. 30, 1966, at Atl.)
   Cleveland 49, New York 40 (Dec. 4, 1966, at Cle.)

Ten Highest-Scoring Games by Opponents
1. 58 - Houston 58, Cleveland 14 (Dec. 9, 1990, at Hou.)
2. 56 - San Francisco 56, Cleveland 28 (Oct. 9, 1949, at S.F.)
3. 55 - Pittsburgh 55, Cleveland 27 (Oct. 17, 1954, at Pit.)
   Green Bay 55, Cleveland 7 (Nov. 12, 1967, at G.B. [Milwaukee])
5. 51 - Minnesota 51, Cleveland 3 (Nov. 9, 1969, at Min.)
   Pittsburgh 51, Cleveland 35 (Oct. 7, 1979, at Cle.)
7. 49 - Green Bay 49, Cleveland 17 (Oct. 15, 1961, at Cle.)
   St. Louis 49, Cleveland 13 (Sept. 26, 1965, at Cle.)
9. 48 - New York 48, Cleveland 7 (Dec. 6, 1959, at N.Y.)
   Cincinnati 48, Cleveland 16 (Dec. 17, 1978, at Cin.)

Ten Highest-Scoring Games Between Both Teams
1. 89 - Cleveland 49, New York 40 (Dec. 4, 1966, at Cle.)
2. 86 - Pittsburgh 51, Cleveland 35 (Oct. 7, 1979, at Cle.)
3. 84 - San Francisco 56, Cleveland 28 (Oct. 9, 1949, at S.F.)
4. 82 - Pittsburgh 55, Cleveland 27 (Oct. 17, 1954, at Pit.)
   Cleveland 48, New York 34 (Dec. 18, 1960, at N.Y.)
6. 80 - Cleveland 66, Brooklyn 14 (Dec. 8, 1946, at Bro.)
7. 79 - Cleveland 42, Washington 37 (Nov. 26, 1967, at Cle.)
8. 77 - Cleveland 49, Chi. Cardinals 28 (Dec. 2, 1951, at Cle.)
9. 76 - Cleveland 62, New York 14 (Dec. 6, 1953, at Cle.)
   Cleveland 45, Los Angeles 31 (Nov. 24, 1957, at Cle.)

Cleveland Browns Facts & Trivia

Ten Lowest-Scoring Games Between Both Teams
1. 6 - N.Y. Giants 6, Cleveland 0 (Oct. 1, 1950, at Cle.)
   Cleveland 6, Philadelphia 0 (Nov. 21, 1954, at Cle.)
3. 7 - Cleveland 7, New York 0 (Oct. 12, 1946, at N.Y.)
   Cleveland 7, New York 0 (Oct. 25, 1953, at N.Y.)
   Cleveland 7, San Francisco 0 (Dec. 1, 1974, at Cle.)
6. 8 - Dallas 6, Cleveland 2 (Dec. 12, 1970, at Cle.)
7. 9 - Cleveland 6, New York 3 (Sept. 29, 1957, at Cle.)
   Los Angeles 9, Cleveland 0 (Nov. 27, 1977, at Cle.)
   Cleveland 6, Kansas City 3 (Sept. 4, 1988, at K.C.)
10. 10 - Cleveland 10, N.Y. Giants 0 (Nov. 18, 1951, at N.Y.)
   Cleveland 10, Chi. Cardinals 0 (Dec. 7, 1952, at Chi.)
   Cleveland 7, Oakland 3 (Nov. 18, 1973, at Oak.)

Ten Most One-Sided Victories
1. 59 - Cleveland 62, Washington 3 (Nov. 7, 1954, at Cle.)
2. 52 - Cleveland 66, Brooklyn 14 (Dec. 8, 1946, at Bro.)
3. 51 - Cleveland 51, Pittsburgh 0 (Sept. 10, 1989, at Pit.)
4. 48 - Cleveland 55, Brooklyn 7 (Sept. 12, 1947, at Bro.)
   Cleveland 62, New York 14 (Dec. 6, 1953, at Cle.)
6. 47 - Cleveland 61, Los Angeles 14 (Oct. 14, 1949, at L.A.)
7. 45 - Cleveland 45, Washington 0 (Oct. 14, 1951, at Cle.)
8. 44 - Cleveland 44, Miami 0 (Sept. 6, 1946, at Cle.)
9. 42 - Cleveland 42, Baltimore 0 (Dec. 7, 1947, at Bal.)
   Cleveland 49, Philadelphia 7 (Oct. 19, 1952, at Phi.)
   Cleveland 42, Chicago 0 (Dec. 11, 1960, at Cle.)

Ten Most One-Sided Defeats
1. 48 - Green Bay 55, Cleveland 7 (Nov. 12, 1967, at G.B. [Milw.]
   Minnesota 51, Cleveland 3 (Nov. 9, 1969, at Min.)
3. 44 - Houston 58, Cleveland 14 (Dec. 9, 1990, at Hou.)
4. 42 - Buffalo 42, Cleveland 0 (Nov. 4, 1990, at Cle.)
5. 41 - New York 48, Cleveland 7 (Dec. 6, 1959, at N.Y.)
6. 36 - St. Louis 49, Cleveland 13 (Sept. 26, 1965, at Cle.)
   Pittsburgh 42, Cleveland 6 (Oct. 5, 1975, at Cle.)
8. 35 - Los Angeles 42, Cleveland 7 (Dec. 12, 1965, at L.A.)
   Pittsburgh 35, Cleveland 0 (Dec. 23, 1990, at Pit.)
10. 34 - Kansas City 34, Cleveland 0 (Sept. 30, 1984, at K.C.)
   San Francisco 41, Cleveland 7 (Nov. 11, 1984, at Cle.)

6. Highest-Scoring, Lowest-Scoring, Most One-Sided Games (Postseason)

Five Highest-Scoring Games
1. 56 - Cleveland 56, Detroit 10 (NFL Championship, Dec. 26, 1954, at Cle.)
2. 49 - Cleveland 49, Buffalo 7 (AAFC Championship, Dec. 19, 1948, at Cle.)
3. 38 - Cleveland 38, Los Angeles 14 (NFL Championship, Dec. 26, 1955, at L.A.)
   Cleveland 38, Dallas 14 (Eastern Conference Championship, Dec. 28, 1969, at Dal.)
   Cleveland 38, Indianapolis 21 (AFC Divisional Playoff, Jan. 9, 1988, at Cle.)

Five Highest-Scoring Games by Opponents
1. 59 - Detroit 59, Cleveland 14 (NFL Championship, Dec. 29, 1957, at Det.)
2. 52 - Dallas 52, Cleveland 14 (Eastern Conference Championship, Dec. 24, 1967, at Dal.)
3. 38 - Denver 38, Cleveland 33 (AFC Championship, Jan. 17, 1988, at Den.)
4. 37 - Denver 37, Cleveland 21 (AFC Championship, Jan. 14, 1990, at Den.)
5. 34 - Baltimore 34, Cleveland 0 (NFL Championship, Dec. 29, 1968, at Cle.)

Five Highest-Scoring Games Between Both Teams
1. 73 - Detroit 59, Cleveland 14 (NFL Championship, Dec. 29, 1957, at Det.)
2. 71 - Denver 38, Cleveland 33 (AFC Championship, Jan. 17, 1988, at Den.)
3. 66 - Cleveland 56, Detroit 10 (NFL Championship, Dec. 26, 1954, at Cle.)
   Dallas 52, Cleveland 14 (Eastern Conference Championship, Dec. 24, 1967, at Dal.)
5. 64 - Cleveland 34, Buffalo 30 (AFC Divisional Playoff, Jan. 6, 1990, at Cle.)

Cleveland Browns Facts & Trivia

Five Lowest-Scoring Games
1. 0 - New York 10, Cleveland 0 (Eastern Conference Playoff, Dec. 21, 1958, at N.Y.)
   Baltimore 34, Cleveland 0 (NFL Championship, Dec. 29, 1968, at Cle.)
3. 3 - Baltimore 20, Cleveland 3 (AFC Divisional Playoff, Dec. 26, 1971, at Cle.)
4. 7 - Detroit 17, Cleveland 7 (NFL Championship, Dec. 28, 1952, at Cle.)
   Minnesota 27, Cleveland 7 (NFL Championship, Jan. 4, 1970, at Min.)

Five Lowest-Scoring Games by Opponents
1. 0 - Cleveland 27, Baltimore 0 (NFL Championship, Dec. 27, 1964, at Cle.)
2. 3 - Cleveland 14, New York 3 (AAFC Championship, Dec. 14, 1947, at N.Y.)
   Cleveland 8, N.Y. Giants 3 (American Conference Playoff, Dec. 17, 1950, at Cle.)
4. 7 - Cleveland 49, Buffalo 7 (AAFC Championship, Dec. 19, 1948, at Cle.)
   Cleveland 21, San Francisco 7 (AAFC Championship, Dec. 11, 1949, at Cle.)

Five Lowest-Scoring Games Between Both Teams
1. 10 - New York 10, Cleveland 0 (Eastern Conference Playoff, Dec. 21, 1958, at N.Y.)
2. 11 - Cleveland 8, N.Y. Giants 3 (American Conference Playoff, Dec. 17, 1950, at Cle.)
3. 17 - Cleveland 14, New York 3 (AAFC Championship, Dec. 14, 1947, at N.Y.)
4. 23 - Cleveland 14, New York 9 (AAFC Championship, Dec. 22, 1946, at Cle.)
   Baltimore 20, Cleveland 3 (AFC Divisional Playoff, Dec. 26, 1971, at Cle.)

Five Most One-Sided Victories
1. 46 - Cleveland 56, Detroit 10 (NFL Championship, Dec. 26, 1954, at Cle.)
2. 42 - Cleveland 49, Buffalo 7 (AAFC Championship, Dec. 19,

Cleveland Browns Facts & Trivia

1948, at Cle.)
3. 27 - Cleveland 27, Baltimore 0 (NFL Championship, Dec. 27, 1964, at Cle.)
4. 24 - Cleveland 38, Los Angeles 14 (NFL Championship, Dec. 26, 1955, at L.A.)
Cleveland 38, Dallas 14 (Eastern Conference Championship, Dec. 28, 1969, at Dal.)

Five Most One-Sided Defeats
1. 45 - Detroit 59, Cleveland 14 (NFL Championship, Dec. 29, 1957, at Det.)
2. 38 - Dallas 52, Cleveland 14 (Eastern Conference Championship, Dec. 24, 1967, at Dal.)
3. 34 - Baltimore 34, Cleveland 0 (NFL Championship, Dec. 29, 1968, at Cle.)
4. 20 - Minnesota 27, Cleveland 7 (NFL Championship, Jan. 4, 1970, at Min.)
Pittsburgh 29, Cleveland 9 (AFC Divisional Playoff, Jan. 7, 1995, at Pit.)

7. Season Point Differentials

Five Best Season Point Differentials

1. +286 (423-137) (1946)
2. +225 (410-185) (1947)
3. +199 (389-190) (1948)
4. +186 (348-162) (1953)
5. +179 (331-152) (1951)

Five Worst Season Point Differentials

1. -234 (228-462) (1990)
2. -154 (218-372) (1975)
3. -99 (276-375) (1981)
4. -93 (251-344) (1974)
5. -67 (289-356) (1995)

8. Streaks

Five Longest Winning Streaks in a Season
1. 14 - Sept. 3 - Dec. 5, 1948 (0-0 to 14-0)
2. 11 - Oct. 7 - Dec. 16, 1951 (0-1 to 11-1)
   Sept. 27 - Dec. 6, 1953 (0-0 to 11-0)
4. 8 - Oct. 24 - Dec. 12, 1954 (1-2 to 9-2)
   Oct. 20 - Dec. 8, 1968 (2-3 to 10-3)

Five Longest Losing Streaks in a Season
1. 9 - Sept. 21 - Nov. 16, 1975 (0-0 to 0-9)
2. 8 - Oct. 14 - Dec. 9, 1990 (2-3 to 2-11)
3. 6 - Nov. 5 - Dec. 9, 1995 (4-4 to 4-10)
4. 5 - Nov. 22 - Dec. 20, 1981 (5-6 to 5-11)
   Sept. 30 - Oct. 28, 1984 (1-3 to 1-8)

Five Longest Winning Streaks to Start a Season
1. 14 - Sept. 3 - Dec. 5, 1948
2. 11 - Sept. 27 - Dec. 6, 1953
3. 7 - Sept. 6 - Oct. 20, 1946
4. 6 - Sept. 15 - Oct. 20, 1963
5. 5 - Sept. 5 - Oct. 5, 1947
   Sept. 28 - Oct. 26, 1958

Five Longest Losing Streaks to Start a Season
1. 9 - Sept. 21 - Nov. 16, 1975
2. 3 - Sept. 3 - 16, 1984
3. 2 - Sept. 17 - 24, 1967
   Sept. 7 - 15, 1980
   Sept. 7 - 13, 1981
   Sept. 6 - 14, 1992

Five Longest Winning Streaks to End a Season
1. 14 - Sept. 3 - Dec. 5, 1948 (0-0 to 14-0)
2. 11 - Oct. 7 - Dec. 16, 1951 (0-1 to 11-1)
3. 6 - Oct. 29 - Dec. 10, 1950 (4-2 to 10-2)
4. 5 - Nov. 10 - Dec. 8, 1946 (7-2 to 12-2)
   Nov. 21 - Dec. 19, 1971 (4-5 to 9-5)
   Nov. 23 - Dec. 21, 1986 (7-4 to 12-4)

Cleveland Browns Facts & Trivia

Five Longest Losing Streaks to End a Season
1. 5 - Nov. 22 - Dec. 20, 1981 (5-6 to 5-11)
2. 4 - Nov. 27 - Dec. 18, 1977 (6-4 to 6-8)
3. 3 - Dec. 8 - 22, 1991 (6-7 to 6-10)
   Dec. 13 - 27, 1992 (7-6 to 7-9)
5. 2 - Dec. 9 - 16, 1973 (7-3-2 to 7-5-2)
   Dec. 7 - 15, 1974 (4-8 to 4-10)
   Dec. 9 - 16, 1979 (9-5 to 9-7)
   Dec. 23 - 30, 1990 (3-11 to 3-13)

9. The Last Time the Browns Beat (Current Teams) ...

* Denotes only victory

Team	At Home	Away
Arizona	Sept. 18, 1994	Oct. 23, 1988
Atlanta	Dec. 16, 1990	Nov. 18, 1984
Buffalo	Nov. 15, 1987	Dec. 7, 1986
Chicago	Nov. 29, 1992	Nov. 30, 1969
Cincinnati	Dec. 17, 1995	Oct. 29, 1995
Dallas	Dec. 4, 1988	Dec. 10, 1994
Denver	Oct. 1, 1989	Oct. 8, 1990
Detroit	Sept. 28, 1986	*Sept. 11, 1983
Green Bay	Oct. 18, 1992	Nov. 4, 1956
Houston	Nov. 27, 1994	Sept. 17, 1995
Indianapolis	Sept. 19, 1988	Sept. 25, 1994
Jacksonville	Never	Never
Kansas City	Sept. 24, 1995	Sept. 4, 1988
Miami	Nov. 10, 1986	*Oct. 25, 1970
Minnesota	Dec. 17, 1989	*Oct. 26, 1986
New England	Nov. 6, 1994	Oct. 25, 1992
New Orleans	Dec. 5, 1993	Oct. 8, 1978
N.Y. Giants	Sept. 30, 1973	Dec. 1, 1985
N.Y. Jets	Oct. 2, 1994	Sept. 2, 1979
Oakland	Never	Sept. 19, 1993
Philadelphia	Oct. 16, 1988	Nov. 13, 1994
Pittsburgh	Oct. 24, 1993	Sept. 10, 1989

St. Louis	Oct. 26, 1987	Dec. 26, 1993
San Diego	Dec. 21, 1986	Oct. 20, 1991
San Francisco	Sept. 13, 1993	Nov. 15, 1981
Seattle	*Dec. 24, 1994	Nov. 12, 1989
Tampa Bay	Sept. 10, 1995	Nov. 5, 1989
Washington	Sept. 28, 1969	Nov. 27, 1988

10. Cleveland Municipal Stadium/Cleveland Stadium Football Seating Capacities, 1946-95

1946	80,000
1947	77,563
1948-51	77,707
1952-61	78,207
1962-64	78,166
1965	77,096
1966	77,124
1967-74	79,282
1975-76	80,165
1977	80,233
1978-80	80,385
1981-82	80,322
1983-91	80,098
1992-95	78,512

11. Attendance

(From 1946-72, Browns home attendance figures were based on the number of tickets purchased; from 1973-95, they were based on the number of tickets used) (From 1946 to November 3, 1980, standing-room-only [SRO] tickets for Browns home games were included in attendance figures; from November 23, 1980, to 1995, they were not included)

Ten Highest Home Attendance Figures, 1946-November 3, 1980
1. 85,703 - Cleveland 31, N.Y. Jets 21 (Sept. 21, 1970)
2. 84,850 - Cleveland 42, Dallas 10 (Nov. 2, 1969)
3. 84,721 - Cleveland 30, Dallas 21 (Oct. 23, 1966)
4. 84,684 - Cleveland 35, Pittsburgh 23 (Oct. 5, 1963)
5. 84,349 - Cleveland 15, Pittsburgh 7 (Oct. 3, 1970)
6. 84,285 - Oakland 34, Cleveland 20 (Oct. 4, 1971)
7. 84,213 - New York 33, Cleveland 6 (Oct. 27, 1963)
8. 84,078 - Cleveland 42, Pittsburgh 31 (Oct. 18, 1969)
9. 83,943 - Green Bay 21, Cleveland 20 (Sept. 18, 1966)
10. 83,819 - Kansas City 31, Cleveland 7 (Oct. 8, 1972)

Ten Highest Home Attendance Figures, November 23, 1980-1995
1. 79,700 - Cleveland 17, Cincinnati 7 (Sept. 15, 1983)
2. 79,543 - Cleveland 34, Pittsburgh 10 (Sept. 20, 1987)
3. 79,483 - Houston 9, Cleveland 3 (Sept. 13, 1981)
4. 79,253 - Cleveland 31, Cincinnati 7 (Nov. 23, 1980)
5. 79,147 - Cleveland 23, Cincinnati 16 (Oct. 30, 1988)
6. 79,042 - Cleveland 17, Pittsburgh 7 (Sept. 16, 1985)
7. 78,986 - Cleveland 42, Baltimore 28 (Oct. 25, 1981)
8. 78,904 - San Diego 44, Cleveland 14 (Sept. 7, 1981)
9. 78,860 - Dallas 26, Cleveland 14 (Sept. 1, 1991)
10. 78,840 - Pittsburgh 17, Cleveland 7 (Oct. 15, 1989)

Ten Lowest Home Attendance Figures
1. 16,506 - Cleveland 35, Chicago 2 (Nov. 6, 1949)
2. 20,564 - Cleveland 17, Philadelphia 14 (Dec. 2, 1956)
3. 20,621 - Cleveland 21, Baltimore 0 (Sept. 11, 1949)
4. 21,908 - Cleveland 20, Washington 14 (Nov. 19, 1950)
5. 22,511 - Cleveland 7, Buffalo 7 (Nov. 13, 1949)
6. 22,878 - Washington 20, Cleveland 17 (Nov. 25, 1956)
7. 24,101 - Cleveland 31, Chi. Cardinals 7 (Oct. 10, 1954)

Cleveland Browns Facts & Trivia

8. 24,499 - Cleveland 27, Chi. Cardinals 16 (Nov. 29, 1953)
9. 24,559 - Cleveland 7, San Francisco 0 (Dec. 1, 1974)
10. 25,158 - Cleveland 62, Washington 3 (Nov. 7, 1954)

Ten Highest Away Attendance Figures
1. 78,266 - Buffalo 22, Cleveland 13 (Nov. 1, 1981)
2. 77,045 - Cleveland 42, New Orleans 7 (Oct. 1, 1967)
3. 76,251 - Cleveland 24, Dallas 17 (Nov. 21, 1965)
4. 75,891 - N.Y. Giants 13, Cleveland 10 (Sept. 22, 1991)
5. 75,806 - Denver 30, Cleveland 7 (Nov. 13, 1988)
6. 75,504 - Dallas 26, Cleveland 14 (Nov. 24, 1966)
7. 75,462 - Kansas City 34, Cleveland 0 (Sept. 30, 1990)
8. 75,313 - Cleveland 28, Miami 0 (Oct. 25, 1970)
9. 75,283 - Detroit 21, Cleveland 10 (Nov. 9, 1975)
10. 74,859 - Denver 23, Cleveland 20 (OT) (Nov. 8, 1981)

Ten Lowest Away Attendance Figures
1. 5,031 - Cleveland 14, Chicago 6 (Nov. 24, 1949)
2. 9,083 - Cleveland 34, Miami 0 (Dec. 3, 1946)
3. 9,821 - Cleveland 31, Brooklyn 21 (Dec. 5, 1948)
4. 14,600 - Cleveland 66, Brooklyn 14 (Dec. 8, 1946)
5. 14,830 - Cleveland 20, New England 10 (Oct. 4, 1987)
6. 15,201 - Cleveland 31, Baltimore 0 (Sept. 24, 1950)
7. 16,263 - Cleveland 24, Philadelphia 9 (Dec. 16, 1951)
8. 18,450 - Cleveland 41, Chicago 21 (Sept. 26, 1947)
9. 18,876 - Cleveland 55, Brooklyn 7 (Sept. 12, 1947)
10. 19,742 - Cleveland 34, Chi. Cardinals 17 (Nov. 4, 1951)

Five Highest Season Average Attendance Figures, 1946-80
(Although SRO tickets were not sold for the last two games of the 1980 season, the '80 season is included since SRO tickets were sold for most - six of the eight - home games that year)
1. 82,623 (1969)
2. 81,054 (1970)
3. 79,612 (1965)
4. 78,476 (1964)
5. 77,830 (1967)

Five Highest Season Average Attendance Figures, 1981-95
1. 77,018 (1988)
2. 76,677 (1989)

3. 75,216 (1981)
4. 72,967 (1986)
5. 71,469 (1991)

Five Lowest Season Average Attendance Figures
1. 30,579 (1954)
2. 31,601 (1949)
3. 33,387 (1950)
4. 36,941 (1956)
5. 38,569 (1951)

12. Attendance (Postseason)

(From 1946-72, Browns home attendance figures were based on the number of tickets purchased; from 1973-95, they were based on the number of tickets used)
(From 1946 to November 3, 1980, standing-room-only [SRO] tickets for Browns home games were included in attendance figures; from November 23, 1980, to 1995, they were not included)

Home Attendance Figures, Highest to Lowest, 1946-79
1. 81,497 - (Eastern Conference Championship, Dec. 21, 1968)
2. 80,628 - (NFL Championship, Dec. 29, 1968)
3. 79,544 - (NFL Championship, Dec. 27, 1964)
4. 74,082 - (AFC Divisional Playoff, Dec. 26, 1971)
5. 50,934 - (NFL Championship, Dec. 28, 1952)
6. 43,827 - (NFL Championship, Dec. 26, 1954)
7. 40,489 - (AAFC Championship, Dec. 22, 1946)
8. 33,054 - (American Conference Playoff, Dec. 17, 1950)
9. 29,751 - (NFL Championship, Dec. 24, 1950)
10. 22,981 -(AAFC Championship, Dec. 19, 1948)
11. 22,550 - (AAFC Championship, Dec. 11, 1949)
12. 17,270 - (AAFC Playoff, Dec. 4, 1949)

Home Attendance Figures, Highest to Lowest, 1980-95
1. 79,915 - (AFC Championship, Jan. 11, 1987)
2. 78,586 - (AFC Divisional Playoff, Jan. 9, 1988)
3. 78,106 - (AFC Divisional Playoff, Jan. 3, 1987)
4. 77,706 - (AFC Divisional Playoff, Jan. 6, 1990)

5. 77,655 - (AFC Divisional Playoff, Jan. 4, 1981)
6. 77,452 - (AFC Wild Card, Jan. 1, 1995)
7. 74,977 - (AFC Wild Card, Dec. 24, 1988)

Away Attendance Figures, Highest to Lowest
1. 87,695 - Los Angeles (NFL Championship, Dec. 26, 1955)
2. 80,010 - Miami (AFC Divisional Playoff, Dec. 24, 1972)
3. 76,046 - Denver (AFC Championship, Jan. 14, 1990)
4. 75,993 - Denver (AFC Championship, Jan. 17, 1988)
5. 75,128 - Miami (AFC Divisional Playoff, Jan 4, 1986)
6. 70,786 - Dallas (Eastern Conference Championship, Dec. 24, 1967)
7. 69,321 - Dallas (Eastern Conference Championship, Dec. 28, 1969)
8. 61,879 - New York (AAFC Championship, Dec. 14, 1947)
9. 61,174 - New York(Eastern Conference Playoff, Dec. 21, 1958)
10. 58,185 - Pittsburgh (AFC Divisional Playoff, Jan. 7, 1995)
11. 57,540 - Los Angeles (NFL Championship, Dec. 23, 1951)
12. 56,555 - L.A. Raiders (AFC First-Round, Jan. 8, 1983)
13. 55,263 - Detroit (NFL Championship, Dec. 21, 1957)
14. 54,577 - Detroit (NFL Championship, Dec. 27, 1953)
15. 50,852 - Green Bay (NFL Championship, Jan. 2, 1966)
16. 47,900 - Minnesota (NFL Championship, Jan. 4, 1970)

13. Shutouts
* Denotes postseason

Cleveland 44, Miami 0 (Sept. 6, 1946, at Cle.)
Cleveland 28, Buffalo 0 (Sept. 22, 1946, at Buf.)
Cleveland 7, New York 0 (Oct. 12, 1946, at N.Y.)
Cleveland 34, Miami 0 (Dec. 3, 1946, at Mia.)
Cleveland 28, Baltimore 0 (Sept. 21, 1947, at Cle.)
Cleveland 42, Baltimore 0 (Dec. 7, 1947, at Bal.)
Cleveland 21, Baltimore 0 (Sept. 11, 1949, at Cle.)
Cleveland 31, Brooklyn-New York 0 (Nov. 20, 1949, at Bro.-N.Y.)
Cleveland 31, Baltimore 0 (Sept. 24, 1950, at Bal.)
N.Y. Giants 6, Cleveland 0 (Oct. 1, 1950, at Cle.)
Cleveland 45, Washington 0 (Oct. 14, 1951, at Cle.)
Cleveland 17, Pittsburgh 0 (Oct. 21, 1951, at Cle.)
Cleveland 10, N.Y. Giants 0 (Nov. 18, 1951, at N.Y.)

Cleveland Browns Facts & Trivia

Cleveland 28, Pittsburgh 0 (Dec. 9, 1951, at Pit.)
Cleveland 10, Chi. Cardinals 0 (Dec. 7, 1952, at Chi.)
Cleveland 27, Green Bay 0 (Sept. 27, 1953, at G.B. [Milwaukee])
Cleveland 7, New York 0 (Oct. 25, 1953, at N.Y.)
Cleveland 6, Philadelphia 0 (Nov. 21, 1954, at Cle.)
Cleveland 16, Philadelphia 0 (Nov. 18, 1956, at Phi.)
Cleveland 24, Pittsburgh 0 (Nov. 10, 1957, at Cle.)
Cleveland 31, Chi. Cardinals 0 (Dec. 1, 1957, at Cle.)
*New York 10, Cleveland 0 (Dec. 21, 1958, at N.Y.)
Cleveland 42, Chicago 0 (Dec. 11, 1960, at Cle.)
*Cleveland 27, Baltimore 0 (Dec. 27, 1964, at Cle.)
Cleveland 24, Chicago 0 (Oct. 22, 1967, at Cle.)
*Baltimore 34, Cleveland 0 (Dec. 29, 1968, at Cle.)
Cleveland 28, Miami 0 (Oct. 25, 1970, at Mia.)
Cleveland 31, Houston 0 (Sept. 19, 1971, at Cle.)
Denver 27, Cleveland 0 (Oct. 24, 1971, at Cle.)
Chicago 17, Cleveland 0 (Oct. 15, 1972, at Cle.)
Pittsburgh 30, Cleveland 0 (Dec. 3, 1972, at Pit.)
Cleveland 20, Houston 0 (Nov. 5, 1972, at Cle.)
Cleveland 7, San Francisco 0 (Dec. 1, 1974, at Cle.)
Los Angeles 9, Cleveland 0 (Nov. 27, 1977, at Cle.)
Cleveland 20, Tampa Bay 0 (Nov. 13, 1983, at Cle.)
Cleveland 30, New England 0 (Nov. 20, 1983, at N.E.)
Seattle 33, Cleveland 0 (Sept. 3, 1984, at Sea.)
Cleveland 34, Cincinnati 0 (Oct. 18, 1987, at Cin.)
Cleveland 51, Pittsburgh 0 (Sept. 10, 1989, at Pit.)
Cincinnati 21, Cleveland 0 (Dec. 3, 1989, at Cle.)
Kansas City 34, Cleveland 0 (Sept. 30, 1990, at K.C.)
Buffalo 42, Cleveland 0 (Nov. 4, 1990, at Cle.)
Pittsburgh 35, Cleveland 0 (Dec. 23, 1990, at Pit.)
Cleveland 20, New England 0 (Sept. 8, 1991, at N.E.)
Cleveland 31, Indianapolis 0 (Dec. 1, 1991, at Ind.)
Denver 12, Cleveland 0 (Sept. 27, 1992, at Cle.)
Cleveland 32, Arizona 0 (Sept. 18, 1994, at Cle.)

Overall Regular Season - 33-11 .750
Home Regular Season - 15-7 .682
Away Regular Season - 18-4 .818
Postseason - 1-2 .333

14. Overtime

* Denotes postseason
Cleveland 30, New England 27 (Sept. 26, 1977, at Cle.)
Cleveland 13, Cincinnati 10 (Sept. 10, 1978, at Cle.)
Pittsburgh 15, Cleveland 9 (Sept. 24, 1978, at Pit.)
Cleveland 37, N.Y. Jets 34 (Dec. 10, 1978, at Cle.)
Cleveland 25, N.Y. Jets 22 (Sept. 2, 1979, at N.Y.)
Cleveland 30, Miami 24 (Nov. 18, 1979, at Cle.)
Pittsburgh 33, Cleveland 30 (Nov. 25, 1979, at Pit.)
Denver 23, Cleveland 20 (Nov. 8, 1981, at Den.)
Cleveland 30, San Diego 24 (Sept. 25, 1983, at S.D.)
Cleveland 25, Houston 19 (Oct. 30, 1983, at Cle.)
Cincinnati 20, Cleveland 17 (Dec. 2, 1984, at Cle.)
St.Louis 27, Cleveland 24 (Sept. 8, 1985, at Cle.)
Cleveland 37, Pittsburgh 31 (Nov. 23, 1986, at Cle.)
Cleveland 13, Houston 10 (Nov. 30, 1986, at Cle.)
*Cleveland 23, N.Y. Jets 20 (2OT) (Jan. 3, 1987, at Cle.)
*Denver 23, Cleveland 20 (Jan. 11, 1987, at Cle.)
San Diego 27, Cleveland 24 (Nov. 1, 1987, at S.D.)
Miami 13, Cleveland 10 (Oct. 8, 1989, at Mia.)
Cleveland 10, Kansas City 10 (Nov. 19, 1989, at Cle.)
Indianapolis 23, Cleveland 17 (Dec. 10, 1989, at Ind.)
Cleveland 23, Minnesota 17 (Dec. 17, 1989, at Cle.)
Cleveland 30, San Diego 24 (Oct. 20, 1991, at S.D.)
Cleveland 29, Cincinnati 26 (Oct. 29, 1995, at Cin.)

Overall Regular Season - 12-8-1 .595
Home Regular Season - 8-2-1 .773
Away Regular Season - 4-6 .400
Postseason - 1-1 .500

Ties
New York 28, Cleveland 28 (Nov. 23, 1947, at N.Y.)
Buffalo 28, Cleveland 28 (Sept. 5, 1949, at Buf.)
Cleveland 7, Buffalo 7 (Nov. 13, 1949, at Cle.)
New York 35, Cleveland 35 (Nov. 27, 1955, at N.Y.)
Washington 30, Cleveland 30 (Nov. 17, 1957, at Was.)
St. Louis 17, Cleveland 17 (Nov. 27, 1960, at St.L.)
New York 7, Cleveland 7 (Dec. 17, 1961, at N.Y.)
Cleveland 14, Philadelphia 14 (Nov. 4, 1962, at Cle.)
Cleveland 33, St. Louis 33 (Sept. 20, 1964, at Cle.)
Cleveland 21, St. Louis 21 (Oct. 26, 1969, at Cle.)
Cleveland 16, San Diego 16 (Oct. 28, 1973, at Cle.)
Kansas City 20, Cleveland 20 (Dec. 2, 1973, at K.C.)
Cleveland 10, Kansas City 10 (OT) (Nov. 19, 1989, at Cle.)

15. Games in Which Both Teams Scored Fewer Than Ten Points
* Denotes postseason

Cleveland 7, New York 0 (Oct. 12, 1946, at N.Y.)
Cleveland 7, Buffalo 7 (Nov. 13, 1949, at Cle.)
N.Y. Giants 6, Cleveland 0 (Oct. 1, 1950, at Cle.)
*Cleveland 8, N.Y. Giants 3 (Dec. 17, 1950, at Cle.)
Cleveland 7, New York 0 (Oct. 25, 1953, at N.Y.)
Cleveland 6, Philadelphia 0 (Nov. 21, 1954, at Cle.)
Chi. Cardinals 9, Cleveland 7 (Sept. 30, 1956, at Chi.)
Cleveland 6, New York 3 (Sept. 29, 1957, at Cle.)
New York 7, Cleveland 7 (Dec. 17, 1961, at N.Y.)
Pittsburgh 9, Cleveland 7 (Nov. 10, 1963, at Pit.)
Dallas 6, Cleveland 2 (Dec. 12, 1970, at Cle.)
Cleveland 7, Oakland 3 (Nov. 18, 1973, at Oak.)
Cleveland 7, San Francisco 0 (Dec. 1, 1974, at Cle.)
Los Angeles 9, Cleveland 0 (Nov. 27, 1977, at Cle.)
Houston 9, Cleveland 3 (Sept. 13, 1981, at Cle.)
Indianapolis 9, Cleveland 7 (Dec. 6, 1987, at Cle.)
Cleveland 6, Kansas City 3 (Sept. 4, 1988, at K.C.)

Overall Regular Season - 7-7-2 .531
Home Regular Season - 3-5-1 .375
Away Regular Season - 4-2-1 .643
Postseason - 1-0 1.000

16. Vs. NFL Champions (1950-69) and Super Bowl Champions (1970-95) of Season at Hand
(Does not include the Browns' four seasons in the AAFC from 1946-49, and the 1950, 1954, 1955, and 1964 seasons since they were the champions those years)

* Denotes postseason

Cleveland 38, Los Angeles 23 (Oct. 7, 1951, at L.A.)
*Los Angeles 24, Cleveland 17 (Dec. 23, 1951, at L.A.)
Detroit 17, Cleveland 6 (Nov. 2, 1952, at Det.)
*Detroit 17, Cleveland 7 (Dec. 28, 1952, at Cle.)
*Detroit 17, Cleveland 16 (Dec. 27, 1953, at Det.)
New York 21, Cleveland 9 (Oct. 14, 1956, at Cle.)

Cleveland 24, New York 7 (Dec. 9, 1956, at N.Y.)
Detroit 20, Cleveland 7 (Dec. 8, 1957, at Det.)
*Detroit 59, Cleveland 14 (Dec. 29, 1957, at Det.)
Cleveland 38, Baltimore 31 (Nov. 1, 1959, at Bal.)
Cleveland 41, Philadelphia 24 (Sept. 25, 1960, at Phi.)
Philadelphia 31, Cleveland 29 (Oct. 23, 1960, at Cle.)
Green Bay 49, Cleveland 17 (Oct. 15, 1961, at Cle.)
*Green Bay 23, Cleveland 12 (Jan. 2, 1966, at G.B.)
Green Bay 21, Cleveland 20 (Sept. 18, 1966, at Cle.)
Green Bay 55, Cleveland 7 (Nov. 12, 1967, at G.B. [Milwaukee])
Cleveland 30, Baltimore 20 (Oct. 20, 1968, at Bal.)
*Baltimore 34, Cleveland 0 (Dec. 29, 1968, at Cle.)
Minnesota 51, Cleveland 3 (Nov. 9, 1969, at Min.)
*Minnesota 27, Cleveland 7 (Jan. 4, 1970, at Min.)
*Miami 20, Cleveland 14 (Dec. 24, 1972, at Mia.)
Miami 17, Cleveland 9 (Oct. 15, 1973, at Cle.)
Pittsburgh 20, Cleveland 16 (Oct. 20, 1974, at Pit.)
Pittsburgh 26, Cleveland 16 (Nov. 17, 1974, at Cle.)
Pittsburgh 42, Cleveland 6 (Oct. 5, 1975, at Cle.)
Pittsburgh 31, Cleveland 17 (Dec. 7, 1975, at Pit.)
Pittsburgh 15, Cleveland 9 (OT) (Sept. 24, 1978, at Pit.)
Pittsburgh 34, Cleveland 14 (Oct. 15, 1978, at Cle.)
Pittsburgh 51, Cleveland 35 (Oct. 7, 1979, at Cle.)
Pittsburgh 33, Cleveland 30 (OT) (Nov. 25, 1979, at Pit.)
*Oakland 14, Cleveland 12 (Jan. 4, 1981, at Cle.)
Cleveland 15, San Francisco 12 (Nov. 15, 1981, at S.F.)
San Francisco 41, Cleveland 7 (Nov. 11, 1984, at Cle.)
Washington 42, Cleveland 17 (Oct. 13, 1991, at Was.)

Overall Regular Season - 6-19 .240
Home Regular Season - 0-10 .000
Away Regular Season - 6-9 .400
Postseason - 0-9 .000 (Postseason wins are not feasible)

17. Games In Domes

Cleveland 21, Houston 10 (Dec. 7, 1970)
Cleveland 37, Houston 24 (Nov. 28, 1971)
Cleveland 23, Houston 17 (Oct. 22, 1972)
Cleveland 23, Houston 13 (Nov. 11, 1973)
Houston 28, Cleveland 24 (Dec. 15, 1974)
Detroit 21, Cleveland 10 (Nov. 9, 1975)
Houston 21, Cleveland 10 (Dec. 21, 1975)
Cleveland 21, Houston 7 (Nov. 7, 1976)

Cleveland Browns Facts & Trivia

Cleveland 24, Houston 23 (Oct. 16, 1977)
Seattle 20, Cleveland 19 (Dec. 18, 1977)
Cleveland 24, New Orleans 16 (Oct. 8, 1978)
Houston 14, Cleveland 10 (Nov. 5, 1978)
Seattle 47, Cleveland 24 (Dec. 3, 1978)
Houston 31, Cleveland 10 (Sept. 30, 1979)
Cleveland 27, Seattle 3 (Oct. 12, 1980)
Cleveland 17, Houston 14 (Nov. 30, 1980)
Houston 17, Cleveland 13 (Dec. 3, 1981)
Seattle 42, Cleveland 21 (Dec. 20, 1981)
Cleveland 21, Seattle 7 (Sept. 12, 1982)
Cleveland 20, Houston 14 (Dec. 26, 1982)
Cleveland 31, Detroit 26 (Sept. 11, 1983)
Houston 34, Cleveland 27 (Dec. 11, 1983)
Seattle 33, Cleveland 0 (Sept. 3, 1984)
Cleveland 27, Houston 20 (Dec. 16, 1984)
Cleveland 21, Houston 6 (Oct. 13, 1985)
Seattle 31, Cleveland 13 (Dec. 8, 1985)
Cleveland 24, Houston 20 (Sept. 14, 1986)
Cleveland 23, Minnesota 20 (Oct. 26, 1986)
Cleveland 24, Indianapolis 9 (Nov. 2, 1986)
New Orleans 28, Cleveland 21 (Sept. 13, 1987)
Cleveland 40, Houston 7 (Nov. 22, 1987)
Houston 24, Cleveland 17 (Nov. 7, 1988)
Cleveland 17, Seattle 7 (Nov. 12, 1989)
Detroit 13, Cleveland 10 (Nov. 23, 1989)
Indianapolis 23, Cleveland 17 (OT) (Dec. 10, 1989)
Cleveland 24, Houston 20 (Dec. 23, 1989)
New Orleans 25, Cleveland 20 (Oct. 14, 1990)
Houston 58, Cleveland 14 (Dec. 9, 1990)
Houston 28, Cleveland 24 (Nov. 17, 1991)
Cleveland 31, Indianapolis 0 (Dec. 1, 1991)
Indianapolis 14, Cleveland 3 (Sept. 6, 1992)
Cleveland 24, Houston 14 (Nov. 8, 1992)
Minnesota 17, Cleveland 13 (Nov. 22, 1992)
Detroit 24, Cleveland 14 (Dec. 13, 1992)
Indianapolis 23, Cleveland 10 (Sept. 26, 1993)
Seattle 22, Cleveland 5 (Nov. 14, 1993)
Atlanta 17, Cleveland 14 (Nov. 28, 1993)
Houston 19, Cleveland 17 (Dec. 12, 1993)
Cleveland 21, Indianapolis 14 (Sept. 25, 1994)
Cleveland 11, Houston 8 (Oct. 13, 1994)
Cleveland 14, Houston 7 (Sept. 17, 1995)
Detroit 38, Cleveland 20 (Oct. 8, 1995)
Minnesota 27, Cleveland 11 (Dec. 9, 1995)
Overall - 25-28 .472

18. Vs. Domed-Stadium Teams at Home * Denotes postseason

Cleveland 28, Houston 14 (Nov. 22, 1970)
Cleveland 31, Houston 0 (Sept. 19, 1971)
Cleveland 20, Houston 0 (Nov. 5, 1972)
Cleveland 42, Houston 13 (Oct. 21, 1973)
Cleveland 20, Houston 7 (Sept. 22, 1974)
Houston 40, Cleveland 10 (Oct. 12, 1975)
Cleveland 17, New Orleans 16 (Nov. 30, 1975)
Cleveland 13, Houston 10 (Dec. 5, 1976)
Houston 19, Cleveland 15 (Dec. 11, 1977)
Houston 16, Cleveland 13 (Oct. 1, 1978)
Seattle 29, Cleveland 24 (Nov. 11, 1979)
Cleveland 14, Houston 7 (Dec. 2, 1979)
Houston 16, Cleveland 7 (Sept. 15, 1980)
Houston 9, Cleveland 3 (Sept. 13, 1981)
Cleveland 20, New Orleans 17 (Oct. 18, 1981)
Minnesota 27, Cleveland 21 (Sept. 4, 1983)
Seattle 24, Cleveland 9 (Oct. 2, 1983)
Cleveland 25, Houston 19 (OT) (Oct. 30, 1983)
New Orleans 16, Cleveland 14 (Oct. 28, 1984)
Cleveland 27, Houston 10 (Nov. 25, 1984)
Cleveland 28, Houston 21 (Dec. 15, 1985)
Cleveland 24, Detroit 21 (Sept. 28, 1986)
Cleveland 13, Houston 10 (OT) (Nov. 30, 1986)
Houston 15, Cleveland 10 (Oct. 11, 1987)
Indianapolis 9, Cleveland 7 (Dec. 6, 1987)
*Cleveland 38, Indianapolis 21 (Jan. 9, 1988)
Cleveland 23, Indianapolis 17 (Sept. 19, 1988)
Seattle 16, Cleveland 10 (Oct. 9, 1988)
Cleveland 28, Houston 23 (Dec. 18, 1988)
*Houston 24, Cleveland 23 (Dec. 24, 1988)
Cleveland 28, Houston 17 (Oct. 29, 1989)
Cleveland 23, Minnesota 17 (OT) (Dec. 17, 1989)
Houston 35, Cleveland 23 (Nov. 18, 1990)
Houston 17, Cleveland 14 (Dec. 15, 1991)
Houston 17, Cleveland 14 (Dec. 20, 1992)
Houston 27, Cleveland 20 (Nov. 21, 1993)
Cleveland 17, New Orleans 13 (Dec. 5, 1993)
Cleveland 34, Houston 10 (Nov. 27, 1994)
Cleveland 35, Seattle 9 (Dec. 24, 1994)
Houston 37, Cleveland 10 (Nov. 5, 1995)
Regular Season - 21-17 .553
Postseason - 1-1 .500

19. Postseason

Cleveland 14, New York 9 (AAFC Championship, Dec. 22, 1946, at Cle.)
Cleveland 14, New York 3 (AAFC Championship, Dec. 14, 1947, at N.Y.)
Cleveland 49, Buffalo 7 (AAFC Championship, Dec. 19, 1948, at Cle.)
Cleveland 31, Buffalo 21 (AAFC Playoff, Dec. 4, 1949, at Cle.)
Cleveland 21, San Francisco 7 (AAFC Championship, Dec. 11, 1949, at Cle.)
Cleveland 8, N.Y. Giants 3 (Am. Conference Playoff, Dec. 17, 1950, at Cle.)
Cleveland 30, Los Angeles 28 (NFL Championship, Dec. 24, 1950, at Cle.)
Los Angeles 24, Cleveland 17 (NFL Championship, Dec. 23, 1951, at L.A.)
Detroit 17, Cleveland 7 (NFL Championship, Dec. 28, 1952, at Cle.)
Detroit 17, Cleveland 16 (NFL Championship, Dec. 27, 1953, at Det.)
Cleveland 56, Detroit 10 (NFL Championship, Dec. 26, 1954, at Cle.)
Cleveland 38, Los Angeles 14 (NFL Championship, Dec. 26, 1955, at L.A.)
Detroit 59, Cleveland 14 (NFL Championship, Dec. 29, 1957, at Det.)
New York 10, Cleveland 0 (East. Conf. Playoff, Dec. 21, 1958, at N.Y.)
Cleveland 27, Baltimore 0 (NFL Championship, Dec. 27, 1964, at Cle.)
Green Bay 23, Cleveland 12 (NFL Championship, Jan. 2, 1966, at G.B.)
Dallas 52, Cleveland 14 (East. Conf. Championship, Dec. 24, 1967, at Dal.)
Cleveland 31, Dallas 20 (East. Conf. Championship, Dec. 21, 1968, at Cle.)
Baltimore 34, Cleveland 0 (NFL Championship, Dec. 29, 1968, at Cle.)
Cleveland 38, Dallas 14 (East. Conf. Championship, Dec. 28, 1969, at Dal.)
Minnesota 27, Cleveland 7 (NFL Championship, Jan. 4, 1970, at Min.)
Baltimore 20, Cleveland 3 (AFC Divisional Playoff, Dec. 26, 1971, at Cle.)
Miami 20, Cleveland 14 (AFC Divisional Playoff, Dec. 24, 1972, at Mia.)
Oakland 14, Cleveland 12 (AFC Divisional Playoff, Jan. 4, 1981, at Cle.)
L.A. Raiders 27, Cleveland 10 (AFC First-Round, Jan. 8, 1983, at L.A.)
Miami 24, Cleveland 21 (AFC Divisional Playoff, Jan. 4, 1986, at Mia.)
Cleveland 23, N.Y. Jets 20 (2OT) (AFC Div. Playoff, Jan. 3, 1987, at Cle.)
Denver 23, Cleveland 20 (OT) (AFC Championship, Jan. 11, 1987, at Cle.)
Cleveland 38, Indianapolis 21 (AFC Div. Playoff, Jan. 9, 1988, at Cle.)
Denver 38, Cleveland 33 (AFC Championship, Jan. 17, 1988, at Den.)
Houston 24, Cleveland 23 (AFC Wild Card, Dec. 24, 1988, at Cle.)
Cleveland 34, Buffalo 30 (AFC Divisional Playoff, Jan. 6, 1990, at Cle.)
Denver 37, Cleveland 21 (AFC Championship, Jan. 14, 1990, at Den.)
Cleveland 20, New England 13 (AFC Wild Card, Jan. 1, 1995, at Cle.)
Pittsburgh 29, Cleveland 9 (AFC Divisional Playoff, Jan. 7, 1995, at Pit.)

Overall - 16-19 .457
Home - 13-6 .684
Away - 3-13 .188

BROWNIE POINTS
(The author ranks the games)

1. Ten Most Thrilling Recent Victories, 1976-95

1. Cleveland 28, Pittsburgh 23 (Oct. 24, 1993, at Cle.)
- Eric Metcalf stuns the Steelers and lifts the Browns into first place.

2. Cleveland 19, Dallas 14 (Dec. 10, 1994, at Dal.)
- Jay Novacek slips at the end as Christmas comes early for Cleveland, a five-point - er, five-*inch* -winner.

3. Cleveland 27, Cincinnati 24 (Dec. 21, 1980, at Cin.)
- A classic seesaw battle ends with the Bengals on the Cleveland 13-yard line and the Browns in the playoffs for the first time in eight years.

4. Cleveland 24, Houston 20 (Dec. 23, 1989, at Hou.)
- The Browns, riding a Mack Truck on the Road to New Orleans, mistakenly turn onto 'What's Clay Matthews Thinking?' Avenue, but find their way back, and eventually make the correct turn - onto Division Title Boulevard.

5. Cleveland 30, Denver 29 (Oct. 8, 1990, at Den.)
- Jerry Kauric's one moment of glory as a Brown - a last-second field goal - almost makes up for the entire Season From Hell.

6. Cleveland 19, L.A. Raiders 16 (Sept. 19, 1993, at L.A.)
- Eric Metcalf scores on a one-yard sweep with no time left, capping an incredible comeback from a 16-3 deficit with under five minutes to go.

7. Cleveland 25, N.Y. Jets 22 (OT) (Sept. 2, 1979, at N.Y.)
- Brian Sipe drives the Browns 68 yards in less than 30 seconds to the tying field goal with four ticks showing on the clock in this drama-filled contest. Then, late in sudden death, Oliver Davis intercepts a Matt Robinson pass and returns it 33 yards to the Jets' 31, leading to Don Cockroft's game-winning trey with 15 seconds

left.

8. Cleveland 26, Green Bay 21 (Oct. 19, 1980, at Cle.)
- Sipe to Logan for 46 yards with 16 seconds to go.

9. Cleveland 24, Philadelphia 19 (Nov. 4, 1979, at Phi.)
- Down, 19-10, late in the game, the Kardiac Kids rally and take the lead with under a minute left. The Eagles then drive to the Cleveland one with but a second to go. Ron Jaworski is picked off by Charlie Hall.

10. Cleveland 35, N.Y. Giants 33 (Dec. 1, 1985, at N.Y.)
- Gary Danielson leads a memorable comeback that stands when Giants kicker Eric Schubert misfires from 34 yards out on the final play of the game.

2. Ten Most Heartbreaking Defeats, 1976-95

1. Minnesota 28, Cleveland 23 (Dec. 14, 1980, at Min.)
- A fourth-quarter lead turns into a nightmare in Bloomington.

2. Pittsburgh 15, Cleveland 9 (OT) (Sept. 24, 1978, at Pit.)
- Pittsburgh's Larry Anderson fumbles the overtime kickoff, and the Browns recover deep in Steelers territory. Anderson, though, is ruled down prior to the miscue - an obviously blatant mistake by the officials - and the ball is awarded to Pittsburgh. Terry Bradshaw leads his team down the field to victory on his flea-flicker touchdown pass to Bennie Cunningham.

3. Pittsburgh 33, Cleveland 30 (OT) (Nov. 25, 1979, at Pit.)
- Leads of 20-6, 27-13, and 30-20 vanish; Matt Bahr's 37-yard field goal with nine seconds left in sudden death dooms the Browns once again.

4. Pittsburgh 16, Cleveland 13 (Nov. 16, 1980, at Pit.)
- A no-call on Theo Bell's illegal pick allows Lynn Swann's late touchdown catch to stand as the Three Rivers Jinx lives on.

Cleveland Browns Facts & Trivia

5. Cincinnati 23, Cleveland 21 (Nov. 3, 1991, at Cin.)
- The Browns blow numerous scoring opportunities. Matt Stover's 34-yard field goal attempt is blocked with no time left as Cincinnati gains its first win of the year in nine games.

6. Houston 28, Cleveland 24 (Nov. 17, 1991, at Hou.)
- Cleveland takes the lead on a long catch-and-run from Bernie Kosar to Reggie Langhorne on fourth down with 4:17 remaining. Then, after the Browns are forced to punt with just over two minutes left, Warren Moon drives his team down the field like a hot knife through butter, and flips the winning touchdown pass to Drew Hill from a yard out with nine seconds left.

7. Houston 17, Cleveland 14 (Dec. 20, 1992, at Cle.)
- Cody Carlson hooks up with Lorenzo White for a long pass play with little time left. That sets up the winning touchdown, dumping the Browns' playoff hopes into Lake Erie.

8. L.A. Raiders 21, Cleveland 20 (Oct. 20, 1985, at Cle.)
- Down by six and facing the roaring Dawg Pound on fourth down, Marc Wilson finds Todd Christensen from eight yards out with 29 seconds left, sending the Browns reeling into a four-game losing streak.

9. New England 17, Cleveland 16 (Oct. 7, 1984, at Cle.)
- Although not fired until two weeks later, this defeat very well could be the one that costs Sam Rutigliano his job. The Browns blow a 16-3 third-quarter lead, but down by one, have a golden opportunity with the ball on the Patriots' 21-yard line with 23 seconds left. All they have to do is run the clock down and have reliable Matt Bahr attempt a very makeable field goal. Instead, Paul McDonald is picked off.

10. N.Y. Giants 16, Cleveland 13 (Dec. 4, 1994, at Cle.)
- Dave Brown does his best John Elway imitation, directing a late drive, culminated by Brad Daluiso's 33-yard field goal with 19 seconds left.

3. Ten Least-Expected Victories, 1976-95

1. Cleveland 27, Pittsburgh 24 (Oct. 5, 1986, at Pit.)
- Sure, the Steelers were nowhere near the Steelers of old, but besides the Browns having more talent, name one reason that warrants anyone believing they could keep the Jinx from reaching 17.

2. Cleveland 18, Pittsburgh 16 (Oct. 10, 1976, at Cle.)
- It wasn't much of a surprise the Browns entered the game with a 1-3 record, but it was a shocker the two-time defending champion did. Despite Pittsburgh's poor record, Cleveland's "Turkey" of a win is still impressive.

3. Cleveland 19, Dallas 14 (Dec. 10, 1994, at Dal.)
- Almost no one predicted the Browns to go into Big D and defeat the two-time defending champion.

4. Cleveland 30, Denver 29 (Oct. 8, 1990, at Den.)
- The Browns rally from nine down late, lifting an 18-year-old Mile High monkey off their back.

5. Cleveland 26, Dallas 7 (Sept. 24, 1979, at Cle.)
- The Kardiac Kids, winners of each of their first three games by a field goal, shed their image and shock America's Team.

6. Cleveland 26, Philadelphia 7 (Nov. 13, 1994, at Phi.)
- The Browns, who had played a relatively soft schedule prior to this game, mesmerize the 7-2 Eagles.

7. Cleveland 23, San Francisco 13 (Sept. 13, 1993, at Cle.)
- The Browns hold Jerry Rice at "Bay" and pull off the upset.

8. Cleveland 15, San Francisco 12 (Nov. 15, 1981, at S.F.)
- One final Kardiac comeback gives the Browns a victory over the eventual Super Bowl Champion.

9. Cleveland 17, Houston 14 (Nov. 30, 1980, at Hou.)
- Clarence Scott's late interception preserves this upset in a battle for first.

10. Cleveland 34, Cincinnati 3 (Dec. 14, 1986, at Cin.)
- Despite the Browns' superior record to the Bengals' - 10-4 to 9-5 - most observers viewed
Cincinnati as the superior team. All of that changes, though, with this rout in Riverfront.

4. Ten Least-Expected Defeats, 1976-95

1. Green Bay 17, Cleveland 14 (Oct. 19, 1986, at Cle.)
- With the Browns leading, 14-3, and at the Green Bay 19 with less a minute to go in the first half, defensive back Mark Lee cuts in front of Brian Brennan in the end zone and intercepts a Bernie Kosar pass. The Browns collapse in the second half, handing Green Bay its first win of the year in seven games.

2. Jacksonville 23, Cleveland 15 (Oct. 22, 1995, at Cle.)
- The first-year Jaguars shock the tumbling Browns more than two weeks *before* the announcement of their impending move to Maryland.

3. Houston 34, Cleveland 27 (Dec. 11, 1983, at Hou.)
- A demoralizing loss for Cleveland, which entered the game 8-6 and in desperate need of a victory to strengthen its fading playoff hopes. Mike Pruitt's big day on the ground (153 yards, three touchdowns) is offset by a rare case of fumble-itis. After going all season without coughing one up, the big fullback fumbles twice, and has a hand in two other turnovers. The win is just Houston's second and final one of the year.

4. N.Y. Giants 16, Cleveland 13 (Dec. 4, 1994, at Cle.)
- Turnovers and penalties - and a late collapse by the defense - drop the Browns into second place, a game behind the division-leading Steelers.

5. Indianapolis 9, Cleveland 7 (Dec. 6, 1987, at Cle.)
- The low point (save for the strike) of an otherwise successful season.

6. Pittsburgh 17, Cleveland 7 (Oct. 15, 1989, at Cle.)
- Anemic is the best way to describe the Browns' offense.

7. San Diego 24, Cleveland 14 (Sept. 23, 1990, at Cle.)
- Riding the crest of five straight playoff appearances and still considered a top team entering this early-season battle, the Browns fall in what turns out to be a shocker - and a foresight of things to come.

8. Kansas City 39, Cleveland 14 (Dec. 12, 1976, at K.C.)
- A successful turnaround season ends on a sour note.

9. Cincinnati 48, Cleveland 16 (Dec. 17, 1978, at Cin.)
- The Browns entered the game 8-7, hoping for a winning record in Sam Rutigliano's first year as coach. However, the 3-12 Bengals make the Browns look 3-12.

10. Cincinnati 23, Cleveland 21 (Nov. 3, 1991, at Cin.)
- The Browns basically commit suicide, making enough mistakes, it seems, for an entire season, handing the Bengals their first win of the year on a silver platter.

5. Most Memorable Games vs. Current Teams, 1976-95

# Denotes only game

Arizona
*Home - Lost, 27-24 (OT) (Sept. 8, 1985)
- After losing game after game in heartbreaking fashion in 1984, it's hard to believe the '85 season could start off the same way.
*Away - Won, 29-21 (Oct. 23, 1988)
- Bernie Kosar's return from injury a success.

Atlanta
*Home - Won, 38-3 (Nov. 8, 1987)
- Complete domination.
*Away - Won, 23-7 (Nov. 18, 1984)
- Eleven sacks by the Browns - a team record.

Cleveland Browns Facts & Trivia

Buffalo
*Home - Lost, 42-0 (Nov. 4, 1990)
- Bud Carson's last stand.
*Away - Won, 13-10 (Nov. 4, 1984)
- Earnest Byner *recovers* a fumble and runs to victory.

Chicago
*Home - Won, 27-7 (Oct. 23, 1989)
- Bernie Kosar hooks up with Webster Slaughter for a 97-yard touchdown as the Browns' offense finally comes to life.
*Away - Lost, 41-31 (Sept. 7, 1986)
- A shootout at Soldier leaves the Browns looking like a MASH unit.

Cincinnati
*Home - Won, 26-10 (Dec. 17, 1995)
- With emotions running high - on the field and off - the Browns win what many people believe at the time to be the final home game in franchise history.
*Away - Won, 27-24 (Dec. 21, 1980)
- Ron Bolton tackles Steve Kreider at the Cleveland 13 as time expires, and the Browns are looking *down* at Pittsburgh and Houston in the standings at season's end for once.

Dallas
*Home - Won, 26-7 (Sept. 24, 1979)
- The undefeated Browns shine in the national spotlight.
*Away - Won, 19-14 (Dec. 10, 1994)
- Football truly is a game of inches.

Denver
*Home - Won, 16-13 (Oct. 1, 1989)
- Finally, and by inches no less, on Matt Bahr's long field goal as time expires.
*Away - Won, 30-29 (Oct. 8, 1990)
- Jerry Kauric (who?) boots the game-winning field goal as time runs out for Cleveland's first win in Denver in 18 years.

Detroit
*Home - #Won, 24-21 (Sept. 28, 1986)
- The Ice Cube freezes the Lions' special teams.

Cleveland Browns Facts & Trivia

*Away - Won, 31-26 (Sept. 11, 1983)
- Brian Sipe resembles his old self.

Green Bay
*Home - Won, 26-21 (Oct. 19, 1980)
- Down by one, Brian Sipe finds Dave Logan for a long touchdown in the final minute.
*Away - #Lost, 35-21 (Nov. 6, 1983, at Milwaukee)
- Bob Golic's touchdown off a short interception return is just about the only bright spot.

Houston
*Home - Won, 28-23 (Dec. 18, 1988)
- Don Strock leads his team back from a 23-7 third-quarter deficit to a playoff berth in a driving snowstorm.
*Away - Won, 17-14 (Nov. 30, 1980)
- The Browns take a giant step toward their first division title in nine years. An estimated crowd (a raucous one, too) of 15,000 greets the team at Hopkins International Airport that evening.

Indianapolis
*Home - Won, 13-10 (Sept. 16, 1979)
- Brian Sipe leads a comeback from 10-0 down.
*Away - Lost, 23-17 (OT) (Dec. 10, 1989)
- Bahr's blunders force overtime, Bernie's blunder ends it.

Jacksonville
*Home - #Lost, 23-15 (Oct. 22, 1995)
- The expansion Jaguars administer an embarrassing blow in a black eye of a season.
*Away - #Lost, 24-21 (Dec. 24, 1995)
- The Browns lose what many people believe at the time to be the final game in the history of the franchise.

Kansas City
*Home - Won, 44-7 (Oct. 30, 1977)
- The Browns rack up more than 500 yards total offense.
*Away - Won, 27-24 (Sept. 9, 1979)
- Brian Sipe to Reggie Rucker with 54 seconds to go.

Miami

Cleveland Browns Facts & Trivia

*Home - Won, 30-24 (OT) (Nov. 18, 1979)
- The Kardiac Kids strike again.
*Away - Lost, 38-31 (Dec. 12, 1988)
- The Browns tie it with 59 seconds left, Miami wins it with 34 to go.

Minnesota
*Home - Won, 23-17 (OT) (Dec. 17, 1989)
- Mike Pagel-to-Van Waiters wins it on a fake field goal.
*Away - Lost, 28-23 (Dec. 14, 1980)
- The miracle at the Met.

New England
*Home - Won, 30-27 (OT) (Sept. 26, 1977)
- The teams swap treys in the final minute of regulation before Don Cockroft's 35-yarder in sudden death wins it.
*Away - Won, 19-17 (Oct. 25, 1992)
- A six-yard touchdown pass from Mike Tomczak to Scott Galbraith on fourth down with 31 seconds left.

New Orleans
*Home - Lost, 16-14 (Oct. 28, 1984)
- Morten spoils Marty's debut.
*Away - Lost, 28-21 (Sept. 13, 1987)
- The Browns lose despite Bernie Kosar's big rushing day - a three-yard touchdown run.

N.Y. Giants
*Home - #Lost, 16-13 (Dec. 4, 1994)
- A gut-wrenching defeat to an inferior team.
*Away - Won, 35-33 (Dec. 1, 1985)
- Gary Danielson, aching arm and all, leads the Browns back from 12 down late.

N.Y. Jets
*Home - Won, 37-34 (OT) (Dec. 10, 1978)
- The Kardiac in Cleveland continues to surface.
*Away - Won, 25-22 (OT) (Sept. 2, 1979)
- The Jets are "Kardiaced" once again.

Oakland
*Home - Lost, 21-20 (Oct. 20, 1985)

Cleveland Browns Facts & Trivia

- Marc Wilson's eight-yard touchdown pass to Todd Christensen on fourth down wins it with 29 seconds left.
*Away - Won, 19-16 (Sept. 19, 1993)
- Eric Metcalf scores on a sweep with no time left, ending an amazing comeback and touching off a wild celebration along the Browns' sideline.

Philadelphia
*Home - Lost, 32-30 (Nov. 10, 1991)
- A 23-0 lead vanishes.
*Away - Won, 24-19 (Nov. 4, 1979)
- The Kardiac Kids rally from nine down late in the game. Charlie Hall's interception at the Cleveland one wins it with no time left.

Pittsburgh
*Home - Won, 28-23 (Oct. 24, 1993)
- Eric Metcalf leaves the Steelers in a trance.
*Away - Won, 27-24 (Oct. 5, 1986)
- The Jinx is history.

St. Louis
*Home - Won, 30-17 (Oct. 26, 1987)
- Felix Wright's two interceptions - the latter for a touchdown - highlight this Monday night victory.
*Away - Lost, 20-17 (Sept. 9, 1984)
- The Browns squander a 17-10 lead; Mike Lansford's late field goal wins it.

San Diego
*Home - Lost, 44-14 (Sept. 7, 1981)
- A foresight of things to come in '81.
*Away - Won, 30-24 (OT) (Sept. 25, 1983)
- A rousing return to the Kardiac yesteryear.

San Francisco
*Home - Won, 23-13 (Sept. 13, 1993)
- The Browns excel in all three phases of the game in pulling off this Monday night upset.
*Away - Lost, 20-17 (Oct. 28, 1990)
- Mike Pagel leads the Browns back from 14 down to tie late, but a big play leads to doomsday.

Cleveland Browns Facts & Trivia

Seattle
*Home - Lost, 29-24 (Nov. 11, 1979)
- The Browns fail to protect a late lead.
*Away - Won, 27-3 (Oct. 12, 1980)
- The Browns are a fine-tuned engine on this day.

Tampa Bay
*Home - Won, 20-0 (Nov. 13, 1983)
- First shutout victory in nine years.
*Away - Won, 42-31 (Nov. 5, 1989)
- Eric Metcalf has a day the Browns dreamed of when they drafted him some six months before.

Washington
*Home - Lost, 13-9 (Oct. 14, 1979)
- Joe Theismann to Clarence Harmon for 15 yards with 27 seconds to go.
*Away - Won, 17-13 (Nov. 27, 1988)
- Earnest Byner's 27-yard touchdown run with 1:49 left in the game gives the Browns their first win over the Redskins since 1971.

6. Five Most Memorable Monday Night Games

1. Cleveland 31, N.Y. Jets 21 (Sept. 21, 1970, at Cle.)
- The inaugural game on ABC's *Monday Night Football* sees Cleveland's Homer Jones return the second-half kickoff 94 yards for a touchdown. Linebacker Billy Andrews intercepts a Joe Namath pass and returns it for a late score, sealing the victory.

2. Cleveland 26, Dallas 7 (Sept. 24, 1979, at Cle.)
- The unbeaten Kardiac Kids fail to live up to their billing, erupting for 20 points in the first half - of the first *quarter* - cruising to victory over America's Team.

3. Cleveland 30, Denver 29 (Oct. 8, 1990, at Den.)
- Down by nine late in the game, Bernie Kosar leads two brilliant drives, culminating in a touchdown and the game-winning field goal as time runs out. The victory is Cleveland's first in Mile High Stadium since 1972.

4. Cleveland 21, San Diego 17 (Nov. 13, 1972, at S.D.)
- Phipps to Pitts for 38 yards with 41 seconds to go.

5. Cleveland 30, New England 27 (OT) (Sept. 26, 1977, at Cle.)
- The Browns' first Monday nighter in four years results in a thriller on the lakefront. Don Cockroft's 37-yard field goal with under a minute left gives Cleveland a three-point lead. The Patriots answer, though, as John Smith connects on a 34-yarder as time runs out. Cockroft's 35-yarder 4:45 into sudden death wins it.

7. Postseason Games, Most Memorable to Least, 1970-95

1. Denver 23, Cleveland 20 (OT) (AFC Championship, Jan. 11, 1987, at Cle.) - The Drive.

2. Cleveland 23, N.Y. Jets 20 (2OT) (AFC Divisional Playoff, Jan. 3, 1987, at Cle.) - Bernie Kosar leads his team back from 10 down frighteningly late.

3. Oakland 14, Cleveland 12 (AFC Divisional Playoff, Jan. 4, 1981, at Cle.) - Red Right 88.

4. Denver 38, Cleveland 33 (AFC Championship, Jan. 17, 1988, at Den.) - With the Browns down, 28-10, the Bernie-and-Byner Show takes center stage, and even with Byner's late blunder (i.e., The Fumble), the game probably goes down as one of the greatest in history.

5. Cleveland 34, Buffalo 30 (AFC Divisional Playoff, Jan. 6, 1990, at Cle.) - An offensive bloodbath on the lakefront. Ronnie Harmon's dropped pass saves the game, Clay Matthews's interception seals it.

6. Miami 24, Cleveland 21 (AFC Divisional Playoff, Jan. 4, 1986, at Mia.) - A huge lead disappears, and turns into heartbreak in the Orange Bowl.

Cleveland Browns Facts & Trivia

7. Miami 20, Cleveland 14 (AFC Divisional Playoff, Dec. 24, 1972, at Mia.) - Mike Phipps's 27-yard touchdown pass to Fair Hooker gives underdog Cleveland a one-point lead with 8:11 left in the game. Miami marches right back, though, and the Browns fall to the unbeaten Dolphins.

8. Cleveland 38, Indianapolis 21 (AFC Divisional Playoff, Jan. 9, 1988, at Cle.) - Felix Wright's third-quarter interception of an Eddie-Johnson-in-his-face Jack Trudeau deep in Cleveland territory with the score tied ignites the Browns, who control the game thereafter.

9. Denver 37, Cleveland 21 (AFC Championship, Jan. 14, 1990, at Den.) - The Browns, down, 24-7, in the third quarter, rally and trail by only three in the fourth, but that's as close as they get.

10. Houston 24, Cleveland 23 (AFC Wild Card, Dec. 24, 1988, at Cle.) - A pair of personal fouls on Earnest Byner help cost the Browns a trip to Buffalo.

11. Cleveland 20, New England 13 (AFC Wild Card, Jan. 1, 1995, at Cle.) - The Browns hold off a late Patriots' attempt at tying the game.

12. L.A. Raiders 27, Cleveland 10 (AFC First-Round, Jan. 8, 1983, at L.A.) - Down by only three in the third, the Browns drive to the Raiders' 14; then Charles White fumbles the game away.

13. Baltimore 20, Cleveland 3 (AFC Divisional Playoff, Dec. 26, 1971, at Cle.) - Two golden scoring opportunities in the early going slip away and the Browns never recover.

14. Pittsburgh 29, Cleveland 9 (AFC Divisional Playoff, Jan. 9, 1995, at Pit.) - Utter domination from the outset. The score is not indicative of how soundly the Browns are beaten.

8. Five Coulda-Been Matchups That Woulda Been Great, 1970-95

1. Cleveland at San Diego (AFC Championship, Jan. 11, 1981)
- This dreamy matchup between the Kardiac Kids and Air Coryell is thwarted by Oakland's Mike Davis.

2. Pittsburgh at Cleveland (AFC Championship, Jan. 14, 1990)
- If not for a touch of John Elway magic the week before, this salivating matchup would have occurred.

3. Denver at Cleveland (Sept. 28, 1987)
- The Browns had been waiting for this - a rematch of the AFC Championship nine months earlier -since the schedule came out five months before. The game, to have been showcased on *Monday Night Football*, is the one Browns game the entire city of Cleveland had hungered for - but also the one Browns game canceled by the players' strike.

4. Miami at Cleveland (AFC Wild Card, Jan. 1, 1995)
- Had the Dolphins lost to the Lions in their regular-season finale, Bernie Kosar's return to Cleveland - albeit as Dan Marino's backup - may have been comparable, at least in terms of newsworthiness, to the release of Kosar one year before (just think if Marino had gone down!).

5. Cleveland vs. N.Y. Giants (Super Bowl XXI, Jan. 25, 1987, at Pasadena, Calif.)
- Two franchises whose storied rivalry in the 1950s and early 1960s was one of the fiercest could have made their initial Super Bowl appearances against one another, but Denver's "drive" to Pasadena ruins it.

BROWNS TRIVIA

1. Players

Running Backs

1. Who were the Browns' starting running backs in the team's first-ever regular-season game?

2. Name the Brown who was the team leader in rushing yards in 1946 and was inducted into the Pro Football Hall of Fame in 1968.

3. Who led Cleveland in rushing touchdowns in 1946?

4. What was Marion Motley's average yards per carry in 1946?

5. What was the closest Marion Motley came to attaining the 1,000-yard milestone in rushing for one season?

6. Name the only two years of his eight with the Browns that Marion Motley failed to lead the team in rushing yards.

7. Who led the Browns in rushing yards in 1954?

8. Who rushed for a team-leading 44 yards in the Browns' 56-10 destruction of the Lions in the 1954 NFL title game?

9. What running back from the University of Maryland was second on the Browns in rushing yards in 1955?

10. Preston Carpenter was the Browns' leader in rushing yards in 1956. How many yards did he have?

11. What rookie out of the University of Syracuse led the Browns in rushing yards in 1957 and was inducted into the Pro Football Hall of Fame in 1971?

12. How many yards did Jim Brown rush for in 1957?

13. How many touchdowns did Jim Brown rush for in 1957?

14. What two awards did the Associated Press bestow upon Jim Brown for his performance in 1957?

Cleveland Browns Facts & Trivia

15. The United Press honored Jim Brown with an award in 1957. What award was it?

16. Jim Brown rushed for a career-high 237 yards in a game twice in his career. Against what teams did he accomplish this feat?

17. Who was Cleveland's leading yard-gainer on the ground in the team's 59-14 bashing at the hands of the Lions in the 1957 NFL Championship game?

18. How many yards did Jim Brown rush for in 1958?

19. Who was second on the Browns in rushing yards in 1958?

20. Jim Brown's performance in the Browns' 38-31 victory at Baltimore on November 1, 1959, was one for the record books. Why?

21. Against what team did Bobby Mitchell run for a 90-yard touchdown on November 15, 1959?

22. What team was Bobby Mitchell traded to three days prior to the close of the 1961 season?

23. What year was Bobby Mitchell inducted into the Hall of Fame?

24. How many touchdowns did Jim Brown rush for in 1962?

25. What was Jim Brown's highest rushing yardage total for one season?

26. How many yards did Jim Brown average per carry in 1963?

27. How many yards receiving did Jim Brown have in 1963?

28. What second-year running back had a 73-yard run on December 8, 1963, in a 38-10 loss to the Lions in Tiger Stadium?

29. How many times did Jim Brown win the NFL rushing yardage title?

30. What were the only two seasons in which Jim Brown failed to rush for at least 1,000 yards?

31. What was the only season that Jim Brown failed to win the NFL rushing yards title?

32. How many yards did Jim Brown rush for in his career?

Cleveland Browns Facts & Trivia

33. In how many games did Jim Brown rush for at least 200 yards?

34. What was Jim Brown's yards per carry average for his career?

35. Who was the Browns' rushing yardage leader every season from 1966-72 and was inducted into the Pro Football Hall of Fame in 1994?

36. How many 1,000-yard seasons did Leroy Kelly have?

37. How many rushing touchdowns did Leroy Kelly have in 1966?

38. How many rushing touchdowns did Leroy Kelly have in 1967?

39. How many rushing touchdowns did Leroy Kelly have in 1968?

40. What Ohio State product led the Browns in rushing touchdowns with seven in 1970?

41. The year 1973 was Leroy Kelly's last, and Greg Pruitt's first, with the Browns. Neither, though, was Cleveland's leading ground gainer yardage-wise that season. Who was?

42. How many rushing touchdowns did Browns rushing yards leader Ken Brown have in 1973?

43. What speedster from the University of Oklahoma led the Browns in rushing yards every season from 1975-78?

44. Against what team did Greg Pruitt rush for a career-high 214 yards on December 14, 1975?

45. How many yards did Greg Pruitt rush for in 1976?

46. What was Greg Pruitt's longest run from scrimmage as a Brown?

47. Who was the Browns' first-round selection out of Purdue in the 1976 NFL Draft?

48. Are Mike Pruitt and Greg Pruitt related?

49. What player out of Kent State was third on the Browns with 356 rushing yards in 1976?

50. In what years did Mike Pruitt gain at least 1,000 yards on the ground?

51. What was Mike Pruitt's highest total for rushing yards in one season?

Cleveland Browns Facts & Trivia

52. Mike Pruitt's longest run from scrimmage was a 77-yarder in a 19-14 loss at Oakland on December 9, 1979. Did Pruitt score on the play?

53. What Cleveland native rushed the ball 14 times for 11 yards, yet a pair of touchdowns, in his only season in the NFL, 1979?

54. Where does Mike Pruitt rank on the all-time Browns' rushing yardage list?

55. What Heisman Trophy winner from the University of Southern California was the Browns' first selection in the 1980 NFL Draft?

56. What running back rushed for 137 yards in a 44-17 defeat at Pittsburgh on October 16, 1983, becoming the first visiting running back to top the century mark in Three Rivers Stadium in six years?

57. What Brown led the team in rushing yards in 1984 but had no rushing touchdowns?

58. Besides Boyce Green, there were two other running backs who led the Browns in rushing yards in a season without scoring a touchdown via the ground. Name them.

59. What rookie, a 10th-round draft choice out of East Carolina, rushed for 188 yards in a season-ending 27-20 victory at Houston on December 16, 1984?

60. What teammates in 1985 became the third running back tandem in NFL history to rush for 1,000 yards in the same season?

61. How many yards did Kevin Mack rush for in 1985?

62. How many yards did Earnest Byner rush for in 1985?

63. Against what team did Earnest Byner rush for a Browns postseason record 161 yards in an AFC Divisional Playoff game on January 4, 1986?

64. After the 1985 season, how many times did Kevin Mack rush for 1,000 yards in a season?

65. After the 1985 season, how many times did Earnest Byner rush for 1,000 yards in a season with the Browns?

66. How many times did Kevin Mack lead the Browns in rushing yardage for a season?

67. How many yards did Kevin Mack rush for in his career?

68. How many times did Earnest Byner lead the Browns in rushing yards for a season?

69. How many yards did Earnest Byner rush for in his career with the Browns?

70. What running back from Louisiana State scored the first points in the AFC Championship game at home against the Denver Broncos on January 11, 1987?

71. What was the score of the AFC Championship game in Denver on January 17, 1988, in which the Browns lost, 38-33, at the point when Earnest Byner was stripped of the football at the Broncos' three-yard line by Denver cornerback Jeremiah Castille?

72. What rookie led the Browns in rushing yards in 1989?

73. What running back, a 1990 second-round draft pick out of the University of Michigan, had two touchdowns rushing but nine receiving - many in spectacular fashion - in 1991?

74. Leroy Hoard led the Browns in rushing yardage in 1994 and 1995. His 1994 total was the highest for a Browns player since Kevin Mack and Earnest Byner both eclipsed the 1,000-yard mark in 1985. How many yards did Hoard rush for in '94?

75. How many touchdowns did "Touchdown" Tommy Vardell, the Browns' first-round selection in the 1992 NFL Draft out of Stanford, score his rookie year?

Quarterbacks

1. Who was the first player the Cleveland Browns ever signed to a contract?

2. Who was the starting quarterback in the Browns' debut against the Miami Seahawks on September 6, 1946?

3. Cliff Lewis connected with Mac Speedie for a touchdown pass in the opening minutes of the Browns' first-ever game against the Miami Seahawks. How many yards did the play cover?

Cleveland Browns Facts & Trivia

4. Who replaced Cliff Lewis as the Browns' starting quarterback shortly into the team's first game on September 6, 1946, against the Miami Seahawks in Cleveland Municipal Stadium?

5. How many touchdown passes did Otto Graham have in 1947?

6. How many touchdown passes and interceptions did Otto Graham have in 1948?

7. Otto Graham attempted 17 passes in Cleveland's 21-7 victory over the San Francisco 49ers in the 1949 AAFC Championship game. How many of those attempts did he complete?

8. Otto Graham threw for nearly 2,000 yards in 1950, the Browns' first season in the NFL. In addition to his 14 touchdown passes, how many interceptions did he have?

9. How many touchdown passes did Otto Graham throw for in the Browns' 30-28 NFL title-game victory in 1950 over the Rams?

10. How many yards did Otto Graham pass for in 1952?

11. What were Otto Graham's passing statistics in the Browns' 17-16 loss to the Lions in the 1953 NFL Championship game?

12. What wire service voted Otto Graham the NFL's Most Valuable Player for 1953?

13. How many touchdowns was Otto Graham responsible for in the Browns' 56-10 rout of the Lions in the 1954 league championship game?

14. Otto Graham announced after the 1953 season that the next season would be his last. However, Graham changed his mind and decided to return for one more year. When did he announce his   decision to come back?

15. Where does Otto Graham rank in the all-time Browns' passing yardage category?

16. What year was Otto Graham inducted into the Pro Football Hall of Fame?

17. How many touchdown passes and interceptions did the Browns' trifecta at the quarterback position in 1956 of George Ratterman, Vito "Babe" Parilli, and Tommy O'Connell have?

Cleveland Browns Facts & Trivia

18. What quarterback from Penn State was the Browns' No. 2 draft choice in 1957?

19. How many interceptions did Milt Plum and Tommy O'Connell account for in Cleveland's 59-14 NFL Championship-game loss to the Lions in Briggs Stadium in Detroit on December 29, 1957?

20. What two years did Milt Plum lead the NFL in passing?

21. How many touchdown passes and interceptions did Milt Plum have in 1960 and 1961?

22. What quarterback from Purdue who would go on to a Hall of Fame career and be part of a Super Bowl winning team attempted 28 passes for the Browns in 1960 and 1961 combined?

23. What fourth-round draft pick of the Browns in 1958 who was traded to Detroit on July 12, 1960, returned to the team on March 28, 1962, as part of a deal that sent Milt Plum to the Lions?

24. What four-year veteran quarterback was brought to Cleveland in a trade with the Los Angeles Rams on July 12, 1962?

25. Who won the Browns' starting quarterback job during the 1962 preseason, Jim Ninowski or Frank Ryan?

26. How far into the 1962 season did Jim Ninowski last until he was replaced by Frank Ryan as Browns starting quarterback?

27. Why was Jim Ninowski succeeded by Frank Ryan during the Browns' victory over the Steelers on October 28, 1962?

28. How many touchdowns and interceptions did Frank Ryan throw in 1963?

29. Frank Ryan hit wide receiver Gary Collins for three touchdown strikes in the second half of the Browns' upset win over the visiting Colts in the 1964 NFL Championship game. For how many yards did each play go?

30. How many yards, touchdowns, and interceptions did Frank Ryan throw for in 1966?

31. How many yards did Frank Ryan throw for in a 38-10 rout of the St. Louis Cardinals on December 17, 1966?

32. The Browns were destroyed by the Cowboys, 52-14, in the Eastern

Cleveland Browns Facts & Trivia

Conference Championship game on Christmas Eve 1967 in front of 70,786 fans in the Cotton Bowl in Dallas. Down, 52-7, in the fourth quarter, Frank Ryan completed a long touchdown pass to Paul Warfield. For how many yards did the play go?

33. How many yards did Frank Ryan throw for in his career with the Browns?

34. What quarterback was obtained from the Pittsburgh Steelers as part of a five-player trade on May 14, 1968?

35. What team did Bill Nelsen make his first start against for the Browns?

36. How many yards was Bill Nelsen's longest pass completion as a Brown?

37. To what receiver did Bill Nelsen complete an 82-yard touchdown pass against the St. Louis Cardinals on December 14, 1969?

38. What quarterback from Purdue did the Browns acquire on draft day 1970 by trading the great Paul Warfield to Miami for the Dolphins' first-round draft choice the night before?

39. Who won the starting quarterback job when the 1970 season began, Bill Nelsen or Mike Phipps?

40. The Browns won the 1971 AFC Central Division title despite Bill Nelsen's sub par year. How many touchdowns and interceptions did the veteran have that season?

41. Mike Phipps's finest season as a Brown (save for his brief appearance in 1976) came in 1972 when the Browns finished 10-4 and won the AFC Wild Card spot. How many touchdown passes and interceptions did Phipps have that year?

42. On December 24, 1972, the Browns squared off against the undefeated, heavily-favored Miami Dolphins in the Orange Bowl in an AFC Divisional Playoff contest. The Browns surprised everyone by taking a one-point lead late in the game on a 27-yard touchdown strike from Mike Phipps to what wide receiver?

43. How many interceptions did Mike Phipps throw in the Browns' 20-14 loss to the Miami Dolphins in an AFC Divisional Playoff on December 24, 1972?

44. How many touchdown passes and interceptions did Mike Phipps have

in 1973?

45. How many touchdown passes and interceptions did Mike Phipps have in 1974?

46. How many touchdown passes and interceptions did Mike Phipps have in 1975?

47. How many touchdown passes and interceptions did Mike Phipps have in his Browns career?

48. What team did the Browns trade Mike Phipps to in 1977 for that team's fourth-round draft pick the same year and first-round pick in 1978?

49. What 1972 13th-round draft choice out of San Diego State burst upon the scene on October 27, 1974, by leading the Browns to a comeback victory over the Denver Broncos?

50. Brian Sipe was lost for the remainder of the 1977 season when he suffered a separated left shoulder in a loss to what team on November 13?

51. What quarterback from Texas Southern led the Browns to a 21-7 victory over the New York Giants on November 20, 1977, in the Meadowlands?

52. What were Brian Sipe's passing statistics in 1980, the Browns' Kardiac Kids year?

53. What Oakland Raider intercepted Brian Sipe's infamous pass that shut the door on the Browns' Kardiac Kids season of 1980?

54. What five national awards did Brian Sipe win for his performance in 1980?

55. How many yards did Brian Sipe pass for in his Browns career?

56. What fourth-round draft choice in 1980 out of Southern California made his first start on December 19, 1982, in a home game against home against the Steelers, replacing a struggling Brian Sipe?

57. The Browns qualified for the playoffs in 1982 with a 4-5 record, matching up with the top-seeded Los Angeles Raiders in an AFC First-Round contest in the Los Angeles Memorial Coliseum. Down, 10-3, Paul McDonald hit what veteran wide receiver on a 43-yard touchdown play that tied the game at 10 late in the first half?

58. What were Paul McDonald's passing statistics in his only full season as starting quarterback in 1984?

59. Who was Cleveland's second-string quarterback in 1984?

60. What star quarterback raised in Boardman, Ohio, and who led the Miami Hurricanes to the national championship in 1983 did the Browns acquire in the 1985 supplemental draft, thanks to some slick maneuvering from Executive Vice President of Football Operations Ernie Accorsi?

61. What quarterback who played for the Browns for three seasons was the starter when the 1985 season began?

62. What happened on Bernie Kosar's first professional snap?

63. How many yards passing did Bernie Kosar have in the Browns' 24-21 loss to the Miami Dolphins in the AFC Divisional Playoffs on January 4, 1986, in the Orange Bowl?

64. How many passing yards did Bernie Kosar have in 1986?

65. What NFL Playoff record did Bernie Kosar achieve in the Browns' dramatic 23-20 double overtime victory over the New York Jets in an AFC Divisional Playoff on January 3, 1987, in Cleveland Stadium?

66. Where were the Browns playing when Bernie Kosar's arm was injured in the opening game of the 1988 season?

67. What veteran quarterback, signed for emergency purposes due to a string of injuries at the position, led the Browns to a thrilling 28-23 victory over Houston at home in the snow that put the team in the playoffs on the final Sunday of the 1988 season?

68. Who replaced Bernie Kosar as starting quarterback for the Browns' home game against the Buffalo Bills on November 4, 1990?

69. What former Cincinnati Bengal passed for three touchdowns to Eric Metcalf in a 28-16 triumph over the Los Angeles Raiders on September 20, 1992, in Los Angeles?

70. What former Ohio State quarterback started eight games for the Browns in 1992, directing the team to four wins and four losses?

71. What shocking event in Browns history occurred on November 8, 1993?

Cleveland Browns Facts & Trivia

72. What former teammate of Bernie Kosar's at the University of Miami, and ex-Tampa Bay Buccaneer, led the Browns to a playoff berth in 1994 by throwing for 2,575 yards and completing over 55 percent of his passes?

73. What quarterback who had led the Washington Redskins to victory in Super Bowl XXVI three years before relieved concussion-prone Vinny Testaverde for a few games in 1994?

74. Who did head coach Bill Belichick start in place of AFC passing leader Vinny Testaverde - to give the team a spark, Belichick said - for the October 29, 1995, road game against the Bengals?

75. What were Eric Zeier's passing statistics in the Browns' 29-26 overtime win against the Bengals on October 29, 1995, in Cincinnati?

Wide Receivers/Tight Ends

1. Who led the Browns in receptions and receiving yards in 1946?

2. Who led the Browns in touchdown receptions in 1946?

3. Who led the Browns in receptions and receiving yards in 1947?

4. Who led the Browns in touchdown receptions in 1947?

5. How many yards receiving did Dante Lavelli have on October 14, 1949, on the road against the Los Angeles Dons?

6. How many receiving yards did Mac Speedie have on November 20, 1949, on the road against the Brooklyn-New York Yankees?

7. What were Mac Speedie's receiving statistics for 1949?

8. What were Mac Speedie's receiving statistics in 1952?

9. What were Dante Lavelli's receiving statistics for 1954?

10. What receiver from North Texas State had five receptions for 94 yards, including a pair of touchdown catches, in the Browns' 56-10 destruction of the Lions in the 1954 NFL title game?

11. Who led the Browns in receptions and receiving yards in 1955?

12. What were Dante Lavelli's receiving statistics in Cleveland's 38-14 victory over the Los Angeles Rams in the NFL Championship game on

Cleveland Browns Facts & Trivia

December 26, 1955, in Los Angeles?

13. What year was Dante Lavelli enshrined into the Pro Football Hall of Fame?

14. Ray Renfro led the Browns in touchdown receptions in 1958. How many did he have?

15. Ray Renfro led the Browns in touchdown receptions in 1959. How many did he have?

16. Who led the Browns with 616 receiving yards in 1960?

17. What 1959 first-round draft pick led the Browns in receiving yards in 1962?

18. What second-year receiver out of Maryland led the Browns with 43 receptions, 674 yards receiving, and 13 touchdown catches in 1963?

19. What were Gary Collins's receiving statistics in 1964?

20. Who was Cleveland's top pick in the 1964 NFL Draft?

21. Paul Warfield led the Browns in receptions, receiving yards, and touchdown receptions in his rookie year of 1964. What were his totals for each category?

22. Gary Collins had five receptions for 130 yards and three touchdowns in Cleveland's 27-0 upset victory over the visiting Baltimore Colts in the NFL Championship game on December 27, 1964. For how many yards did Collins's three touchdown catches go?

23. Who led the Browns with 10 touchdown receptions in 1965?

24. What were Paul Warfield's receiving statistics for 1965?

25. How many receptions and receiving yards did Gary Collins and Paul Warfield combine for in the Browns' loss to the Packers in the 1965 NFL Championship game?

26. What tight end out of Massachusetts was the Browns' top pick in the 1966 draft?

27. What were Milt Morin's receiving statistics his rookie year of 1966?

28. Milt Morin was on the receiving end of an 87-yard pass play from Bill

Nelsen on November 24, 1968, against Philadelphia. Did the play go for a touchdown?

29. In 1968, Paul Warfield became the first Browns' player since Mac Speedie in 1947 to do what?

30. What was Paul Warfield's longest reception as a Cleveland Brown?

31. The Browns had 24 touchdown receptions as a team in 1969. For how many of those were Gary Collins and Paul Warfield responsible?

32. Where does Gary Collins rank on the all-time Browns' receptions list?

33. What team was Paul Warfield traded to in 1970?

34. What 1969 fifth-round draft pick from Arizona State led the Browns in receptions and receiving yards in 1971?

35. Who caught Mike Phipps's game-winning 38-yard touchdown pass with under a minute to go in the Browns' 21-17 victory in San Diego on Monday night, November 13, 1972?

36. Frank Pitts led the Browns in receptions, receiving yards, and touchdown receptions in 1972. How many of each did Pitts have?

37. Who caught Mike Phipps's 27-yard touchdown pass that put the Browns ahead of the unbeaten Miami Dolphins, 14-13, in the fourth quarter of a 1972 AFC Divisional Playoff in the Orange Bowl?

38. What Browns wide receiver, the team's top pick in the 1973 NFL Draft, led Cleveland in receiving yards in 1974?

39. Who was the receiver the Browns obtained from New England on a draft day deal in 1975?

40. Reggie Rucker was the Browns' leader in receptions and receiving yards in 1975. What were his totals for each category?

41. Reggie Rucker was Cleveland's co-leader with just three touchdown catches in 1975 with what rookie tight end, a third-round draft choice from Southern Methodist?

42. What were Paul Warfield's receiving statistics upon returning to the Browns in 1976 after a six-year absence?

43. How many yards did Paul Warfield average per reception in his eight

years with the Browns?

44. What year was Paul Warfield inducted into the Pro Football Hall of Fame?

45. What tight end from Florida State led the 1977 Browns in touchdown catches with five?

46. What player who was a wide receiver at Alabama did the Browns turn into one of the finest tight ends of all time with their second pick of the 1978 draft?

47. Who led the Browns in receptions, receiving yards, and touchdown receptions in 1978?

48. Who was the Browns' top pick in the 1979 NFL Draft, a wide receiver from Houston who spent seven rather unproductive seasons in Cleveland?

49. What 1976 third-round draft choice had team highs of 59 receptions and 982 yards receiving in 1979, with seven touchdown catches?

50. What fifth-year receiver had two third-quarter touchdown receptions that helped the Browns to a season-ending 27-24 victory in Cincinnati that clinched Cleveland's first AFC Central Division title in nine years?

51. What receiver was wide open in the middle of the end zone as Brian Sipe, who opted for tight end Ozzie Newsome instead, was intercepted by Mike Davis in the final minute of the Browns' 14-12 loss to the Oakland Raiders in an AFC Divisional Playoff on January 4, 1981?

52. Ozzie Newsome led Cleveland in receptions in 1981, breaking Mike Pruitt's team record of 63, set one year before. How many catches did "The Wizard of Oz" have?

53. Ozzie Newsome was the Browns' leader in receiving yards and touchdown receptions in 1981. How many of each did he have?

54. What two players were co-leaders for the Browns in touchdown receptions in 1982?

55. What were Reggie Rucker's career receiving statistics with the Browns?

56. What wide receiver acquired in a trade with the New York Jets on July 19, 1983, stung his old team by making a diving touchdown catch from Brian Sipe in a 10-7 victory over the New Yorkers on October 9, 1983, in Cleveland Stadium?

Cleveland Browns Facts & Trivia

57. Ozzie Newsome made a spectacular, diving catch from Brian Sipe that went for 19 yards and a touchdown, giving the Browns a 7-0 lead in a game Cleveland would eventually win, 17-7, on Thursday night, September 15, 1983, at home. Who was the Browns' opponent that night?

58. On December 18, 1983, the Browns took an early lead on visiting Pittsburgh when Brian Sipe hooked up with what wide receiver from the University of Miami on a 64-yard pass play (clue: Sylvester Stallone)?

59. What receiver did the Browns acquire from the Miami Dolphins in 1984 for a 1985 draft pick?

60. What 1983 second-round draft choice did the Browns trade to the Los Angeles Rams for a second-round pick in the 1984 draft?

61. What team did the Browns trade Dave Logan to in 1984?

62. Although the Browns lost, 24-20, at home to the New York Jets on October 14, 1984, Ozzie Newsome caught 14 passes. How many yards receiving did he have?

63. How many yards receiving did Ozzie Newsome have in 1984?

64. Who was on the receiving end of a 72-yard third-quarter scoring play, the Browns' only pass play of the entire second half, that helped lift them to a 24-6 victory over the Bengals?

65. Who led the Browns in receptions, receiving yards, and touchdown catches in 1986?

66. What 1986 top draft pick from San Diego State caught Bernie Kosar's 37-yard touchdown pass that beat the Steelers in sudden death on November 23, 1986?

67. How many receptions did Reggie Langhorne have in 1986?

68. Who turned Bernie Kosar's underthrown pass late in the 1986 AFC Championship game against the Broncos into a spectacular 48-yard touchdown catch-and-run, giving the Browns a 20-13 lead?

69. Who led the Browns in receiving yards and touchdown receptions in 1987?

70. What lofty receiver from Auburn, the Browns' second pick in the 1989 draft, failed to live up to expectations as he suffered through an injury-prone career with Cleveland, in which he caught 36 balls in three seasons as an active member of the team?

71. What lanky receiver with the same first and last name of a popular music star led the Browns with 756 receiving yards and eight touchdown receptions in 1993?

72. What former Michigan receiver whom the Browns selected second in the 1994 NFL Draft led the team with 48 receptions and 828 receiving yards his rookie year?

73. Who caught seven passes for 122 yards in the Browns' 20-13 victory over New England in an AFC Wild Card game on New Year's Day 1995?

74. What veteran free agent wide receiver who had put up big numbers with the Colts and Falcons previously did the Browns sign prior to the 1995 season?

75. What Browns receiver caught 56 passes for 709 yards and four touchdowns in 1995?

Offensive Linemen

1. Name the Ohio State product who was the Browns' starting left tackle from 1948-59 and is also the team's all-time scoring leader because of his kicking duties.

2. Lou Groza played 21 seasons for the Browns during the period 1946-67. In what season did he not play?

3. Lou Groza scored one touchdown in his 21 years in the NFL. When did this occur?

4. In what year was Lou Groza inducted into the Pro Football Hall of Fame?

5. What Marshall product played center for the Browns from 1946-56?

6. What year was Frank Gatski inducted into the Pro Football Hall of Fame?

7. What position on the offensive line did Abe Gibron play in his seven-year career with the Browns from 1950-56?

8. What years was tackle John Sandusky a member of the Browns?

9. What future Pittsburgh Steelers head coach who attended the University of Dayton played right guard (and some linebacker) for the

Cleveland Browns Facts & Trivia

Browns from 1953-59?

10. What University of Kansas product, inducted into the Hall of Fame in 1984, played on the defensive line in his first year with Cleveland in 1954, then was switched to right tackle for the remainder of his career, which lasted through 1962?

11. What left guard out of Baylor, a member of the Browns from 1956-62, was traded to the Dallas Cowboys for tackle Monte Clark on April 30, 1963?

12. What stalwart from the University of Mississippi was a standout in his 15-year career with Cleveland from 1958-73 (he missed the 1972 season with a broken leg), spent mainly as a right guard?

13. What Colorado product chosen in the fifth round of the 1959 NFL Draft played for the Browns for nine years and starred mainly as a left guard?

14. What Ohio State product was a mainstay at left tackle for Cleveland for most of his career, which lasted from 1959-71?

15. Who was the Browns' starting center from 1960-66?

16. What University of Pittsburgh product, a sixth-round draft pick by the Browns in 1966, was Cleveland's starting center the majority of the time beginning his rookie year, for seven seasons?

17. What player from the University of Texas who was a right tackle for most of his career with Cleveland was the Browns' second pick in the 1970 draft?

18. What Louisiana State product, a sixth-round draft choice in 1967, played right tackle his rookie year, then switched to left guard and eventually right guard the remainder of his career with the Browns?

19. What fifth-round draft pick in 1976 out of Southern Methodist played for the Browns for six seasons, mostly at left guard?

20. What three "D's" on the offensive line were voted to the 1980 Pro Bowl?

21. What left tackle, a sixth-round draft choice in 1971, caught a touchdown pass from Paul McDonald - the only touchdown of his career - in a 25-19 victory over Houston on October 30, 1983, in Cleveland Stadium?

22. What seventh-round selection in the 1979 NFL Draft suffered a season-

Cleveland Browns Facts & Trivia

ending knee injury in the final preseason game of 1984, a 20-19 loss to the Eagles in Veterans Stadium on August 23?

23. What Boston University product played mostly at left tackle for the Browns in a career that lasted from 1983-91?

24. Mike Baab was a fifth-round draft choice in 1982 out of Texas who played center for the Browns through 1987 and again in 1990 and 1991. What team did Baab play for in 1988 and 1989?

25. Who took Mike Baab's place as the Browns' starting center in 1988 and 1989 when Baab was a member of the New England Patriots?

26. George Lilja played for three years on the Browns' offensive line as a guard, tackle, and center. He appeared in all 16 games in both 1985 and 1986. In how many games did he play in 1984?

27. What years did Rickey Bolden play for the Browns?

28. What University of Florida product started at right guard for Cleveland from 1985-89 and started at right tackle in 1991 and 1992?

29. Who started at left guard for the Browns in 1987 and 1988?

30. What was the name of the 6-foot-5, 320-pound man whose only action in the NFL came as a "replacement" Browns offensive tackle during the 1987 players' strike?

31. Who played right guard and right tackle in 1989 and 1990 before settling in as the Browns' starting left tackle in 1991, and remained there until the team left for Baltimore in 1996?

32. What 1991 second-round draft pick from Auburn was a major disappointment in his three seasons with the Browns, including the role of starting right guard his first two years?

33. What 11-year veteran center of the Bears signed with the Browns just prior to the start of the 1992 season?

34. What University of Michigan product was Cleveland's top pick in the 1993 NFL Draft and was the Browns' starting center from 1993-95?

35. What 1993 fifth-round draft choice of out of Grambling played in all 48 games for the Browns from 1993-95 at left guard and left tackle, but started only three of them?

Defensive Backs

1. Who intercepted 10 passes in the Browns' first season of 1946?

2. What defensive back returned an interception 76 yards for a touchdown in the Browns' first-ever game, a 44-0 whitewashing of the Miami Seahawks on September 6, 1946, in Cleveland Municipal Stadium?

3. What Browns player from Northwestern intercepted five passes as a defensive back in 1946?

4. Who intercepted nine passes for the Browns in 1948?

5. What cornerback led the Browns in interceptions in 1950?

6. What Cleveland Brown led the NFL with two interception returns for touchdowns in 1951?

7. How many interceptions did Warren Lahr have in his Browns career?

8. What ninth-round draft pick of the Browns in 1951 out of John Carroll University (Ohio) went on to become the winningest head coach in NFL history?

9. What safety out of Louisiana State, Cleveland's top pick in the 1951 NFL Draft, led the Browns with seven interceptions in 1954, two of which were returned for touchdowns, which led the league?

10. Who led the Browns with seven interceptions in 1956?

11. What two players tied for the Browns' lead in interceptions with four in both 1957 and 1958?

12. How many interceptions did Ken Konz have in his Browns career?

13. What former University of Florida player was a Brown for eight years and the team's starting left cornerback from 1959-65?

14. What 11th-round draft choice of Cleveland in 1960 who was a quarterback at Mississippi was transformed into a right safety by the Browns?

15. Against what team did Bobby Franklin become the third player in NFL annals to return two interceptions for touchdowns on December 11, 1960, in Cleveland Stadium?

Cleveland Browns Facts & Trivia

16. Who led the Browns in interceptions in 1961?

17. Who led the Browns in interceptions in 1962?

18. How many interceptions did safety Larry Benz have in 1963?

19. How many interceptions did Bernie Parrish have in his Browns career?

20. How many interceptions did Ross Fichtner have in his Browns career?

21. What right cornerback out of Grambling tied Ross Fichtner for the team lead with eight interceptions in 1966?

22. Right cornerback Ben Davis led the Browns with eight interceptions in 1968. He was the NFL leader in interception return yardage with how many?

23. What years did defensive back Erich Barnes play for the Browns?

24. What year did Erich Barnes lead the Browns in interceptions?

25. Who was the Browns' seventh-round draft selection in 1969 out of Florida State who was a Cleveland defensive back through 1974?

26. What year did Walt Sumner lead the Browns in interceptions?

27. What Browns' first-round draft choice in 1971 out of Kansas State started at left cornerback from his rookie year through 1978 and strong safety from 1979-83?

28. Clarence Scott was the Browns' leader in interceptions with five in 1973 and four in 1981. He was co-leader with linebacker Charlie Hall in 1975. How many thefts did Scott have that year?

29. How many interceptions did Clarence Scott have in his career?

30. Who is the Browns' all-time leader in interceptions?

31. How many times did Thom Darden lead Cleveland in interceptions for a season?

32. Who tied a Browns' record by intercepting 10 passes in 1978?

33. Against what team did Thom Darden return a first-quarter interception 39 yards for a touchdown on Monday night, September 24, 1979?

Cleveland Browns Facts & Trivia

34. Who intercepted a Jim Plunkett pass and returned it 42 yards to give the Browns a 6-0 lead on the Oakland Raiders in an AFC Divisional Playoff in Cleveland on January 4, 1981?

35. What fourth-year cornerback was a major factor in the start of the "Dawg Pound" era by barking to fans in the Cleveland Stadium bleachers section during a home game late in the 1984 season?

36. What cornerback position did Hanford Dixon play, left or right?

37. Hanford Dixon led the Browns in interceptions twice in his career - 1984 and 1986. Both times he had five thefts. In 1984, though, he was co-leader with whom?

38. Strong safety Al Gross, who led the Browns in interceptions in 1985 with five, returned one 37 yards for a touchdown. It occurred on December 1 against what team?

39. What Louisville product who had played in the United States Football League came to the Browns to pair up with right cornerback Hanford Dixon in 1984 to form the "Corner Brothers" duo?

40. What Ohio State product from nearby Canton, Ohio, and a graduate of Canton's McKinley High School, was Cleveland's starting strong safety in 1986 and 1987?

41. What 1984 first-round draft pick was the Browns' starting free safety for two seasons before dying from a drug overdose some three-and-a-half weeks before the 1986 training camp began?

42. Frank Minnifield's four interceptions in 1987 tied for the team lead with what free safety?

43. Against what team did Felix Wright steal the show with a pair of first-half interceptions in the Browns' 30-17 victory at home on Monday night, October 26, 1987?

44. Left cornerback Frank Minnifield put the finishing touches on a 38-21 victory over the Indianapolis Colts in an AFC Divisional Playoff contest on January 9, 1988, in Cleveland Stadium. How did he do this?

45. Felix Wright led the Browns in interceptions each season from 1988-90. His highest theft total came in 1989 when he led the league. How many did he have?

46. What 1991 No. 1 draft pick led the Browns in interceptions in 1993 and

1994, tying Cardinals cornerback Aeneas Williams for the league lead in 1994?

47. Miami Dolphins quarterback Dan Marino suffered a torn right Achilles tendon late in the first half of the Browns' 24-14 loss on October 10, 1993, in Cleveland. Replacing Marino was Scott Mitchell, whose first pass was intercepted by Browns cornerback Najee Mustafaa. What happened immediately after Mustafaa's pick?

48. Against what team did free safety Eric Turner return an interception 93 yards for a touchdown on September 18, 1994?

49. What 1994 first-round draft selection from Alabama was Cleveland's starting left cornerback in 1994 and 1995?

50. Who led the Browns in interceptions in 1995?

Linebackers

1. What University of Indiana product and future head coach of the Patriots, Bills, and Broncos was a Browns linebacker from 1946-49?

2. What William & Mary product was a Browns linebacker from 1949-53?

3. What future New York Jets head coach was a starting linebacker for the Browns from 1952-61?

4. What Auburn product was Cleveland's starting right linebacker in 1952, his third and final year with the team, after spending 1950 and 1951 as a reserve?

5. Chuck Noll was drafted out of Dayton by Cleveland in the 20th round of the 1953 NFL Draft. The future Pittsburgh Steelers' head coach spent seven seasons with the Browns. In what three years was he the Browns' starting left linebacker?

6. Who was Cleveland's starting left linebacker in 1954?

7. What years did Galen Fiss play for the Browns?

8. What Ohio University product started for the Browns from 1957-66, the majority of the time at middle linebacker?

9. Galen Fiss had a big day in the opening game of the 1962 season on September 16 in Cleveland with two key defensive gems late in the

contest. First, he deflected a pass to teammate Vince Costello, setting up the go-ahead touchdown, and then intercepted a pass, leading to Lou Groza's game-icing 29-yard field goal in the Browns' 17-7 victory. Who did the Browns defeat that day?

10. How many interceptions did Vince Costello have in his Browns career?

11. What team was Vince Costello traded to on September 11, 1967, less than a week before the start of the 1967 season?

12. What seventh-round draft pick in 1965 out of Western Kentucky replaced Vince Costello at middle linebacker during the 1966 season, and spent eight years with Cleveland, mostly at the same position?

13. Against what team did Dale Lindsey up Cleveland's lead to 17-10 by intercepting a pass in the third quarter, and returning it 27 yards for a score in the Browns' 31-20 victory in the 1968 Eastern Conference Championship game on December 21 in Cleveland?

14. Jim Houston was the Browns' top pick out of Ohio State in the 1960 NFL Draft. How many interceptions did Houston return for touchdowns in his career?

15. Who returned an interception 70 yards for a score to give the Browns a 14-0 first-quarter lead over the Washington Redskins on November 26, 1967, in a game the Browns would eventually win, 42-37?

16. Jim Houston intercepted a pass and returned it 79 yards for a touchdown to seal a victory over the New York Giants on December 3, 1967. What was the name of the quarterback who threw the ball?

17. What linebacker out of Duke was the Browns' top pick in the 1967 NFL Draft?

18. What second-round draft pick in 1968 from Louisiana State played for the Browns at left linebacker and right linebacker - as a starter most of the time - through 1977?

19. Who was the Browns' 13th-round draft pick out of Southeast Louisiana in 1967 who manned the right linebacker position for most of his eight-year career with Cleveland?

20. Against what team did Billy Andrews make a diving interception and return it 25 yards for a score with 35 seconds left, sealing a 31-21 victory at home on September 21, 1970?

Cleveland Browns Facts & Trivia

21. What third-round draft pick out of Houston in 1971 was the Browns' starting left (and left outside) linebacker from 1972-80?

22. On November 4, 1979, linebacker Charlie Hall intercepted a pass on the Browns' one-yard   line with no time left to preserve a come-from-behind 24-19 victory over what NFC team?

23. What linebacker from Miami University did the Browns acquire in a trade with the San Diego Chargers on September 6, 1973?

24. What 12th-round pick out of Virginia in the 1975 draft was a solid starter as a middle and inside linebacker for nine seasons with the Browns?

25. What linebacker was obtained from the Oakland Raiders in a trade on April 8, 1976, and spent four years with the Browns, starting on the right side the first three?

26. Who did the Browns select with their top pick in the 1978 NFL Draft?

27. How many years did Clay Matthews spend with the Browns?

28. Clay Matthews was responsible for one of the more infamous plays in Browns history. It occurred on Saturday evening, December 23, 1989, in the Astrodome in Houston. What happened?

29. Clay Matthews made a game-winning interception of Jim Kelly at the Cleveland one with three seconds left to seal an AFC Divisional Playoff win over the Bills on January 6, 1990, in Cleveland. What was the final score?

30. What team did Clay Matthews, a free agent, sign with prior to the 1994 season?

31. Left inside linebacker Robert L. Jackson had two interceptions in his career. They came in the same year. What year?

32. Who was the Browns' starting left outside linebacker in 1981?

33. Who was Cleveland's top pick in the 1982 NFL Draft?

34. Chip Banks returned one interception for a touchdown in his career. When did it occur?

35. Left outside linebacker Chip Banks recorded his highest number of quarterback sacks as a Brown in 1985. How many did he have?

36. What Cleveland native and former Ohio State star did the Browns

acquire the rights to on April 23, 1982, in a trade with the Bills for high draft choices in 1983, 1984, and 1985?

37. For what team did Tom Cousineau play from 1979-81, the time in between his Ohio State and Browns days?

38. Tom Cousineau's career-high interceptions total came in 1983. How many did he have that year?

39. In 1984 and 1985, the Browns had one of their strongest sets of linebackers ever. Who were the four starters for most of those two seasons?

40. Eddie Johnson, a seventh-round selection out of Louisville in 1981, was a member of the Browns for 10 seasons, through 1990. In how many of those years was he a starter?

41. What late-round draft pick in 1982 out of the University of Miami spent five years with the Browns, at times starting at left inside linebacker and right inside linebacker?

42. What former Virginia Tech player was a solid starter, mostly at middle linebacker, for most of his eight-year career with the Browns that lasted from 1986-93?

43. Marty Schottenheimer billed the Browns' first selection of the 1987 draft, a linebacker from Duke, as a "Mad dog in a meat house." Who was this thought-to-be star who simply didn't pan out?

44. What Fresno State product who started at various times as Cleveland's left outside linebacker and right outside linebacker from 1988-90 began his career as a Browns replacement player during the 1987 players' strike?

45. The Browns' top pick in the 1988 draft was a University of Florida product who lasted two years in the NFL, both with the Browns. Who was he?

46. The Browns' third choice in the 1988 NFL Draft was not spectacular but had some success with Cleveland, starting at various times throughout his four-year career with the Browns. Name this former Indiana standout.

47. Who returned an interception 30 yards for the game-winning touchdown 7:40 into sudden death to give the Browns a 30-24 victory over the Chargers on October 20, 1991, in San Diego?

48. What member of the 1988 Notre Dame national championship team

and former nearby Akron (Ohio) St. Vincent-St. Mary High School standout started at right outside linebacker for the Browns in 1994?

49. What former New York Giants star who had spent 1993 with the Washington Redskins did the Browns sign as a free agent in 1994?

50. What former Ohio State Buckeye and New York Giant led the Browns in tackles in 1995 with 195?

Defensive Linemen

1. Who were the Browns' starting defensive ends in their first-ever game on September 6, 1946, at home against the Miami Seahawks?

2. What former Ohio State star played middle guard for the Browns from 1946-53 and was inducted into the Pro Football Hall of Fame in 1977?

3. Who was Cleveland's left defensive end the majority of his Browns career, which lasted from 1946-53?

4. What Ohio University product was a Browns defensive tackle from 1946-48?

5. What former Michigan Wolverine was the Browns' starting right defensive end from 1950-57 and was a Hall of Fame inductee in 1976?

6. What Boston College product began his Browns career in 1950 by playing the right defensive tackle position and ended it by manning the left defensive tackle position?

7. What years did Bob Gain play for the Browns?

8. Name Cleveland's starting left defensive end for most of the period from 1954-56 who was the Browns' eighth-round draft choice out of Texas in 1953.

9. What Brown University product was the starting left defensive tackle in 1953, his first year with the Browns, then switched to right defensive tackle the next five years?

10. What future Kansas City Chiefs head coach was a standout on the Browns' defensive line at both end positions from 1957-67?

11. What Browns first-round draft pick out of Ohio State in 1960 began his career as a left end but spent most of his career manning the left

linebacker position?

12. Name the 1960 fourth-round draft choice from Ohio State who spent a year with the Browns at right end before being shipped to the Minnesota Vikings on August 31, 1961, as part of an eight-player deal?

13. What right defensive end was acquired by the Browns from the Detroit Lions on March 28, 1962, as part of a six-player deal?

14. How many seasons did Bill Glass play for the Browns?

15. What Maryland product whose older brother was a Browns running back in the 1950s started at left defensive tackle for Cleveland in 1964 and 1965?

16. What second-round draft choice in 1963 from Michigan State was Cleveland's starting right defensive tackle most of the time in his stay with the Browns, which lasted through 1969?

17. Name the second-round draft pick out of Los Angeles State in 1965 who was Cleveland's regular at left defensive tackle for the most part from 1966-76?

18. Name the Browns' No. 1 draft pick in 1968 out of Trinity (Texas) who started at right defensive tackle at times for two seasons before being traded to Kansas City almost two weeks prior to the 1970 season opener, for the Chiefs' third-round draft choice in 1971.

19. What Oklahoma State product, a second-round draft selection by Cleveland in 1970, succeeded Marvin Upshaw at right defensive tackle his rookie year, and was a fixture there until Week 11 in 1979 when he suffered a staph infection that ended his season, and for all intents and purposes, his career (which officially lasted through 1981)?

20. Who played with the Browns from 1967-71, starting at right defensive end for most of the period, was traded to the New York Giants on June 15, 1972, then was traded back to the Browns for the 1979 season before being released?

21. What defensive end, an Ohio State product and graduate of nearby Canton (Ohio) McKinley High School, spent three seasons with the Browns from 1972-74 after two years with the Bengals?

22. Who was the Browns' first-round draft selection in 1975 from the University of Houston who started at right defensive end his rookie year, and started at the same position a good deal of the time the next three

years before spending his final NFL season, 1979, in Cincinnati?

23. What defensive end lifted Pittsburgh Steelers quarterback Terry Bradshaw and slammed him head first to the ground in the fourth quarter of the Browns' 18-16 upset of the two-time defending champion Steelers on October 10, 1976, in Cleveland Municipal Stadium?

24. Mike St. Clair, a fourth-round pick out of Grambling by the Browns in the 1976 draft, started at two positions on the defensive line in his four years with the team. What positions were they?

25. What burly defensive end who was United Press International's AFC Defensive Player of the Year in 1977 with Denver was acquired by Cleveland on August 12, 1979, from the Broncos in exchange for the Browns' second- and fifth-round draft picks in 1980?

26. How many seasons did Lyle Alzado spend in Cleveland?

27. What Notre Dame product started at nose tackle for seven seasons from 1982-88?

28. What 1983 third-round draft pick from the University of California started at left defensive end for the Browns from 1983-87?

29. What member of the 1980 NFC Champion Philadelphia Eagles joined the Browns in 1984 and started at right defensive end from 1985-88, and was the left defensive tackle in 1989?

30. What University of Pittsburgh product, who excelled both at football and basketball as a Panther, started at left defensive end for the Browns in 1987 and 1988?

31. Name the Browns' second-round draft pick in 1988 out of Clemson who was the team's starting right defensive tackle from 1989-94.

32. What fifth-round draft choice in 1990 from Syracuse started at left defensive end for Cleveland from his rookie year through 1995?

33. What third-round draft pick in 1990 out of Tennessee State started at right defensive end for the Browns from his rookie season through 1995?

34. Name the defensive tackle who was used as a running back in a September 13, 1993, Monday night home victory over the 49ers, plunging in for a one-yard touchdown in the early stages of the second quarter.

35. Who led the Browns with eight quarterback sacks in 1995?

Punters

1. Who was the Browns' punter the majority of the time in the 1946 and 1948 seasons?

2. Who punted for the Browns most of the time in 1947 and 1949?

3. Who was Cleveland's only punter from 1950-55?

4. Horace Gillom is responsible for the longest punt in Browns history. It came on November 28, 1954, in a 16-7 victory on the road against the New York Giants. How long was Gillom's punt?

5. Horace Gillom's 3,321 punting yards in 1951 rank tied for seventh on the Browns' all-time list for most punting yards in one season. With whom is he tied?

6. Horace Gillom ranks second on the Browns' all-time list in punting yards with 21,207. Who does he rank behind?

7. Horace Gillom led the NFL in average yards per punt in both the 1951 and 1952 seasons. What were his averages those years?

8. The Browns went through a number of punters - seven, actually - from 1956-61. Name them.

9. What 1962 first-round draft choice out of Maryland, a standout receiver, was also the Browns' usual punter from his rookie year through 1967?

10. What year did Gary Collins lead the NFL in punting yards average?

11. Where does Gary Collins rank in the all-time Browns' punting yards category?

12. Who took over for Gary Collins as the Browns' main punter in 1968?

13. For how many seasons was Don Cockroft the Browns' No. 1 punter?

14. Don Cockroft twice had punts of 71 yards, the longest of his career. One came in 1970, the other in 1973. Against what teams did he do this?

15. Don Cockroft averaged 40.5 yards per punt in each of four seasons. Which ones?

Cleveland Browns Facts & Trivia

16. Don Cockroft holds four of the Browns' top nine positions in the team's category of punting yardage for a season. Which positions does he hold?

17. Don Cockroft led the NFL in number of punts in 1973. How many did he have?

18. Don Cockroft led the NFL in number of punts in 1974. How many did he have?

19. Don Cockroft's punting yardage total in 1974 ranks second for most punting yards in one season for the Browns. How many yards did he have?

20. Don Cockroft ranks first in career punting yards for the Browns. How many did he have?

21. Who was the Browns' punter in 1977?

22. Name the Browns' punter from 1978-80.

23. What was Johnny Evans's yards per punt average in 1979?

24. How many punting yards did Johnny Evans have in his career?

25. What University of Arkansas product averaged 43.4 yards per punt for the Browns in 1984?

26. Who punted the ball 164 times in the 1985 and 1986 seasons combined?

27. In 1988, Max Runager accounted for the fewest punting yards by a Browns punter since 1962 (not counting the strike seasons of 1982 and 1987). How many did Runager have?

28. Bryan Wagner led the NFL in 1989 in three categories - punts, punting yards, and what else?

29. Bryan Wagner led the NFL in what inauspicious category in 1990?

30. Who was the Browns' punter from 1991-93?

31. Brian Hansen punted 82 times for 3,632 yards in 1993 for a 44.3-yard average, the highest average by a Browns punter in how many years?

32. Brian Hansen's 3,632 yards punting in 1993 ranks where on the all-time Browns' list for punting yards in a season?

Cleveland Browns Facts & Trivia

33. Brian Hansen's two longest punts for the Browns went for 73 and 72 yards, respectively. The first one came on September 27, 1992, and the second occurred a year later on October 17, 1993. Who were Cleveland's opponents those days?

34. Name the former Ohio Stater who was Cleveland's punter in 1994 and 1995.

35. How many yards per punt did Tom Tupa average in 1995?

Kickers

1. What former Ohio State Buckeye is Cleveland's all-time leading scorer?

2. Lou Groza is the Browns' all-time leader in postseason scoring. How many points did Groza accumulate in postseason play?

3. Lou Groza played a total of 21 seasons with the Browns, from 1946-67 (a 22-year period). He retired for one of those seasons. Which one?

4. Who was the Browns' kicker in 1960 when Lou Groza was retired that season?

5. Lou Groza kicked a 53-yard field goal on October 10, 1948, in a 30-17 Browns victory over whom?

6. Lou Groza nailed the game-winning field goal with 28 seconds left to lift the Browns to a dramatic 30-28 victory over the Los Angeles Rams in the 1950 NFL title game on December 24 in Cleveland. How long was Groza's winning kick?

7. Against what team did Lou Groza kick a 51-yard field goal on October 28, 1962?

8. What were the most points Lou Groza scored in one season?

9. How many extra points and extra point attempts did Lou Groza have in his career?

10. How many field goals and field goal attempts did Lou Groza have in his career?

11. Who took over for Lou Groza as Cleveland's kicker in 1968, outdueling

Cleveland Browns Facts & Trivia

the veteran in training camp of that year?

12. What years did Don Cockroft kick for the Browns?

13. Don Cockroft was perfect on extra point attempts in three seasons. Which seasons?

14. What season did Don Cockroft connect on the fewest number of field goals in his career, 12?

15. One of Don Cockroft's most memorable field goals came on November 19, 1972, with 13 seconds left in a game against the Pittsburgh Steelers in Cleveland Municipal Stadium. Cockroft's trey was the game-winner in the Browns' 26-24 victory that lifted them into a first-place tie with Pittsburgh in the AFC Central Division with a record of 7-3. How long was the winning field goal?

16. In the final game of his 13-year career - on January 4, 1981, in an AFC Divisional Playoff against the Oakland Raiders at home - Don Cockroft had a miserable day in treacherous conditions. Temperature at game time was 1 degree with the wind chill making it feel like minus-37; the field was a sheet of ice. The Browns lost, 14-12. What were Cockroft's statistics that day?

17. What was the longest field goal Don Cockroft ever kicked?

18. How many points did Don Cockroft score in his career?

19. Who succeeded Don Cockroft as the Browns' kicker in 1981?

20. How long did Dave Jacobs last with the Browns?

21. Who did the Browns acquire in a trade with San Francisco on October 6, 1981?

22. In his sixth game as a Brown, Matt Bahr booted a game-winning 24-yard field goal with 43 seconds left to give the Browns a 15-12 victory over what West Coast team?

23. Against what AFC team did Matt Bahr tear ligaments in his right knee while making a game-saving tackle off a return of his own kickoff with the Browns leading, 31-28 - ending his season - on November 23, 1986?

24. What years did Matt Bahr play with the Browns?

25. Where does Matt Bahr rank on the all-time Browns' scoring list?

26. What was Matt Bahr's longest field goal as a Brown?

27. Who redeemed himself following a missed 23-yard field goal attempt in the first overtime by kicking the Browns into the 1986 AFC Championship game by connecting on the winning field goal from 27 yards out 2:02 into the second overtime, that gave the Browns a 23-20 double-overtime triumph over the New York Jets in a divisional playoff on January 3, 1987, in Cleveland?

28. Who kicked the longest field goal in Browns history?

29. Who was the Browns' leading scorer in 1987?

30. What player kicked the winning field goal as time ran out to give the Browns a stunning 30-29 victory over the Denver Broncos in Mile High Stadium on Monday night, October 8, 1990?

31. What kicker from Louisiana State did the Browns sign as a Plan B free agent in 1991?

32. Matt Stover's two longest field goals as a Brown came against the same team in the same venue. Name the team.

33. How many field goals of 50 yards or more did Matt Stover connect on in his five-year career with Cleveland from 1991-95?

34. Matt Stover's point totals in 1995 and 1994 rank third and fourth, respectively, on the all-time Browns' scoring list. How many points did he account for those years?

35. Matt Stover accounted for the Browns' last point - a conversion kick - in the first 50 years of the franchise. Where did the historic extra point occur?

Punt Returners

1. Who returned the most punts for the Browns in each of the franchise's first two seasons of 1946 and 1947?

2. Who led the Browns in average yards per punt return in 1946?

3. Who returned a punt 82 yards for a touchdown in a 55-7 rout of the Brooklyn Dodgers on September 12, 1947, in Ebbets Field?

4. Name the Duke University product who led the Browns with 26 punt

Cleveland Browns Facts & Trivia

returns and 258 punt return yards in 1948.

5. Where does Cliff Lewis rank in all-time Browns punt return yards?

6. Who led the Browns in punt returns and punt return yardage in 1950?

7. What No. 1 draft pick in 1950 out of Oregon State was the Browns' leader in average yards per punt return in 1951 and 1952?

8. Who led the Browns in punt return yards in 1953, 1954, and 1957?

9. What were Ken Konz's punt return statistics in 1956?

10. Bobby Mitchell returned three punts for touchdowns in his four-year career with the Browns. For how many yards did his longest go?

11. How many yards did Bobby Mitchell average per punt return in his four seasons with Cleveland from 1958-61?

12. Where does Bobby Mitchell rank on the Browns' all-time list of punt return yardage?

13. Who led the Browns in punt return yards and average yards per punt return in 1962?

14. Who led the Browns in punt return yards and average yards per punt return in 1963?

15. What future Browns offensive coordinator and interim head coach returned five punts for 41 yards in 1963?

16. Who had nine punt returns for 171 yards, a 19-yard average, in 1964, the latter two statistics which led the team?

17. Against what team did Leroy Kelly return a punt 68 yards for a touchdown on October 25, 1964?

18. Who led the Browns with 10 punt returns in 1964?

19. Name the Brown who led the NFL with a 15.6-yard punt return average in 1965.

20. Leroy Kelly led the league with two touchdowns off punt returns in 1965. Against what teams did they come?

21. Against what team did Ben Davis return a punt 52 yards for a

Cleveland Browns Facts & Trivia

touchdown on November 5, 1967?

22. What seventh-round draft pick in 1969 out of Florida State led the Browns with 88 punt return yards his rookie year?

23. Who led the Browns with 15 punt returns and 133 punt return yards in 1970?

24. Who led the Browns in punt returns, punt return yardage, and average yards per punt return in 1971?

25. Where does Leroy Kelly rank on the all-time Browns' punt return yardage list?

26. Who led the Browns in punt returns and punt return yardage in 1973, 1974, and 1975?

27. Greg Pruitt's punt return yardage total in 1974 ranks fifth on the all-time Browns' list. How many yards did Pruitt have that year?

28. Greg Pruitt returned a punt 72 yards late in a home game on October 27, 1974, that led to the winning score. Against what team did this occur?

29. What first-round draft pick in 1973 from Arizona State returned 31 punts for 205 yards, a 6.6-yard average, in 1976, leading the Browns in the first two categories?

30. What Boise State product led the Browns in punt returns, punt return yardage, and average yards per punt return in 1977?

31. What 1978 fifth-round draft choice out of Memphis State led the AFC with 16 fair catches his rookie year?

32. Who led the Browns in punt returns and punt return yards in 1979, 1981, and 1983?

33. How many yards did Dino Hall average per punt return in 1979?

34. Where does Dino Hall rank all-time in Browns punt return yards?

35. Where does Keith Wright rank all-time in Browns punt return yards?

36. Who led the Browns in punt returns and punt return yardage in 1982?

37. What Boston College product scored on a 37-yard punt return against the New York Jets in the 1985 season finale on December 22 in the

Meadowlands?

38. What speedster from Baylor was the Browns' leader in punt returns, punt return yardage, and average yards per punt return each season from 1986-89?

39. Gerald McNeil returned a punt for a touchdown in the Browns' 24-21 victory over the Detroit Lions on September 28, 1986, in Cleveland Stadium. How long was the "Cube's" return?

40. Gerald McNeil's punt return yardage total in 1989 ranks first all-time in Browns annals. How many did he have that season?

41. Gerald McNeil ranks first in career punt return yards for the Browns. How many did he have?

42. Whose mental miscue on a punt return deep in Browns territory late in a November 10, 1991, contest at home against Philadelphia led to the Eagles' winning touchdown in a 32-30 defeat, a game in which the Browns once led, 23-0?

43. What No. 1 draft pick in 1989 out of the University of Texas led the NFL in punt returns in 1992 with 44 and led the AFC in punt return yards that year with 429?

44. Against what team did Eric Metcalf score on a 75-yard punt return on November 29, 1992?

45. Sunday, October 24, 1993, will burn brightly in Eric Metcalf's mind forever. Why?

46. Where do Eric Metcalf's 464 punt return yards in 1993 rank in the category of most punt return yards in a season for the Browns?

47. Eric Metcalf's average yards per punt return in 1993 led the AFC. What was it?

48. Eric Metcalf returned an NFL-best two punts for touchdowns in 1994, the first one going for 92 yards, the longest in the AFC that season. The second went for 73 yards. Both returns came against the same team. What team?

49. Where does Eric Metcalf rank in the category of all-time Browns punt return yardage?

50. Name the first-round draft pick out of Michigan who scored on a 69-

yard punt return during the Browns' 22-19 loss to Buffalo in Cleveland Stadium on Monday night, October 2, 1995.

Kickoff Returners

1. Who led the Browns in kickoff returns and kickoff return yardage in the team's first season of 1946?

2. Who led the Browns in kickoff returns and kickoff return yards in 1947 and 1948?

3. What Tulane product who played for the Browns from 1948-55 returned a kickoff 46 yards in Cleveland's 49-7 destruction of Buffalo in the 1948 AAFC Championship game in Cleveland?

4. Who led the Browns in kickoff returns in 1949?

5. Who led the Browns in kickoff return yardage in 1949?

6. Who returned nine kickoffs for 189 yards in 1949?

7. What University of Kentucky product led the Browns in kickoff returns, kickoff return yards, and average yards per kickoff return in 1950?

8. What first-round draft choice in 1950 out of Oregon State led the Browns in kickoff returns and kickoff return yardage in 1951, 1952, and 1953?

9. What University of Pittsburgh product led the NFL in 1954 with a 29.5-yard kickoff return average?

10. Who is responsible for the longest kickoff return in Browns history?

11. What rookie returned a kickoff for 102 yards for a touchdown on October 26, 1958, in Chicago against the Cardinals?

12. Bobby Mitchell led Cleveland with 11 kickoff returns in 1959. For how many yards did his 11 returns go?

13. Bobby Mitchell returned three kickoffs for touchdowns in his career with the Browns from 1958-61. Two were against Philadelphia - a 98-yarder on November 23, 1958, and a 91-yarder on November 19, 1961. Against what team did the other occur?

Cleveland Browns Facts & Trivia

14. How many yards per kickoff return did Bobby Mitchell average in 1961?

15. How many kickoff return yards did Bobby Mitchell accumulate in his four years with the Browns?

16. Who led the Browns in kickoff return yardage in 1962?

17. Two players tied for the Browns' lead with 24 kickoff returns in 1964. Who were they?

18. Who led the Browns in 1965 with 24 kickoff returns and 621 return yards?

19. How many yards per kickoff return did Walter Roberts average in 1965?

20. Walter Roberts returned 20 kickoffs for how many yards in 1966?

21. Who led the Browns in kickoff returns and kickoff return yardage in 1967?

22. Who led the Browns in kickoff returns, kickoff return yards, and average yards per kickoff return in 1968?

23. Who led the Browns in kickoff returns and kickoff return yards in 1969?

24. Who returned the second-half kickoff 94 yards for a touchdown in the Browns' home game against the New York Jets on September 21, 1970, the first-ever ABC *Monday Night Football* contest?

25. How many kickoff return yards did Frank Pitts have in 1971?

26. Who led the Browns in kickoff returns, kickoff return yards, and average yards per kickoff return in 1972?

27. What University of Oklahoma product was the AFC leader in average yards per kickoff return in 1974?

28. On November 10, 1974, Greg Pruitt returned the opening kickoff 88 yards - longest in the AFC that year - for a touchdown to ignite the Browns' 21-14 victory over what team?

29. What Brown returned the opening kickoff 92 yards in Cleveland's 35-23 upset of Cincinnati on November 23, 1975, in Cleveland?

30. Who led the Browns with 24 kickoff returns and 551 kickoff return yards

in 1976?

31. What fifth-round draft pick in 1978 out of Memphis State led the AFC with a 26.3-yard kickoff return average his rookie year?

32. Where does Keith Wright rank on the all-time Browns' kickoff return yardage list?

33. Who became the first Brown to attain 1,000 yards in kickoff returns for one season in 1979 with 1,014?

34. Dino Hall is the Browns' all-time leader in kickoff return yards. How many did he have?

35. What Brown was the AFC leader in average yards per kickoff return in 1985?

36. Where does Glen Young rank on the all-time Browns' kickoff return yardage list?

37. Who led the NFL with 47 kickoff returns in 1986 and returned one for 100 yards - longest in the league that season - against Pittsburgh in Three Rivers Stadium on October 5 of that year?

38. How many kickoff return yards did Gerald McNeil have in 1986?

39. Who led the Browns in kickoff returns and kickoff return yardage in 1988?

40. What rookie from the University of Texas led the Browns in kickoff returns, kickoff return yards, and average yards per kickoff return in 1989?

41. Eric Metcalf led the NFL in four kickoff return categories in 1990. Which ones?

42. Eric Metcalf became the only player in Browns annals to return a kickoff for a touchdown in postseason play when he burned what team for a 90-yard score in an AFC Divisional Playoff on January 6, 1990, in Cleveland?

43. Where does Eric Metcalf rank on the Browns' career kickoff return yards list?

44. Who led the Browns in kickoff returns, kickoff return yardage, and average yards per kickoff return in 1992?

45. What were Randy Baldwin's kickoff return statistics in 1992?

46. Who had the third most kickoff returns for Cleveland in 1993 behind Randy Baldwin and Eric Metcalf, respectively?

47. Who returned a kickoff 85 yards for a touchdown in the Browns' 28-20 victory over the Bengals in Cincinnati in the 1994 season opener on September 4?

48. Randy Baldwin led the AFC in average yards per kickoff return in 1994. What was Baldwin's average?

49. How many kickoff return yards did Randy Baldwin have in his Browns career?

50. Who led the Browns in kickoff returns, kickoff return yardage, and average yards per kickoff return in 1995?

2. Head Coaches

Paul Brown

1. When and where was Paul Brown born?

2. Where was Paul Brown raised?

3. What high school did Paul Brown attend?

4. What position did Paul Brown play for the Massillon Washington High School Tigers his last two years there?

5. Paul Brown attended Ohio State University his freshman year of college, but from what school did he graduate?

6. Where was Paul Brown's first football coaching job?

7. What took up much of Paul Brown's time while he coached at Severn Prep (Maryland)?

Cleveland Browns Facts & Trivia

8. What Ohio high school hired Paul Brown as its head football coach in 1932?

9. What was the Massillon Washington Tigers' record in Paul Brown's first year as their head coach?

10. What was Massillon Washington High's record under Paul Brown in the six seasons from 1933-38 combined?

11. Paul Brown's final season as head coach at Massillon Washington was 1940. What was Brown's record in his nine seasons in charge in Tigertown?

12. During his head coaching tenure at Massillon Washington High School, Paul Brown received head coaching offers from several small colleges throughout Ohio. He turned them all down because his No. 1 goal was to be the head coach at what football tradition-rich university?

13. What university hired Paul Brown as its head coach in 1941?

14. Who did Paul Brown replace as Ohio State's head coach in 1941?

15. What was Ohio State's record in Paul Brown's first year as head coach there?

16. How did the Ohio State Buckeyes fare in Paul Brown's second season as their head coach in 1942?

17. Calls to military service destroyed Ohio State's 1943 team, Brown's last. What was the Buckeyes' record that year?

18. What did Paul Brown do after his short stay as Ohio State University's head coach?

19. What was the Great Lakes Naval Training Center football team's record in Paul Brown's two seasons as head coach there?

20. In between his two seasons as head coach at the Great Lakes Naval Training Center, Paul Brown was hired to coach what professional team beginning in 1946?

21. What wealthy Cleveland businessman hired Paul Brown to be the first head coach of the Cleveland entry in the AAFC?

22. Name the first player Paul Brown ever signed to the Cleveland entry in the AAFC.

Cleveland Browns Facts & Trivia

23. After whom were the Browns named?

24. In what division did the Browns compete during their first three years in the AAFC?

25. In what division did the Browns compete in their last year in the AAFC, which disbanded following the 1949 season?

26. What team did Cleveland defeat in the 1946 and 1947 AAFC Championship games?

27. What was the Browns' overall record in their four years in the AAFC, including postseason?

28. What team was Cleveland's first opponent in the NFL?

29. The Browns won the NFL title in 1950. What team did they defeat in the championship game?

30. After winning the 1950 NFL Championship, Cleveland won two more NFL titles with Paul Brown as head coach. In what years?

31. When did Paul Brown's final postseason game as head coach of the Browns take place?

32. Under what circumstances did Paul Brown leave the Browns' organization?

33. What was Paul Brown's regular-season record as Cleveland's coach?

34. What was Paul Brown's postseason record as Cleveland's coach?

35. When was Paul Brown's death?

Other Head Coaches

1. Who replaced Paul Brown as head coach of the Browns?

2. Did Blanton Collier assume the duties of general manager when he was hired as Browns coach like Paul Brown did?

3. Blanton Collier was an assistant coach for the Browns before succeeding Paul Brown as head coach. What positions did Collier coach?

Cleveland Browns Facts & Trivia

4. Where did Blanton Collier begin his coaching career?

5. Where did Blanton Collier graduate from college?

6. Where did Blanton Collier meet Paul Brown for the first time?

7. What was the Browns' record in Blanton Collier's first season as their head coach?

8. How did the Browns do in Blanton Collier's second season as head coach?

9. In how many NFL Championship games did the Browns appear in Blanton Collier's eight seasons as the team's head coach?

10. In what stadium did Blanton Collier coach his final game as head man of the Browns?

11. What was Blanton Collier's overall record as Browns head coach?

12. What was Blanton Collier's postseason record as head coach of the Browns?

13. Name the only head coach in Browns history who had prior NFL head coaching experience.

14. How many times did the Philadelphia Eagles qualify for the postseason with Nick Skorich as their head coach?

15. What was Nick Skorich's record as the Philadelphia Eagles' head coach?

16. In what small southern Ohio town was Nick Skorich born?

17. At what large Ohio university did Nick Skorich excel as a guard?

18. Nick Skorich was an offensive guard for three seasons in the NFL. For what team?

19. Nick Skorich was an assistant coach for three NFL teams other than the Browns. Name the three clubs.

20. Who did the Browns defeat in Nick Skorich's first game as Browns head coach?

21. What was the Browns' record in Nick Skorich's first year as head coach

Cleveland Browns Facts & Trivia

in 1971?

22. On Christmas Eve 1972, the Browns were leading the undefeated, eventual Super Bowl Champion Miami Dolphins late in an AFC Divisional Playoff game. The Dolphins pulled the game out, however. What was the final score?

23. When was Nick Skorich fired as Browns head coach?

24. What former Green Bay Hall of Fame offensive tackle succeeded Nick Skorich as Cleveland's head coach in 1975?

25. What southern university did Forrest Gregg play for?

26. What extra duty did Forrest Gregg take on in 1969 and 1970, his final two seasons in Green Bay?

27. For what AFC West team was Forrest Gregg the offensive line coach in 1972 and 1973?

28. Prior to Forrest Gregg's hiring as the Cleveland Browns' head coach in 1975, for what team was he offensive line coach the year before?

29. How many consecutive games did the Browns lose to begin Forrest Gregg's tenure as head coach?

30. After nine losses to open the 1975 season, the Browns finally broke into the win column. Their victim was the Cincinnati Bengals. What was the Bengals' record going into the game?

31. Forrest Gregg began his head coaching career with the Browns by losing his first nine games to open the 1975 season. He ended his career with the Browns by dropping five of his last six games in 1977 (he was fired with one game to go that season), giving him a 1-14 record in those 15 games. What was Gregg's record in the 26 games in between?

32. Forrest Gregg was fired following a 19-15 home loss to what AFC Central team on December 11, 1977, in front of only 30,898 fans, with one game remaining on the schedule?

33. Who was the Browns' head coach in the 1977 season finale in Seattle?

34. Name the Brooklyn, New York, native who was introduced to the media as the Brown' sixth -and fifth full-time - head coach on December 28, 1977.

35. Sam Rutigliano played for a national championship team in college.

Cleveland Browns Facts & Trivia

What school?

36. After his playing days at the University of Tennessee, where did Sam Rutigliano play - and letter - in football?

37. From what Ivy League School did Sam Rutigliano earn a master's degree in education?

38. For what two northeastern universities was Sam Rutigliano an assistant football coach?

39. What former Browns linebacker and NFL head coach was the University of Maryland's mentor when Rutigliano arrived in College Park?

40. When Lou Saban left the University of Maryland head coaching job to take the same position with the Denver Broncos, he took aide Sam Rutigliano with him. Name the three other NFL teams Rutigliano was an assistant coach for before his appointment as Browns head coach.

41. The Browns defeated the San Francisco 49ers, 24-7, at home on September 3, 1978, in Sam Rutigliano's debut as head coach. Who led the 49ers in rushing yards that day?

42. What award was bestowed upon Sam Rutigliano after both the 1979 and 1980 seasons?

43. What play that occurred toward the end of the Browns' 14-12 divisional playoff loss to the Oakland Raiders on January 4, 1981, will Sam Rutigliano be remembered for most?

44. Under what circumstances did Sam Rutigliano leave the Browns?

45. Who replaced Sam Rutigliano as Browns head coach midway through the 1984 season?

46. What two teams did Marty Schottenheimer play linebacker for in his six-year professional career from 1965-70?

47. Where did Marty Schottenheimer graduate from college?

48. Who ruined Marty Schottenheimer's debut as Browns head coach on October 28, 1984, by kicking a 53-yard field goal with no time left to give his team a 16-14 victory in Cleveland Stadium?

49. Marty Schottenheimer replaced Sam Rutigliano as head coach at the midway point of the 1984 season when the Browns had a 1-7 record. How

Cleveland Browns Facts & Trivia

did the team fare in the second half of the year?

50. How many AFC Central Division titles did the Browns win under Marty Schottenheimer?

51. What was Marty Schottenheimer's record as Browns head coach?

52. What was Marty Schottenheimer's postseason record as Browns head coach?

53. Under what circumstances did Marty Schottenheimer leave Cleveland?

54. Who succeeded Marty Schottenheimer as the Browns' eighth head coach on January 27, 1989?

55. What defense for another team that turned out to be one of the best ever did Bud Carson design as an assistant coach in the 1970s?

56. For what AFC East team was Bud Carson defensive coordinator from 1985-88?

57. What team was Bud Carson's first game as Browns coach against?

58. What team was Bud Carson's second game as Browns coach against?

59. What was Cleveland's record in Bud Carson's first year as Browns coach?

60. Who did the Browns defeat in the AFC Divisional Playoffs on January 6, 1990, in Cleveland Stadium?

61. The Browns lost to the Denver Broncos, 37-21, in the AFC Championship game for the third time in four years on January 14, 1990, in Mile High Stadium in Denver. What was the score after three quarters?

62. After a season-opening victory over Pittsburgh, the Browns found the going rough in 1990, Bud Carson's second year at the helm. In fact, Carson was fired after nine games with the team in last place in the AFC Central at 2-7. What team delivered the crushing blow to Carson's head coaching career?

63. Who became the Browns' interim head coach when Bud Carson was fired on November 5, 1990?

64. Who did Art Modell announce as the Browns' tenth - and eighth full-time - head coach on February 5, 1991?

65. What UCLA product was the Browns' first draft pick with Bill Belichick as head coach?

66. The Browns lost their first game under Bill Belichick by the score of 26-14 on September 1, 1991, in Cleveland Stadium. Who defeated the Browns that day?

67. The Browns had a 13-13 record in game Nos. 1-13 in 1991 and 1992 combined. What was their record in games 14-16 in those two seasons combined?

68. With the Browns 5-3 and tied for first place, what ninth-year quarterback was released by the team at the strong urging of Bill Belichick on November 8, 1993?

69. Bill Belichick Infamous Moment No. 1: it occurred on November 22, 1992, in Minneapolis. What happened?

70. Bill Belichick's fourth Browns team, the 1994 edition, finished 11-5 and qualified for the postseason as a wild card team. Cleveland led the league in fewest points allowed that year. How many points did the Browns yield?

71. Who did the Browns defeat, 20-13, in an AFC Wild Card game on New Years Day 1995?

72. Who destroyed the Browns, 29-9, in an AFC Divisional Playoff game on January 7, 1995?

73. Bill Belichick Infamous Moment No. 2: it occurred on December 3, 1995, in San Diego. What happened?

74. The Browns finished the 1995 season 5-11 but began the year with a successful September. What was the team's record after the season's first month?

75. What was Bill Belichick's record as Browns coach?

3. Browns vs. ...

Browns vs. Giants

1. What was the result of the first-ever Browns-Giants game?

2. The Browns lost to the Giants twice during the 1950 regular season. The two teams finished tied for first place in the American Conference at 10-2. In a playoff on December 17 to decide the conference representative in the NFL Championship game, the Browns defeated the Giants in a defensive struggle in Cleveland. What was the final score?

3. The Browns lost a crucial game to the Giants in the 1952 season finale to the Giants on December 14 in the Polo Grounds by a score of 37-34. A victory would have clinched the American Conference title for Cleveland. The Browns, though, still won the conference championship. Why?

4. The Browns entered their December 6, 1953, matchup with the New York Giants in Cleveland with a perfect 10-0 record, as opposed to the Giants' 3-7 mark. The Browns easily dismantled the visitors, 62-14. Who was the Browns' starting quarterback that day?

5. The Browns and Giants played to a 35-35 tie on November 27, 1955, in New York. The Browns had a chance to take the lead with 30 seconds left in the game, but Lou Groza's short field goal try was blocked. What Giants defensive tackle was the culprit?

6. On September 29, 1957, in the season opener, a 47-yard field goal into the wind late in the fourth quarter was the game-winner as the Browns dealt the visiting Giants a 6-3 defeat. Just minutes before, though, the Giants themselves had a golden opportunity to break the 3-3 tie, but Ben Agajanian misfired on a short field goal try. Exactly how short was it?

7. The Browns and Giants waged a titanic battle in the 1958 season finale on December 14 in New York. The Browns entered the game 9-2, the Giants 8-3. A win, or tie, would have given Cleveland the Eastern Conference Championship. But with the score, 10-10, on the ice-covered field of Yankee Stadium, New York took a 13-10 lead with 2:07 to play, and hung on for the victory. Who kicked the winning field goal that not only gave the Giants the win, but forced a playoff between the two teams a week later in the same venue?

8. In the Browns' 10-0 loss to the Giants in the 1958 Eastern Conference Playoff on December 21 in Yankee Stadium, the great Jim Brown was held

to just 18 yards rushing. How many yards rushing did the Browns have overall?

9. The Giants destroyed the Browns by a score of 48-7 on December 6, 1959, in Yankee Stadium. The lopsided victory by the Giants was a sidelight, however, to what occurred with two minutes remaining in the game. What happened?

10. The Browns, tied with the Eagles at 7-3, needed a win over the 8-2 Giants on November 26, 1961, to move into a tie for first place in the Eastern Conference with the New Yorkers (and, as it turned out, Philadelphia, too). Were the Browns successful?

11. The Browns needed a victory over the struggling Giants on the final day of the 1964 season to clinch the Eastern Conference title. Cleveland erupted in Yankee Stadium for a 32-point triumph. What was the final score?

12. The Browns entered their December 1, 1968, home game against the New York Giants in first place in the Century Division with an 8-3 record, but with St. Louis hot on their trail. The Giants entered at 7-4 and with an outside shot at catching the front-running Dallas Cowboys in the Capitol Division. How did the Browns fare that day?

13. The Giants invaded Cleveland Municipal Stadium for a September 30, 1973, battle with the Browns. The Browns won. What was the final score (clue: there were 22 points scored)?

14. The Browns' 21-7 victory over the New York Giants on November 20, 1977, in Giants Stadium was orchestrated by what quarterback?

15. The Browns staged an amazing comeback win in the Meadowlands on December 1, 1985, when down by 12 late in the game, injured quarterback Gary Danielson gave it all he had and led the team to a 35-33 victory (Danielson was knocked out of the game, however, with the Browns trailing, 33-28; Bernie Kosar finished for him). The Giants had a chance at the end but New York's kicker misfired on a 34-yard field goal try as time expired. What was the kicker's name?

16. The Browns' 16-13 loss to the Giants on December 4, 1994, was Cleveland's first home game against the New Yorkers in how many years?

17. The Browns have shut out the Giants twice. What years?

18. How many times have the Giants bageled the Browns?

Cleveland Browns Facts & Trivia

19. How many times have the Browns swept the season series from the Giants?

20. How many times have the Giants swept the season series from the Browns?

21. The Browns once had a six-game winning streak against the Giants. When?

22. The Giants once had a five-game winning streak against Cleveland. When?

23. What is the Browns' lowest point total in a victory over the Giants?

24. What is the Giants' lowest point total in a victory over the Browns?

25. What is the Browns' highest point total in a loss to the Giants?

26. What is the Giants' highest point total in a loss to the Browns?

27. What is the most one-sided Browns' victory over the Giants?

28. What is the most one-sided Giants' victory over the Browns?

29. What is the highest-scoring game between the Browns and Giants?

30. What is the lowest-scoring game between the Browns and Giants?

31. How many times have the Browns and Giants played to a tie?

32. How many times have the Browns and Giants met in postseason play?

33. What is the Browns' record against the Giants (44 games)?

34. What is the Browns' home record against the Giants (22 games)?

35. How many points have the Browns scored and yielded against the Giants?

Cleveland Browns Facts & Trivia

Browns vs. Steelers

1. Who won the first-ever Browns-Steelers game?

2. The Browns lost only two of their first 18 games against Pittsburgh from 1950-58. When did the two defeats occur?

3. Pittsburgh opened the 1959 season with a 17-7 upset of the Browns on Saturday night, September 26 in Forbes Field in Pittsburgh. What quarterback led the Steelers to victory that evening, completing 13 of 20 passes for 209 yards (and also kicked a field goal and two extra points)?

4. The Browns hung on for a thrilling 30-28 victory over Pittsburgh on October 22, 1961, in Forbes Field. Who was the Browns' starting quarterback that day?

5. What Pittsburgh running back rushed for exactly 200 yards in the Steelers' 23-7 victory over the Browns on Saturday night, October 10, 1964, in Cleveland?

6. Pittsburgh's 28-9 victory over the Browns on November 29, 1970, began a streak of 16 consecutive victories over their arch-rivals from down the turnpike in Three Rivers Stadium, the Steelers' new home. What did the streak come to be known as over the years?

7. Don Cockroft kicked the winning field goal with 13 seconds left to give the Browns a thrilling 26-24 victory over Pittsburgh on November 19, 1972, in Cleveland Municipal Stadium in front of 83,009 spectators. How long was the field goal?

8. The Browns invaded Three Rivers Stadium on September 19, 1976, following their season-opening victory over the Jets seven days earlier, after having finished 3-11 the year before. The two-time defending Super Bowl Champion Steelers entered the game having lost their opener in Oakland a week earlier after blowing a 14-point lead late in the game. The Steelers defeated the Browns, 31-14. What was the halftime score?

9. Name the defensive end who sacked Steelers quarterback Terry Bradshaw by lifting him up and slamming him head first to the ground early in the fourth quarter of the Browns' 18-16 upset win on October 10, 1976, in Cleveland Municipal Stadium.

10. The Browns and Steelers butted heads in Three Rivers Stadium on September 24, 1978, in a battle for first place in the AFC Central Division. The two teams, both 3-0 entering the contest, played to a 9-9 tie after

Cleveland Browns Facts & Trivia

regulation. Browns return man Ricky Feacher recovered a fumble on the overtime kickoff deep in Steelers territory. Officials ruled the play dead, although television replays affirmed there had been an obvious fumble on the play. The ball was awarded to Pittsburgh. Moments later, Terry Bradshaw hit tight end Bennie Cunningham for a 37-yard touchdown pass on a flea-flicker for a 15-9 Steelers' victory. Name the Steelers' player who "fumbled" the kickoff.

11. Pittsburgh destroyed the visiting Browns, 44-17, on October 16, 1983, in a battle for first place in the AFC Central Division. Browns quarterback Brian Sipe didn't help matters by tossing how many interceptions?

12. Why was it rather difficult to identify Browns players during Cleveland's 31-14 exhibition loss to Pittsburgh on Saturday night, August 4, 1984, in Cleveland Stadium?

13. Gerald "The Ice Cube" McNeil's 100-yard kickoff return just before halftime lifted the Browns to an exhilarating triumph over the Steelers on October 5, 1986, in Three Rivers Stadium, ending the Three Rivers Jinx. What was the final score?

14. Name the Browns' speedster who returned punts 91 and 75 yards, respectively - the second the game-winner with 2:05 left - to lift the Browns to a memorable 28-23 victory over Pittsburgh on October 24, 1993, in Cleveland Stadium.

15. How many times have the Browns and Steelers met on *Monday Night Football*?

16. How many times have the Browns and Steelers met on a Saturday afternoon?

17. The Browns have shut out the Steelers four times. What years?

18. How many times have the Steelers blanked the Browns?

19. How many times have the Browns swept the season series from the Steelers?

20. How many times have the Steelers swept the season series from the Browns?

21. The Browns once had an eight-game winning streak against the Steelers. When?

22. The Steelers once had a six-game winning streak against Cleveland.

Cleveland Browns Facts & Trivia

When?

23. What is the Browns' lowest point total in a victory over the Steelers?

24. What is the Steelers' lowest point total in a victory over the Browns?

25. What is the Browns' highest point total in a loss to the Steelers?

26. What is the Steelers' highest point total in a loss to the Browns?

27. What is the most one-sided Browns' victory over the Steelers?

28. What is the most one-sided Steelers' victory over the Browns?

29. What is the highest-scoring game between the Browns and Steelers?

30. What is the lowest-scoring game between the Browns and Steelers?

31. How many times have the Browns and Steelers played to a tie?

32. How many times have the Browns and Steelers met in the postseason?

33. What is the Browns' record against the Steelers (92 games)?

34. What is the Browns' home record against the Steelers (46 games)?

35. How many points have the Browns scored and yielded against the Steelers?

Browns vs. Bengals

1. The Bengals defeated the Browns by a score of 31-24 in the first-ever preseason meeting between the teams on August 29, 1970, in brand new Riverfront Stadium in Cincinnati. Two years later, the Ohio rivals began a preseason series that would last through 1974. Where were these three exhibition games played?

2. Who won the first Browns-Bengals game?

3. The Browns defeated the Bengals, 35-23, on November 23, 1975, in Cleveland. What were the teams' records heading into the contest?

4. When was the Bengals' first win in Cleveland?

Cleveland Browns Facts & Trivia

5. What fullback out of Ohio State rushed for 160 yards on 27 carries in the Bengals' 48-16 trouncing of the Browns in the 1978 season finale on December 17 in Cincinnati?

6. What Browns receiver just missed catching a fourth-down pass from Brian Sipe in the end zone in the final minute of play in the Browns' 16-12 loss to the Bengals in Cincinnati on December 16, 1979, in the season finale?

7. What Browns receiver caught two long touchdown passes from Brian Sipe in Cleveland's 27-24 season-ending, division-clinching win in Cincinnati on December 21, 1980?

8. Who kicked a Browns-record 60-yard field goal on October 21, 1984, against the Bengals in Riverfront Stadium?

9. What Browns head coach was fired the day after the team's 12-9 loss to the Bengals on October 21, 1984, in Cincinnati?

10. Besides the obvious, what was special about Gary Danielson's 72-yard touchdown pass to Clarence Weathers in the third quarter of the Browns' 24-6 victory over the Bengals on November 24, 1985, in Cleveland?

11. Although the Browns carried a 10-4 record into their December 14, 1986, meeting in Cincinnati with the Bengals, who were 9-5, most observers believed the home club was the better team. What was the result of the game?

12. What Browns defensive end became a surprise "sprinter" in Cleveland's 38-24 triumph over Cincinnati on December 13, 1987, in Cleveland Stadium?

13. The Browns played Santa Claus a month-and-a-half early when on November 3, 1991, in Riverfront Stadium, they gift-wrapped a victory to Cincinnati by committing miscue after miscue. The Bengals won, 23-21, when Browns kicker Matt Stover had his 34-yard field goal try blocked as time ran out. Who blocked it?

14. Eric Metcalf had quite a year returning punts against the Bengals in 1994. In what fashion?

15. When was the only Saturday meeting between the Browns and Bengals?

16. The Browns and Bengals have squared off twice on Monday night - a 21-14 Bengals' victory on September 25, 1989, in Cincinnati, and a 34-13

Cleveland Browns Facts & Trivia

Bengals' rout on October 22, 1990, in Cleveland. The two teams have played twice on Thursday evening, as well. When were those games played?

17. The Browns have shut out the Bengals once. What year?

18. How many times have the Bengals bageled the Browns?

19. How many times have the Browns swept the season series from the Bengals?

20. How many times have the Bengals swept the season series from the Browns?

21. The Browns once had a seven-game winning streak against the Bengals. When?

22. Three times, the Bengals had a four-game winning streak against Cleveland. When?

23. What is the Browns' lowest point total in a victory over the Bengals?

24. What is the Bengals' lowest point total in a victory over the Browns?

25. What is the Browns' highest point total in a loss to the Bengals?

26. What is the Bengals' highest point total in a loss to the Browns?

27. What is the most one-sided Browns' victory over the Bengals?

28. What is the most one-sided Bengals' victory over the Browns?

29. What is the highest-scoring game between the Browns and Bengals?

30. What is the lowest-scoring game between the Browns and Bengals?

31. How many times have the Browns and Bengals played to a tie?

32. How many times have the Browns and Bengals met in the postseason?

33. What is the Browns' record against the Bengals (51 games)?

34. What is the Browns' home record against the Bengals (25 games)?

35. How many points have the Browns scored and yielded against the Bengals?

Browns vs. AAFC/Rest of NFL

1. What was the result of the first-ever Browns game, which came against the Miami Seahawks on September 6, 1946, in Cleveland?

2. The Browns' all-time record for most points scored in one game came against what team?

3. Who did the Browns defeat in the 1946 and 1947 AAFC Championship games?

4. Who scored on a 99-yard touchdown reception - the longest pass play in Browns history - from Otto Graham in a 28-7 victory over the Buffalo Bills on November 2, 1947, in Buffalo?

5. What was the Browns' all-time record against the Chicago Rockets (eight games)?

6. What was the Browns' all-time record against the original Baltimore Colts (six games)?

7. What team did the Browns tie twice during the 1949 season and then defeat, 31-21, in an AAFC Playoff on December 4 in Cleveland?

8. Who did the Browns defeat in the 1949 AAFC Championship game?

9. The Browns lost four games in the four years the AAFC existed. Who were the only two teams to beat them?

10. Mac Speedie holds the Browns' record for most receiving yards in a single game with 228 on November 20, 1949. Against what team did Speedie achieve this?

11. Who did the Browns play in their first game in the NFL?

12. Otto Graham completed 22 of 35 passes for how many yards in the Browns' 34-24 victory over the Chicago Cardinals on October 15, 1950, in Cleveland?

13. The Browns won the NFL Championship in their first year in the league in 1950. Who did they defeat to win the title?

14. Who scored a team-record six touchdowns in the Browns' 42-21 rout of the Chicago Bears on November 25, 1951, in Cleveland?

Cleveland Browns Facts & Trivia

15. The Browns lost the 1952 and 1953 NFL Championship games to the Detroit Lions but rebounded to win the 1954 title. Who did the Browns defeat to claim the title in '54?

16. The Browns won their first 11 games of the 1953 season, then lost the season finale by a 42-27 count to what team?

17. The Browns have played one regular-season game in Lambeau Field. When was it?

18. The Browns clinched their first-ever losing season on December 16, 1956, by dropping a 24-7 decision to what team in Cleveland Municipal Stadium?

19. How many yards did Browns fullback Jim Brown rush for in his team's 45-31 victory over the Los Angeles Rams on November 24, 1957, in Cleveland?

20. Who defeated the Browns for the 1957 NFL title?

21. The Browns defeated the Baltimore Colts, 38-31, on November 1, 1959, in Baltimore. Who scored all five of Cleveland's touchdowns that day?

22. What team administered a 17-14 upset of Cleveland - rebounding from a 14-0 first-quarter deficit - on December 10, 1961, knocking the Browns out of postseason contention?

23. Against what team did the Browns play to a 33-33 tie on September 20, 1964, in Cleveland Municipal Stadium?

24. Who did the Browns upset in the NFL Championship game on December 27, 1964, in Cleveland?
25. Who defeated the Browns in the 1965 NFL Championship game on January 2, 1966?

26. What team did the Browns oppose for three straight seasons, from 1967-69, in the Eastern Conference Championship game?

27. The Baltimore Colts walloped the Browns in the 1968 NFL title game on December 29 - in Cleveland, no less. What was the final score?

28. What team limited the Browns to 151 total yards and eight first downs in a 51-3 rout on November 9, 1969, and then two months later defeated the Browns again, 27-7, in the NFL title game on January 4, 1970?

29. The Browns were one of the combatants in the first ABC *Monday Night Football* game on September 21, 1970, in Cleveland. Who opposed the Browns that night?

30. After beginning the 1971 season 4-5, the Browns ran off five straight victories, including a 20-13 victory over what NFC East team (clue: "Over-the-Hill Gang")?

31. The Browns won a thrilling Monday night game in San Diego on November 13, 1972, when Mike Phipps hit what wide receiver for a 38-yard touchdown pass with 41 seconds left?

32. The Browns were beaten by the undefeated Miami Dolphins, 20-14, in an AFC Divisional Playoff game on December 24, 1972, in the Orange Bowl. The Browns had taken a 14-13 lead with 8:11 to go when Mike Phipps hit what wide receiver for a 27-yard touchdown strike?

33. The Browns' only win in Oakland came on November 18, 1973. What was the score?

34. What rookie from the University of Oklahoma dashed 65 yards for a fourth-period score that helped the Browns to a 20-20 tie with the Chiefs in Kansas City on December 2, 1973?

35. What rookie quarterback relieved Mike Phipps in the fourth quarter and led the Browns back from a 21-9 deficit to a 23-21 victory over the Denver Broncos on October 27, 1974, in Cleveland Municipal Stadium?

36. The Browns won an awfully exciting game by a score of 30-27 on the evening of September 26, 1977, in Cleveland Municipal Stadium. It was the Browns' first appearance on *Monday Night Football* in four seasons. Who was the Browns' victim that night?

37. Dick Modzelewski was the Browns' head coach for one game. The former Browns' defensive tackle was hired as the interim coach when Forrest Gregg was fired with one game remaining in the 1977 season. Who was the Browns' opponent for Modzelewski's head coaching debut (and farewell)?

38. The Browns lost to the Houston Oilers, 16-13, with the help of a controversial call on October 1, 1978, in Cleveland. Browns cornerback Ron Bolton and the Oilers' Ken Burrough both came down with a long pass at the Cleveland four with under a minute left in the game. Although Bolton argued that he had possession of the ball, officials ruled a simultaneous catch (in that scenario, the ball is awarded to the receiver). Soon after, Tony Fritsch kicked the winning field goal. Name the Oilers' quarterback

who threw the long pass.

39. The Browns opened the 1979 season with a heart-palpitating 25-22 victory over what AFC East team on September 2?

40. The Browns began the 1979 season 4-0. They capped their fine start with a rousing 26-7 victory over the also-undefeated (at least prior to the Browns game) defending NFC Champion Dallas Cowboys - "America's Team" - on Monday night, September 24, in a rocking Cleveland Stadium. The Browns scored 20 points in the first seven minutes of play. Thom Darden's 39-yard interception return of Roger Staubach not only topped off the first-quarter barrage of points by the Browns, but it was also special for another reason. What reason was it?

41. The Browns experienced quite possibly the most devastating defeat in team history on the afternoon of December 14, 1980, in Minnesota. With the Browns leading, 23-22, with four seconds to go in the game - they had led, 23-9, at one point in the fourth quarter - and the Vikings at the Cleveland 46, Tommy Kramer lofted one down the right sideline. The ball was struck by Browns cornerback Ron Bolton but then cascaded into the left hand of a Vikings' receiver as he backpedaled into the end zone, cradling the ball against his body. The Vikings won, 28-23. Name the Minnesota receiver who was in the right place at the right time.

42. Name the Oakland Raiders' strong safety who made a game-saving interception of a Brian Sipe pass late in the game that preserved the Raiders' 14-12 victory over the Browns in an AFC Divisional Playoff game on January 4, 1981, in a frozen Cleveland Stadium.

43. The Browns were trashed, 44-14, in 1981's opening Monday night game on September 7 in Cleveland. What AFC West team did the honors?

44. The Browns pulled a major upset on November 15, 1981, when they defeated the eventual Super Bowl Champion, 15-12, on the road. What team was it?

45. The Browns were horrendous in the 1981 season finale in Seattle, committing 10 turnovers. Did they lose the game?

46. Name the Cleveland tight end who scored the game-winning touchdown on a 48-yard catch-and-run off a Brian Sipe pass to give the Browns a 30-24 sudden death victory over the Chargers on September 25, 1983, in San Diego.

47. What is the Browns' all-time record against the Detroit Lions (15 games)?

Cleveland Browns Facts & Trivia

48. The Browns' 30-0 victory at New England on November 20, 1983, not only gave a boost to their postseason aspirations, but was also history-making. Why?

49. Marty Schottenheimer lost his head coaching debut on October 28, 1984, when what Michigan State University product nailed a 53-yard field goal with no time left to defeat the Browns, 16-14?

50. What is the Browns' all-time record against the Rams (15 games)?

51. The Browns, who finished just 8-8 during the 1985 regular season, were heavy underdogs in their AFC Divisional Playoff matchup with the 12-4 Miami Dolphins in the Orange Bowl on January 4, 1986. The Browns built a 21-3 third-quarter lead, however, thanks largely to Earnest Byner's relentless effort on the ground (he rushed for 161 yards and two touchdowns). The Dolphins woke up, though, and won the game, 24-21. What Dolphins running back scored Miami's last two touchdowns on 31- and one-yard runs?

52. To what NFC Central team did the Browns lose the 1986 season opener in which there were 72 points scored?

53. The Browns orchestrated an incredible comeback in an AFC Divisional Playoff against the New York Jets on January 3, 1987, in Cleveland Stadium. They won, 23-20, in double overtime. From how far back did the Browns have to come?

54. What did Denver Broncos quarterback John Elway do on January 11, 1987, that burned his big grin in the minds of Browns fans forever?

55. The Browns defeated an NFC West team, 38-3, on November 8, 1987, in Cleveland. What team was it?

56. What AFC East team did the Browns defeat, 27-21, on November 15, 1987, in Cleveland?

57. What Denver defensive back stripped Earnest Byner of the football late in the Browns' 38-33 loss to the Broncos in the AFC Championship game on January 17, 1988, in Mile High Stadium?

58. Name the Kansas City safety who blind-sided Bernie Kosar in the Browns' 6-3 opening-day triumph in Arrowhead Stadium on September, 4, 1988, knocking the Browns' quarterback out of action for the next six weeks.

59. The Browns won a thrilling game on the final Sunday of the 1988

season by turning a 23-7 deficit into a 28-23 victory in a snowstorm at home. The next Saturday, they lost, 24-23, again at home. Who were the Browns' opponents in those two games?

60. What team did the Browns defeat by a score of 34-30 in an AFC Divisional Playoff on January 6, 1990, in Cleveland?

61. Bud Carson's final game as Browns head coach came on November 4, 1990, in Cleveland. The Browns suffered their worst shutout loss - and worst home defeat - ever that day to the tune of 42-0. What team administered Carson's crushing blow?

62. The Browns began the 1990 season 2-3. They won just one more game the rest of the year. Against whom did the lone victory occur?

63. What is the Browns' all-time record against the Houston Oilers (51 games)?

64. The Browns blew a 23-0 lead on November 10, 1991, at home against Philadelphia, and lost. What was the final score?

65. What Brown scored four touchdowns in the team's 28-16 victory over the Raiders in Los Angeles on September 20, 1992?

66. What is the Browns' all-time record against the Miami Dolphins (14 games)?

67. Bernie Kosar fired a 30-yard touchdown pass with 35 seconds left in the first half that gave the Browns a 20-13 lead over San Francisco in a Monday night game on September 13, 1993, in Cleveland, a contest the Browns would end up winning, 23-13. What lanky wide receiver made a spectacular catch on Kosar's aerial?

68. What is Cleveland's all-time record against the New Orleans Saints (12 games)?

69. What is the Browns' all-time home record against Seattle (four games)?

70. What is the Browns' all-time record against the Washington Redskins (42 games)?

71. Who was the Browns' starting quarterback in Cleveland's 20-13 loss in Kansas City on November 20, 1994, in a downpour?

72. Name the Dallas Cowboys' tight end who slipped, and fell inside the Browns' one-yard line with no time left after catching a pass from Troy

Aikman, giving Cleveland a 19-14 upset on December 10, 1994, in Texas Stadium?

73. What is the Browns' all-time record against the Green Bay Packers (14 games)?

74. What is the Browns' all-time record against the Tampa Bay Buccaneers (five games)?

75. What is the Browns' all-time record against the Jacksonville Jaguars?

4. Individual Records

Bold - Denotes dates to 1950

Service

1. Who holds the Browns' record for most seasons played?

2. Who holds the Browns' record for most consecutive seasons played?

3. Who holds the Browns' record for most games played?

4. Doug Dieken holds the Browns' all-time record for most consecutive games played. How many did he play in?

5. Who holds the Browns' record for most consecutive starts?

Scoring

1. Who holds the Browns' record for most points scored in a career?

2. Who holds the Browns' record for most points scored in a season?

3. What is the Browns' record for most points scored in a single game?

4. Who holds the Browns' record for most points scored by a rookie in one season?

5. Who holds the Browns' record for most consecutive games scoring?

Cleveland Browns Facts & Trivia

6. Jim Brown holds the Browns' record for most career touchdowns. How many did he score?

7. What is the Browns' record for most touchdowns scored in one season?

8. Who holds the Browns' record for most touchdowns scored in one game?

9. Who holds the Browns' record for most touchdowns in one game by a rookie?

10. Who holds the Browns' record for most seasons scoring 100 points or more?

11. Who holds the Browns' record for most consecutive games scoring at least one touchdown?

12. Who holds the Browns' record for most extra point attempts in a career?

13. Who holds the Browns' record for most extra point tries in one season?

14. Who holds the Browns' record for most extra point attempts in one game?

15. What is the Browns' record for most career extra points?

16. Who holds the Browns' record for most extra points in one season?

17. Lou Groza holds the Browns' record for most extra points in one game with eight on December 6, 1953, against what team?

18. What is the Browns' record for most consecutive extra points made?

19. Who holds the Browns' record for most career field goals?

20. Who holds the Browns' record for most field goals in one season?

21. Who holds the Browns' record for most field goals in one game?

22. What is the Browns' record for most field goals attempted in a career?

23. Who holds the Browns' record for most field goals attempted in a season?

Cleveland Browns Facts & Trivia

24. Who holds the Browns' record for most field goals attempted in one game?

25. Who holds the Browns' record for longest field goal?

26. Who holds the Browns' record for most consecutive games having made at least one field goal?

27. Who holds the Browns' record for most consecutive field goals made?

28. Matt Stover holds the Browns' record for highest career field goal percentage (minimum 50 field goals made). What is it?

29. Who holds the Browns' record for highest field goal percentage in one season (minimum 14 field goal attempts)?

30. Who holds the Browns' record for most safeties in a career?

31. What is the Browns' record for most safeties in one game?

Rushing

1. Who holds the Browns' record for most rushing attempts in a career?

2. Who holds the Browns' record for most rushing attempts in a season?

3. Who holds the Browns' record for most rushing attempts in one game?

4. Jim Brown holds the Browns' record for most career rushing yardage. How many did he have?

5. Jim Brown holds the Browns' record for most rushing yards in one season with 1,863. In what season did he achieve this?

6. Who holds the Browns' record for most rushing yards in one game?

7. Who holds the Browns' record for most seasons of 1,000 or more yards rushing?

8. Who holds the Browns' record for the longest rush from scrimmage?

9. Jim Brown holds the Browns' record for most games with 100 or more yards rushing. How many did he have?

Cleveland Browns Facts & Trivia

10. **Jim Brown holds the Browns' record for most games in one season with 100 or more yards rushing. He did it twice - in 1958 and 1963. In how many games did the great fullback gain at least 100 yards in each of those seasons?**

11. **Who holds the Browns' record for most consecutive games of 100 or more yards rushing?**

12. Who holds the Browns' record for most career rushing touchdowns?

13. Who holds the Browns' record for most rushing touchdowns in one season with 17?

14. Jim Brown holds the Browns' record for most rushing touchdowns in a single game with five. Against what team did he do this?

15. **Who holds the Browns' record for most consecutive games with at least one touchdown rushing?**

16. Who holds the Browns' record for highest career rushing yards average (minimum 450 rushes)?

17. Who holds the Browns' record for highest average yards per rush for one season (minimum 132 rushes)?

18. **Who holds the Browns' record for highest average yards per rush for one game (minimum 11 rushes)?**

Passing

1. Who holds the Browns' record for most career passing attempts?

2. Brian Sipe holds the Browns' record for most pass attempts in one season with 567. What season?

3. Who holds the Browns' record for most pass attempts in a single game?

4. Who holds the Browns' record for most pass completions in a career?

5. Who holds the Browns' record for most pass completions in one season?

6. Brian Sipe holds the Browns' record for most pass completions in a

game with 33. Against what team did he do this?

7. Who holds the Browns' record for most consecutive pass completions?

8. Who holds the Browns' record for longest pass completion?

9. Who holds the Browns' record for most yards passing in a career?

10. Who holds the Browns' record for most yards passing in a season?

11. Who holds the Browns' record for most passing yards in a game?

12. Who holds the Browns' record for most career touchdown passes?

13. Who holds the Browns' record for most touchdown passes in a single season with 30?

14. Who holds the Browns' record for most touchdown passes in one game?

15. Who holds the Browns' record for most consecutive games throwing a touchdown pass?

16. Who holds the Browns' record for most passes had intercepted in a career?

17. Who holds the Browns' record for most passes had intercepted in one season?

18. Brian Sipe holds the Browns' record for most passes had intercepted in one game. He was picked off six times on two occasions - against the same team. What team was it?

19. Who holds the Browns' record for most consecutive pass attempts without being intercepted?

20. Who holds the Browns' record for lowest career interception rate (minimum 750 passes)?

21. Bernie Kosar holds the Browns' record for lowest interception rate for one season, 1.8. In what season did Kosar achieve this?

22. Who holds the Browns' record for highest completion percentage for a career?

23. Bernie Kosar holds the Browns' record for highest completion

percentage in one season when he completed 66.5 percent of his passes one year. In what season did Kosar do this?

24. Who holds the Browns' record for highest completion percentage for one game?

Receiving

1. Who holds the Browns' record for most career receptions?

2. Ozzie Newsome holds the Browns' record for most receptions in a season with 89. He did it twice. In what two seasons did he accomplish this?

3. Ozzie Newsome holds the Browns' record for most receptions in a single game with 14. Against what AFC East team did he do this?

4. Who holds the Browns' record for most receptions by a rookie?

5. Who holds the Browns' record for most consecutive games with at least one reception?

6. Who holds the Browns' record for most career receiving yardage?

7. Who holds the Browns' record for most receiving yards in one season?

8. Who holds the Browns' record for most receiving yards in one game?

9. Who holds the Browns' record for most seasons with 50 or more receptions?

10. Who holds the Browns' record for longest reception?

11. Who holds the Browns' record for most touchdown receptions in a career?

12. Who holds the Browns' record for most touchdown receptions in a season?

13. Who holds the Browns' record for most touchdown receptions in a single game?

14. Who holds the Browns' record for most consecutive games with at least one touchdown reception?

15. Who holds the Browns' record for best career receiving yards average (minimum 100 receptions)?

16. Who holds the Browns' record for best receiving yards average for a season (minimum 16 receptions)?

17. Who holds the Browns' record for best receiving yards average for one game (minimum three receptions)?

18. Who holds the Browns' record for most games with 100 or more yards receiving in a career?

19. Three players hold the Browns' record for most games with 100 or more yards receiving in a season with four. Name the trifecta.

20. What two players hold the Browns' record for most games with at least 100 yards receiving by a rookie?

Interceptions

1. Who holds the Browns' record for most career interceptions?

2. Who holds the Browns' record for most interceptions in one season?

3. Eight players hold the Browns' record for most interceptions in one game with three. They are Tom Colella, Tommy James, Bobby Franklin, Bernie Parrish, Ross Fichtner, Ron Bolton, Hanford Dixon, and Frank Minnifield. Name the only one to do it twice.

4. Who holds the Browns' record for most career interception return yardage?

5. Who holds the Browns' record for most interception return yards in one season?

6. Who holds the Browns' record for most interception return yards in one game?

7. Who holds the Browns' record for longest interception return?

8. Who holds the Browns' record for most career touchdowns off interceptions?

9. Five players hold the Browns' record for most interception returns for touchdowns in a season with two: Warren Lahr, Ken Konz, Bobby Franklin,

Cleveland Browns Facts & Trivia

Jim Houston, and Thane Gash. Who is the only one to do it twice?

10. Who holds the Browns' record for most touchdowns off interceptions in one game?

11. Who holds the Browns' record for highest average gain off interception returns in a career (minimum 10 interceptions)?

12. Who holds the Browns' record for highest average gain off interception returns for one season (minimum three interceptions)?

13. Who holds the Browns' record for highest average gain off interception returns in one game (minimum two interceptions)?

14. Who holds the Browns' record for most consecutive games with an interception?

Punting

1. Who holds the Browns' record for most career punts?

2. Who holds the Browns' record for most punts in one season?

3. What two players share the Browns' record for most punts in a game with 12?

4. Who holds the Browns' record for highest career punting yards average (minimum 100 punts)?

5. Who holds the Browns' record for highest punting yards average for one season?

6. Who holds the Browns' record for highest punting yards average for one game (minimum four punts)?

7. Horace Gillom holds the Browns' record for longest punt ever. He did it on November 28, 1954, against the New York Giants in New York. How far did Gillom's punt travel?

8. Who holds the Browns' record for most punts placed inside the opponents' 20-yard line in a career (note: records kept since 1976)?

9. Who holds the Browns' record for placing most punts inside the opponents' 20-yard line in a season (note: records kept since 1976)?

Punt Returns

1. Who holds the Browns' record for most career punt returns?

2. Who holds the Browns' record for most punt returns in a season?

3. What is the Browns' record for most punt returns in a single game?

4. Who holds the Browns' record for most career punt return yardage?

5. Who holds the Browns' record for most punt return yardage in a season?

6. Who holds the Browns' record for most punt return yards in a game?

7. Who holds the Browns' record for longest punt return?

8. Who holds the Browns' record for best career punt return yards average (minimum 50 punt returns)?

9. Who holds the Browns' record for best punt return yards average for a season?

10. Who holds the Browns' record for best punt return yards average in one game (minimum three punt returns)?

11. Who holds the Browns' record for most career touchdowns off punt returns?

12. Leroy Kelly and Eric Metcalf share the Browns' record for most touchdowns off punt returns in one season with two. One of them did it twice, however. Which one?

13. Eric Metcalf holds the Browns' record for most touchdowns off punt returns in one game with two. He did it against the Pittsburgh Steelers on October 24, 1993, in a 28-23 Browns victory in Cleveland. For how many yards did each of Metcalf's punt returns go?

Kickoff Returns

1. Who holds the Browns' record for most career kickoff returns?

2. Who holds the Browns' record for most kickoff returns in one season?

Cleveland Browns Facts & Trivia

3. Who holds the Browns' record for most kickoff returns in one game?

4. Who holds the Browns' record for most kickoff return yardage in a career?

5. Who holds the Browns' record for most kickoff return yardage in a season?

6. Who holds the Browns' record for most kickoff return yards in a single game?

7. Who holds the Browns' record for longest kickoff return?

8. Who holds the Browns' record for best career average kickoff return yardage (minimum 50 kickoff returns)?

9. Who holds the Browns' record for best average kickoff return yardage in a season?

10. Who holds the Browns' record for best average kickoff return yardage for one game (minimum three kickoff returns)?

11. Who holds the Browns' record for most touchdowns off kickoff returns in a career?

12. Eric Metcalf holds the Browns' record for most touchdowns off kickoff returns in a season with two. In what season did Metcalf do this?

13. What is the Browns' record for most touchdowns off kickoff returns in a single game?

Combined Net Yards

1. Who holds the Browns' record for most career attempts?

2. Who holds the Browns' record for most attempts in a season?

3. What two players share the Browns' record for most attempts in one game?

4. Who holds the Browns' record for most career combined yardage?

5. Who holds the Browns' record for most combined net yards in one

season?

6. Who holds the Browns' record for most combined net yards in a single game?

7. Who holds the Browns' record for highest career yards per gain average (minimum 500 attempts)?

8. Who holds the Browns' record for highest yards per gain average for a season (minimum 150 attempts)?

9. Who holds the Browns' record for highest yards per gain average for one game (minimum 15 attempts)?

Fumbles

1. Who holds the Browns' record for most career fumbles?

2. Who holds the Browns' record for most fumbles in one season?

3. What three players share the Browns' record for most fumbles in one game with four?

4. Who holds the Browns' record for most opponents' fumbles recovered in a career?

5. What two players share the Browns' record for most opponents' fumbles recovered in a season with five?

6. What is the Browns' record for most opponents' fumbles recovered in a game?

7. What four players share the Browns' record for most touchdowns off opponents' fumbles in a career?

8. What is the Browns' record for longest opponents' fumble return?

Quarterback Sacks

1. Who holds the Browns' record for most career quarterback sacks?

2. Who holds the Browns' record for most quarterback sacks in one season?

3. What two players share the Browns' record for most quarterback sacks in one game with four?

4. Who holds the Browns' record for most consecutive games with at least one quarterback sack?

5. Who holds the Browns' record for most sack yards in a career?

6. Who holds the Browns' record for most sack yards in one season?

7. Who holds the Browns' record for most sack yards in a single game?

8. Who holds the Browns' record for most sacks by a rookie?

9. Who holds the Browns' record for most sacks by a rookie in one game?

5. Individual Records (Postseason)

Scoring

1. Who holds the Browns' record for most career postseason points scored?

2. What is the Browns' record for most points scored in a single postseason game?

3. Who holds the Browns' record for most consecutive postseason games scoring?

4. Who holds the Browns' record for most career postseason touchdowns?

5. Who holds the Browns' record for most touchdowns scored in one

postseason game?

6. Who holds the Browns' record for most touchdowns in one postseason game by a rookie?

7. Who holds the Browns' record for most consecutive postseason games scoring at least one touchdown?

8. Who holds the Browns' record for most career postseason extra point attempts?

9. Who holds the Browns' record for most extra point attempts in one postseason game?

10. What is the Browns' record for most career extra points in the postseason?

11. Who holds the Browns' record for most extra points in one postseason game?

12. What is the Browns' record for most consecutive extra points made in the postseason?

13. Who holds the Browns' record for most career postseason field goals?

14. Who holds the Browns' record for most field goals in one postseason game?

15. What is the Browns' record for most career postseason field goals attempted?

16. Who holds the Browns' record for most field goals attempted in one postseason game?

17. Who holds the Browns' record for longest postseason field goal?

18. Who holds the Browns' record for most consecutive postseason games having made at least one field goal?

19. Who holds the Browns' record for most consecutive postseason field goals made?

20. What is the Browns' record for highest career postseason field goal percentage (minimum four field goals made)?

21. Who holds the Browns' record for most career postseason safeties?

Cleveland Browns Facts & Trivia

Rushing

1. Who holds the Browns' record for most career postseason rushing attempts?

2. Who holds the Browns' record for most rushing attempts in one postseason game?

3. Who holds the Browns' record for most career postseason rushing yardage?

4. Who holds the Browns' record for most rushing yards in one postseason game?

5. What three players share the Browns' record for most postseason games with 100 or more yards rushing with two?

6. Who holds the Browns' record for most consecutive postseason games of 100 or more yards rushing?

7. Who holds the Browns' record for most career postseason rushing touchdowns?

8. Who holds the Browns' record for most rushing touchdowns in a postseason game?

9. Who holds the Browns' record for most consecutive postseason games with at least one touchdown rushing?

10. Who holds the Browns' record for highest career postseason rushing yards average (minimum 22 rushes)?

11. Who holds the Browns' record for highest average yards per rush for one postseason game (minimum 11 rushes)?

Passing

1. Who holds the Browns' record for most career postseason passing attempts?

2. Who holds the Browns' record for most pass attempts in a single postseason game?

3. Who holds the Browns' record for most career postseason pass completions?

4. Who holds the Browns' record for most pass completions in a postseason game?

5. Who holds the Browns' record for most career yards passing in the postseason?

6. Who holds the Browns' record for most passing yards in a postseason game?

7. Who holds the Browns' record for most career touchdown passes in the postseason?

8. Who holds the Browns' record for most touchdown passes in one postseason game?

9. Who holds the Browns' record for most consecutive postseason games throwing a touchdown pass?

10. Who holds the Browns' record for most career passes had intercepted in the postseason?

11. Who holds the Browns' record for most passes had intercepted in one postseason game?

12. Who holds the Browns' record for lowest career postseason interception rate (minimum 22 passes)?

13. Who holds the Browns' record for highest career postseason completion percentage (minimum 44 passes)?

14. Who holds the Browns' record for highest completion percentage for one postseason game (minimum 22 passes)?

Receiving

1. Who holds the Browns' record for most career postseason receptions?

2. Who holds the Browns' record for most receptions in a postseason game?

Cleveland Browns Facts & Trivia

3. What three players share the Browns' record for most receptions by a rookie in a postseason game with six?

4. Who holds the Browns' record for most career receiving yardage in postseason play?

5. Who holds the Browns' record for most receiving yards in one postseason game?

6. What three players share the Browns' record for most career postseason touchdown receptions with five?

7. Who holds the Browns' record for most touchdown receptions in a postseason game?

8. Who holds the Browns' record for most consecutive postseason games with at least one touchdown reception?

9. Who holds the Browns' record for best career postseason receiving yards average (minimum six receptions)?

10. Who holds the Browns' record for best receiving yards average for one postseason game (minimum three receptions)?

11. Name the seven players who share the Browns' record for most postseason games with 100 or more yards receiving with one.

Punting

1. Who holds the Browns' record for most career postseason punts?

2. Who holds the Browns' record for most punts in a postseason game?

3. Who holds the Browns' record for most career postseason punting yards?

4. Who holds the Browns' record for highest career punting yards average in postseason play (minimum eight punts)?

5. Who holds the Browns' record for highest punting yards average for one postseason game (minimum four punts)?

6. Team Records

Games Won

1. What is the Browns' record for most victories in one season?

2. What is the Browns' record for most consecutive victories?

3. What is the Browns' record for most consecutive victories to start a season?

4. What is the Browns' record for most consecutive home wins?

5. What is the Browns' record for most consecutive road wins?

Games Lost

1. What Browns team holds the club record for most losses in one season?

2. What is the Browns' record for most consecutive losses?

3. What is the Browns' record for most consecutive losses to start a season?

4. What is the Browns' record for most consecutive losses to end a season?

5. What is the Browns' record for most consecutive home losses?

6. What is the Browns' record for most consecutive road losses?

Scoring

1. What Browns team holds the club record for most points scored in one season?

2. What is the Browns' record for most points scored in one game?

3. What Browns team holds the club record for most points allowed in one season?

Cleveland Browns Facts & Trivia

4. What is the Browns' record for most points allowed in one game?

5. What are the fewest points the Browns scored in one season?

6. What Browns team holds the club record for fewest points allowed in one season?

7. What is the Browns' record for most points scored by both teams in one game?

8. What is the Browns' record for fewest points scored by both teams in one game?

9. What Browns team holds the club record for most touchdowns scored in one season?

10. What is the Browns' record for most touchdowns scored in one game?

11. What Browns team holds the club record for most touchdowns yielded in one season?

12. What is the Browns' record for most touchdowns yielded in one game?

13. The Browns' record for fewest touchdowns in one season is 17. In what year did they do this?

14. What is the Browns' record for fewest touchdowns scored against them in one season?

15. What is the Browns' record for most consecutive quarters not allowing a touchdown?

16. What is the Browns' record for most rushing touchdowns in one season?

17. What is the Browns' record for most rushing touchdowns in a single game?

18. What is the Browns' record for most rushing touchdowns allowed in one season?

19. What is the Browns' record for most rushing touchdowns allowed in one game?

Cleveland Browns Facts & Trivia

20. What two Browns teams hold the club record for fewest rushing touchdowns in a season?

21. What is the Browns' record for fewest touchdowns rushing allowed in one season?

22. What is the Browns' record for most touchdowns rushing by both teams in a game?

23. What is the Browns' record for most consecutive games rushing for at least one touchdown?

24. What Browns team holds the club record for most touchdown passes in one season?

25. What is the Browns' record for most touchdown passes in one game?

26. What is the Browns' record for fewest touchdown passes in one season?

27. What is the Browns' record for most touchdown passes allowed in one season?

28. What is the Browns' record for most touchdown passes allowed in one game?

29. What is the Browns' record for fewest touchdown passes against for one season?

30. What two Browns teams hold the club record for most points after touchdown in one season?

31. What is the Browns' record for most points after touchdown in a game?

32. What is the Browns' record for fewest points after touchdown in one season?

33. What is the Browns' record for most points after touchdown against in one season?

34. What is the Browns' record for most points after touchdown against in one game?

35. What is the Browns' record for fewest points after touchdown against

in one season?

36. What is the Browns' record for most consecutive games scoring at least one touchdown?

37. What two Browns teams share the club record for most field goals in one season?

38. What is the Browns' record for most field goals in one game?

39. What is the Browns' record for fewest field goals in one season?

40. What is the Browns' record for most field goals against in one season?

41. What is the Browns' record for most field goals scored on them in one game?

42. The Browns' record for fewest field goals against in one season is two. What year did this happen?

43. What is the Browns' record for most safeties in one season?

44. What is the Browns' record for most safeties in one game?

45. What is the Browns' record for most safeties against in one season?

46. What is the Browns' record for most safeties by an opponent in one game?

47. What is the Browns' record for most safeties by both teams in a season?

48. What is the Browns' record for most safeties by both teams in one game?

49. What is the Browns' record for most two-point conversions in one season?

50. What is the Browns' record for most two-point conversions in one game?

51. What is the Browns' record for most two-point conversions allowed in one season?

Cleveland Browns Facts & Trivia

52. What is the Browns' record for most two-point conversions allowed in one game?

53. What is the Browns' record for most points scored in the first quarter of a game?

54. What is the Browns' record for most points scored in the second quarter of a game?

55. What is the Browns' record for most points scored in the third quarter of a game?

56. What is the Browns' record for most points scored in the fourth quarter of a game?

57. What is the Browns' record for most points scored in the first half of a game?

58. What is the Browns' record for most points scored in the second half of a game?

59. What is the Browns' record for most consecutive games scoring?

60. What is the Browns' record for most points overcome to win a game?

61. What is the Browns' record for largest blown lead to lose a game?

62. What is the Browns' largest margin of victory?

63. What is the Browns' largest margin of defeat?

First Downs

1. The Browns' record for most first downs in one season is 364. In what year did the Browns total this amount?

2. What is the Browns' record for most first downs in one game?

3. What is the Browns' record for fewest first downs in a season?

4. What is the Browns' record for fewest first downs in one game?

Cleveland Browns Facts & Trivia

5. What is the Browns' record for most first downs allowed in one season?

6. **What is the Browns' record for most first downs allowed in a game?**

7. What is the Browns' record for fewest first downs yielded in one season?

8. **What is the Browns' record for fewest first downs given up in a single game?**

9. **What is the Browns' record for most first downs by both teams in one game?**

10. What Browns team holds the club record for most first downs rushing in one season?

11. **What is the Browns' record for most first downs rushing in one game?**

12. What is the Browns' record for fewest first downs rushing in one season?

13. **What is the Browns' record for fewest first downs rushing in a game?**

14. What is the Browns' record for most first downs rushing allowed in one season?

15. **What is the Browns' record for most first downs rushing allowed in one game?**

16. What Browns team holds the club record for fewest first downs rushing yielded in one season?

17. **What is the Browns' record for fewest first downs rushing by an opponent in a single game?**

18. What Browns team holds the club record for most first downs passing in one season?

19. **The Browns' record for most first downs passing in a single game is 22. Did this occur in a victory or a defeat?**

20. What Browns team holds the club record for fewest first downs passing in one season?

21. What is the Browns' record for fewest first downs passing in one game?

22. What Browns team holds the club record for most first downs passing allowed in one season?

23. What is the Browns' record for most first downs passing by an opponent in one game?

24. What Browns team holds the club record for fewest first downs passing given up in a season?

25. What is the Browns' record for fewest first downs passing by an opponent in one game?

26. What is the Browns' record for most first downs by penalty in one season?

27. What is the Browns' record for most first downs by penalty in one game?

28. What is the Browns' record for fewest first downs by penalty in a season?

29. What is the Browns' record for most first downs by penalty in one season by opponents?

30. What is the Browns' record for most first downs by penalty in one game by an opponent?

31. What is the Browns' record for fewest first downs by penalty in one season by opponents?

Rushing

1. What is the Browns' record for most rushing yards in one season?

2. What is the Browns' record for most rushing yards in a single game?

Cleveland Browns Facts & Trivia

3. What Browns team holds the club record for fewest rushing yards in one season?

4. What is the Browns' record for fewest rushing yards in one game?

5. What is the Browns' record for most rushing yards allowed in one season?

6. What is the Browns' record for most rushing yards given up in one game?

7. What is the Browns' record for fewest rushing yards allowed in one season?

8. What is the Browns' record for fewest rushing yards allowed in one game?

9. What is the Browns' record for fewest yards rushing allowed per game in one season?

10. What Browns team holds the club record for most rushing attempts in one season?

11. What is the Browns' record for most rushing attempts in one game?

12. What Browns team holds the club record for fewest rushing attempts in one season?

13. What is the Browns' record for fewest rushing attempts in one game?

14. What is the Browns' record for most rushing attempts by opponents in one season?

15. What is the Browns' record for most rushing attempts by an opponent in one game?

16. What is the Browns' record for fewest rushing attempts by opponents in one season?

17. What is the Browns' record for fewest rushing attempts by an opponent in one game?

18. What Browns team holds the club record for highest average yards per

gain rushing in one season?

19. What Browns team holds the club record for lowest average yards per gain rushing in one season?

Passing

1. What Browns team holds the club record for most passing yards in one season?

2. What is the Browns' record for most passing yards in one game?

3. What Browns team holds the club record for most average yards per passing attempt for one season?

4. What Browns team holds the club record for fewest passing yards in one season?

5. What is the Browns' record for fewest passing yards in one game?

6. What Browns team holds the club record for most passing yards allowed in one season?

7. What is the Browns' record for most passing yards allowed in one game?

8. What Browns team holds the club record for fewest passing yards allowed in one season?

9. What is the Browns' record for fewest passing yards allowed in one game?

10. What Browns team holds the club record for most pass attempts in one season?

11. What is the Browns' record for most pass attempts in one game?

12. What is the Browns' record for fewest pass attempts in one season?

13. What is the Browns' record for fewest pass attempts in one game?

14. What is the Browns' record for most passes attempted in one season

by opponents?

15. What is the Browns' record for most passes attempted in one game by an opponent?

16. What is the Browns' record for fewest pass attempts by opponents in one season?

17. What is the Browns' record for fewest pass attempts by an opponent in one game?

18. What Browns team holds the club record for most pass completions in a season?

19. What is the Browns' record for most pass completions in one game?

20. What Browns team holds the club record for fewest pass completions in one season?

21. What is the Browns' record for fewest passes completed in one game?

22. What is the Browns' record for most passes completed by opponents in one season?

23. What is the Browns' record for most pass completions by an opponent in a game?

24. What Browns team holds the club record for fewest passes completed by opponents in one season?

25. What is the Browns' record for fewest pass completions in one game by an opponent?

26. What Browns team holds the club record for highest pass completion percentage for one season?

27. What Browns team holds the club record for lowest pass completion percentage for one season?

Interceptions

1. What Browns team holds the club record for most interceptions in one

season?

2. What is the Browns' record for most interceptions in one game?

3. What is the Browns' record for fewest interceptions in a season?

4. What Browns team holds the club record for most interceptions by opponents in one season?

5. What is the Browns' record for most interceptions by an opponent in one game?

6. What is the Browns' record for lowest interception percentage by opponents for one season?

7. What is the Browns' record for fewest interceptions by opponents in one season?

8. What is the Browns' record for most consecutive games without intercepting a pass?

9. What Browns team holds the club record for most interception return yardage in one season?

10. What is the Browns' record for most interception return yards in one game?

11. What is the Browns' record for fewest interception return yardage in one season?

12. What is the Browns' record for most interception return yardage by opponents in one season?

13. What is the Browns' record for most interception return yards in one game by an opponent?

14. What is the Browns' record for fewest interception return yardage by opponents in one season?

15. What is the Browns' record for most interceptions returned for touchdowns in one season?

16. The Browns' record for most interceptions returned for touchdowns in one game is three. Against what team did this happen?

17. What is the Browns' record for most touchdowns off interception returns by opponents in one season?

18. What is the Browns' record for most touchdowns off interception returns by an opponent in one game?

Punting

1. What Browns team holds the club record for most punts in one season?

2. What is the Browns' record for most punts in one game?

3. What is the Browns' record for most punts in a season by opponents?

4. What is the Browns' record for most punts in one game by an opponent?

5. What is the Browns' record for most punts by both teams in one season?

6. What is the Browns' record for most punts by both teams in one game?

7. What is the Browns' record for fewest punts in one season?

8. What is the Browns' record for fewest punts in one season by opponents?

9. What is the Browns' record for fewest punts in one game by both teams?

10. What is the Browns' record for highest punting yards average for one season?

11. What is the Browns' highest punting yards average for one game?

12. What is the Browns' record for highest punting yards average by opponents for one season?

13. What is the Browns' record for highest punting yards average by an opponent for one game (minimum three punts)?

Punt Returns

1. What is the Browns' record for most punt returns in one season?

2. **What is the Browns' record for most punt returns in one game?**

3. What is the Browns' record for fewest punt returns in a season?

4. What Browns team holds the club record for most punt returns by opponents in one season?

5. **What is the Browns' record for most punt returns by an opponent in one game?**

6. What is the Browns' record for fewest punt returns by opponents in one season?

7. What Browns team holds the club record for most punt return yardage in one season?

8. **What is the Browns' record for most punt return yardage in one game?**

9. What Browns team holds the club record for fewest punt return yards in one season?

10. What is the Browns' record for most punt return yardage by opponents in one season?

11. **What is the Browns' record for most punt return yardage by an opponent in one game?**

12. What is the Browns' record for fewest punt return yards by opponents in one season?

13. What is the Browns' record for highest punt return yards average for one season?

14. What is the Browns' record for lowest punt return yards average for one season?

15. What Browns team holds the club record for highest punt return yards average allowed for one season?

16. What Browns team holds the club record for lowest punt return yards

average allowed for one season?

17. What Browns team holds the club record for most touchdowns off punt returns in one season?
18. What is the Browns' record for most punt returns for touchdowns in one game?

19. What is the Browns' record for most touchdowns off punt returns by opponents in one season?

20. What is the Browns' record for most punt returns for touchdowns by an opponent in one game?

Kickoff Returns

1. What Browns team holds the club record for most kickoff returns in one season?

2. What is the Browns' record for most kickoff returns in one game?

3. What Browns team holds the team record for fewest kickoff returns in one season?

4. What is the Browns' record for most kickoff returns by opponents in one season?

5. What is the Browns' record for most kickoff returns in one game by an opponent?

6. What is the Browns' record for fewest kickoff returns by opponents in one season?

7. What Browns team holds the club record for most kickoff return yardage in one season?

8. What is the Browns' record for most kickoff return yardage in one game?

9. What Browns team holds the record for fewest kickoff return yardage in one season?

10. What is the Browns' record for most kickoff return yardage by opponents in one season?

11. What is the Browns' record for most kickoff return yardage by an

opponent in one game?

12. What is the Browns' record for fewest kickoff return yards by opponents in one season?

13. What Browns team holds the club record for highest kickoff return yards average for one season?

14. What Browns team holds the club record for lowest kickoff return yards average for one season?

15. What Browns team holds the club record for highest kickoff return yards average allowed for one season?

16. What Browns team holds the club record for lowest kickoff return yards average allowed for one season?

17. What two Browns teams share the club record for most touchdowns off kickoff returns in one season with two?

18. What is the Browns' record for most touchdowns off kickoff returns in one game?

19. What two Browns teams share the club record for most touchdowns off kickoff returns allowed in one season with two?

20. The Browns' record for most touchdowns off kickoff returns allowed in one game is two. It happened in 1967. What team was it?

Total Net Yards

1. What Browns team holds the club record for most total net yards in one season?

2. What is the Browns' record for most total net yards in one game?

3. What Browns team holds the club record for fewest total net yards in one season?

4. What is the Browns' record for fewest total net yards in one game?

5. What Browns team holds the club record for most total net yards by opponents in one season?

6. What is the Browns' record for most total net yards by an opponent in one game?

7. What Browns team holds the club record for fewest total net yards allowed in one season?

8. What is the Browns' record for fewest total net yards allowed in one game?

9. What is the Browns' record for most consecutive games with 400 or more total net yards?

10. What is the Browns' record for most consecutive games with 300 or more total net yards?

Fumbles

1. What Browns team holds the club record for most fumbles in one season?

2. What is the Browns' record for most fumbles in one game?

3. What Browns team holds the club record for fewest fumbles in one season?

4. What is the Browns' record for most fumbles by opponents in one season?

5. What is the Browns' record for most fumbles by an opponent in one game?

6. What is the Browns' record for fewest fumbles in one season by opponents?

7. What is the Browns' record for most fumbles in one game by both teams?

8. What Browns team holds the club record for most fumbles lost in one season?

9. What is the Browns' record for most fumbles lost in a single game?

10. What is the Browns' record for fewest fumbles lost in one season?

11. What Browns team holds the club record for most opponents' fumbles recovered in one season?

12. What is the Browns' record for most opponents' fumbles recovered in one game?

13. What is the Browns' record for fewest opponents' fumbles recovered in a season?

Quarterback Sacks

1. What Browns team holds the club record for most quarterback sacks allowed in one season?

2. What is the Browns' record for most quarterback sacks allowed in one game?

3. What Browns team holds the team record for fewest quarterback sacks allowed in one season?
4. What Browns team holds the club record for most opponents' quarterbacks sacked in one season?

5. What is the Browns' record for most opponents' quarterbacks sacked in one game?

6. What Browns team holds the club record for fewest opponents' quarterbacks sacked in a game?

7. What is the Browns' record for most consecutive games with at least one opponents' quarterback sacked?

8. What Browns team holds the club record for most yards lost by opponents trying to pass in one season?

9. What is the Browns' record for most yards lost in one game by an opponent trying to pass?

10. What is the Browns' record for most sacks allowed in one game by both teams?

11. What is the Browns' record for fewest sacks allowed in one game by both teams?

7. Team Records (Postseason)

Scoring

1. What Browns team holds the club record for most points scored in one postseason game?

2. What is the Browns' record for most points allowed in one postseason game?

3. What is the Browns' record for most points scored by both teams in one postseason game?

4. What is the Browns' record for fewest points scored by both teams in one postseason game?

5. What is the Browns' record for most touchdowns scored in one postseason game?

6. What is the Browns' record for most touchdowns yielded in one postseason game?

7. What is the Browns' record for most consecutive quarters in postseason play not allowing a touchdown?

8. What is the Browns' record for most rushing touchdowns in a single postseason game?

9. What is the Browns' record for most rushing touchdowns allowed in one postseason game?

10. What is the Browns' record for most touchdowns rushing by both teams in a postseason game?

11. What is the Browns' record for most consecutive postseason games rushing for at least one touchdown?

12. What is the Browns' record for most touchdown passes in one postseason game?

13. What is the Browns' record for most touchdown passes allowed in one postseason game?

Cleveland Browns Facts & Trivia

14. What is the Browns' record for most points after touchdown in a postseason game?

15. What is the Browns' record for most points after touchdown against in one postseason game?

16. What is the Browns' record for most consecutive postseason games scoring at least one touchdown?

17. What is the Browns' record for most field goals in one postseason game?

18. What is the Browns' record for most field goals scored on them in one postseason game?

19. What is the Browns' record for most safeties in one postseason game?

20. What is the Browns' record for most safeties by an opponent in one postseason game?

21. What is the Browns' record for most safeties by both teams in one postseason game?

22. What is the Browns' record for most points scored in the first quarter of a postseason game?

23. What is the Browns' record for most points scored in the second quarter of a postseason game?

24. What is the Browns' record for most points scored in the third quarter of a postgame game?

25. What is the Browns' record for most points scored in the fourth quarter of a postseason game?

26. What is the Browns' record for most points scored in the first half of a postseason game?

27. What is the Browns' record for most points scored in the second half of a postseason game?

28. What is the Browns' record for most consecutive postseason games scoring?

29. What is the Browns' record for most points overcome to win a postseason game?

30. What is the Browns' record for largest blown lead to lose a postseason game?

31. What is the Browns' largest margin of victory in a postseason game?

32. What is the Browns' largest margin of defeat in a postseason game?

Rushing

1. What is the Browns' record for most rushing yards in a single postseason game?

2. What is the Browns' record for fewest rushing yards in one postseason game?

3. What is the Browns' record for most rushing yards given up in one postseason game?

4. What is the Browns' record for fewest rushing yards allowed in one postseason game?

5. What is the Browns' record for most rushing attempts in one postseason game?

6. What is the Browns' record for fewest rushing attempts in one postseason game?

7. What is the Browns' record for most rushing attempts by an opponent in one postseason game?

8. What is the Browns' record for fewest rushing attempts by an opponent in one postseason game?

Passing

1. What is the Browns' record for most passing yards in one postseason game?

2. What is the Browns' record for fewest passing yards in one postseason game?

3. What is the Browns' record for most passing yards allowed in one

postseason game?

4. What is the Browns' record for fewest passing yards allowed in one postseason game?

5. What is the Browns' record for most pass attempts in one postseason game?

6. What is the Browns' record for fewest pass attempts in one postseason game?

7. What is the Browns' record for most passes attempted in one postseason game by an opponent?

8. What is the Browns' record for fewest pass attempts by an opponent in one postseason game?

9. What is the Browns' record for most pass completions in one postseason game?

10. What is the Browns' record for fewest passes completed in one postseason game?

11. What is the Browns' record for most pass completions by an opponent in a postseason game?

12. What is the Browns' record for fewest pass completions in one postseason game by an opponent?

Interceptions

1. What is the Browns' record for most interceptions in one postseason game?

2. What is the Browns' record for most interceptions by an opponent in one postseason game?

3. What is the Browns' record for most consecutive postseason games without intercepting a pass?

4. What is the Browns' record for most interception return yards in one postseason game?

5. What is the Browns' record for most interception return yards in one postseason game by an opponent?

6. The Browns' record for most interceptions returned for touchdowns in one postseason game is one. They did it seven times. They did it once each against the Rams on Dec. 26, 1955, the Raiders on Jan. 4, 1981, and the Colts on Jan. 9, 1988. The Browns did it twice against two other teams. Name the clubs.

7. The Browns' record for most touchdowns off interception returns by an opponent in one postseason game is one. It happened twice. Detroit was one of them. The Lions did it in the NFL Championship game on Dec. 29, 1957, in Detroit. Who was the other team to do it?

Punting

1. What is the Browns' record for most punts in one postseason game?

2. What is the Browns' record for most punts in one postseason game by an opponent?

3. What is the Browns' record for most punts by both teams in one postseason game?

4. What is the Browns' record for fewest punts in one postseason game by both teams?

5. What is the Browns' record for highest punting yards average for one postseason game (minimum three punts)?

6. What is the Browns' record for highest punting yards average by an opponent for one postseason game (minimum three punts)?

Punt Returns
(Does not include game against Buffalo on Dec. 4, 1949)

1. What is the Browns' record for most punt returns in one postseason game?

2. What is the Browns' record for most punt returns by an opponent in one postseason game?

3. What is the Browns' record for most punt return yardage in one postseason game?

4. What is the Browns' record for most punt return yardage by an opponent in one postseason game?

Kickoff Returns

1. What is the Browns' record for most kickoff returns in one postseason game (Does not include game against Buffalo on Dec. 4, 1949)?

2. What is the Browns' record for most kickoff returns in one postseason game by an opponent (does not include game against Buffalo on Dec. 4, 1949)?

3. What is the Browns' record for most kickoff return yardage in one postseason game?

4. What is the Browns' record for most kickoff return yardage by an opponent in one postseason game?

5. The Browns' record for most touchdowns off kickoff returns in one postseason game is one. It happened once. Against whom?

Total Net Yards

1. What is the Browns' record for most total net yards in one postseason game?

2. What is the Browns' record for fewest total net yards in one postseason game?

3. What is the Browns' record for most total net yards by an opponent in one postseason game?

4. What is the Browns' record for fewest total net yards allowed in one postseason game?

5. What is the Browns' record for most consecutive postseason games with 400 or more total net yards?

6. What is the Browns' record for most consecutive postseason games with 300 or more total net yards?

Fumbles

1. What is the Browns' record for most fumbles in one postseason game?

2. What is the Browns' record for most fumbles by an opponent in one postseason game?

3. What is the Browns' record for most fumbles in one postseason game by both teams?

4. What is the Browns' record for most fumbles lost in a single postseason game?

5. What is the Browns' record for most opponents' fumbles recovered in one postseason game?

Quarterback Sacks

(Does not include games against New York on Dec. 22, 1946, and Dec. 14, 1947; Buffalo on Dec. 19, 1948, and Dec. 4, 1949; San Francisco on Dec. 11, 1949; Los Angeles on Dec. 24, 1950; and Detroit on Dec. 28, 1952)

1. What is the Browns' record for most quarterback sacks allowed in one postseason game?

2. What is the Browns' record for most opponents' quarterbacks sacked in one postseason game?

3. What is the Browns' record for most consecutive postseason games with at least one opponents' quarterback sacked?

4. What is the Browns' record for most yards lost in one postseason game by an opponent trying to pass?

5. What is the Browns' record for most sacks allowed in one postseason game by both teams?

6. What is the Browns' record for fewest sacks allowed in one postseason game by both teams?

8. Miscellaneous

Firsts

1. Who was the Browns' first majority owner?

2. Who was the Browns' first head coach?

3. Where was the Browns' first training camp held?

4. Who was the first player the Browns signed to a contract?

5. Who was the Browns' first draft choice?

6. Against what team did the Browns play their first preseason game?

7. Against what team did the Browns play their first game?

8. Who was the Browns' first starting quarterback?

9. Who scored the Browns' first points?

10. Who kicked Cleveland's first field goal?

11. Against what team did the Browns play their first road game?

12. Against what team did the Browns lose their first game?

13. Against whom did the Browns play their first postseason game?

14. Against what team did the Browns play their first postseason game on the road?

15. Who was the Browns' first draft choice as a member of the NFL?

16. Against what team did the Browns play their first preseason game as a member of the NFL?

17. Who was the Browns' first game against as a member of the NFL?

18. Who scored the Browns' first points as a member of the NFL?

19. Who kicked Cleveland's first field goal as a member of the NFL?

20. Against what team did the Browns play their first home game as a member of the NFL?

21. Against whom did the Browns play their first postseason game as a member of the NFL?

22. Against whom did the Browns play their first postseason game on the road as a member of the NFL?

23. Against whom did the Browns play their first game on ABC *Monday Night Football*?

24. Against what team did the Browns play their first *Monday Night Football* game on the road?

25. Against what team did the Browns play their first overtime game?

26. Against what team did the Browns lose their first overtime game?

27. In what year did the Browns miss qualifying for the postseason for the first time?

28. In what year did the Browns post their first losing record?

29. Who was the Browns' first player to rush for 1,000 yards in one season?

30. Who was the Browns' first player to pass for 3,000 yards in a season?

31. Who was the Browns' first player to total 1,000 yards receiving in a season?

32. What seven players were the first Browns to be selected for participation in the annual Pro Bowl?

33. Who was the first Browns' player to be named a conference/league's Rookie of the Year?

34. Who was the first Browns' head coach to be selected a conference/league's Coach of the Year?

35. Who was the first Browns' player to be named a conference/league's Most Valuable Player/Player of the Year (clue: he was the first Browns' player to be inducted into the Pro Football Hall of Fame)?

Cleveland Browns Facts & Trivia

The Last Time ...

1. The last time a Browns' player rushed for 100 yards in one game was

2. The last time a Browns' opposing player rushed for 100 yards in one game was ...

3. The last time a Browns' player passed for 400 yards in a game was ...

4. The last time a Browns' opposing player passed for 400 yards in a game was ...

5. The last time a Browns' player was unsuccessful on an extra point attempt was ...

6. The last time a Browns' opposing player was unsuccessful on an extra point attempt was ...

7. The last time a Browns' player blocked a field goal was ...

8. The last time a Browns' opposing player blocked a field goal was ...

9. The last time a Browns' player returned an interception for a touchdown was ...

10. The last time a Browns' opposing player returned an interception for a touchdown was ...

11. The last time a Browns' defensive player returned a fumble for a touchdown was ...

12. The last time a Browns' opposing defensive player returned a fumble for a touchdown was ...

13. The last time a Browns' player blocked a punt was ...

14. The last time a Browns' opposing player blocked a punt was ...

15. The last time a Browns' player returned a punt for a touchdown was ...

16. The last time a Browns' opposing player returned a punt for a touchdowns was ...

17. The last time a Browns' player returned a kickoff for a touchdown was ...

18. The last time a Browns' opposing player returned a kickoff for a touchdown was ...

19. The last time a Browns' player scored a safety was ...

20. The last time a Browns' opposing player scored a safety was ...

21. The last time the Browns gained 500 combined net yards in one game was ...

22. The last time a Browns' opponent gained 500 combined net yards in one game was ...

23. The last time the Browns posted a shutout was ...

24. The last time the Browns were shut out was ...

Who Am I?

1. I was the Browns' original starting quarterback. Who am I?

2. I led the Browns in rushing yards from 1946-49 and in 1950 and 1952. I was inducted into the Pro Football Hall of Fame in 1968. Who am I?

3. I am an Ohio State product who was the Browns' starting left tackle from 1946-59 and starting place kicker during the same period and from 1961-67. I was enshrined into the Pro Football Hall of Fame in 1974. Who am I?

4. I was the Browns' head coach from 1946-62 who was inducted into the Pro Football Hall of Fame in 1967. Who am I?

5. I am an Ohio State product who had a Hall of Fame career (inducted in 1975) with the Browns as a wide receiver from 1946-56. My 209 yards receiving on October 14, 1949, against the Los Angeles Dons rank second for the Browns in all-time single-game receiving yardage. Who am I?

6. I am an Ohio State product who played middle guard for the Browns from 1946-53. I was inducted into the Pro Football Hall of Fame in 1977. Who am I?

7. I was the Browns' primary quarterback from 1946-55, winning the AAFC's own Most Valuable Player award in 1947 and the United Press's MVP honor in 1948 and 1953. I led the Browns to seven championships in 10 years. Who am I?

Cleveland Browns Facts & Trivia

8. I played center for the Browns from 1946-56 and was inducted into the Hall of Fame in 1985. My nickname was "Gunner." Who am I?

9. I rank third on both the all-time Browns' receiving yardage (5,602) and receptions (349) lists. Who am I?

10. I was a halfback who was the Browns' top draft pick in 1948 who never made the regular squad. Who am I?

11. I rank second in career interceptions for the Browns with 44. Who am I?

12. I returned an interception 39 yards late in the fourth quarter for the final touchdown of the game in the Browns' 49-7 rout of the Buffalo Bills in the 1948 AAFC Championship game. Who am I?

13. I ran the ball 16 times for 63 yards and caught one pass for 10 yards in the Browns' 21-7 victory over the San Francisco 49ers in the 1949 AAFC title game. Who am I?

14. I was the Browns' starting right defensive end from 1950-57 and was enshrined into the Pro Football Hall of Fame in 1976. Who am I?

15. I tied an NFL record for most touchdowns in one game by scoring six against the Chicago Bears on November 25, 1951. Who am I?

16. I was Cleveland's top draft choice in 1952 out of Tennessee who was a member of the Browns for just my rookie year as the starting safety. Who am I?

17. I played on the Browns' defensive line in 1952 and from 1954-64. I was a five-time Pro Bowler from 1957-59 and in 1961 and 1962. Who am I?

18. I was a Cleveland wide receiver from 1952-63 and rank fourth on the all-time Browns' list of receiving yards with 5,508. Who am I?

19. I was drafted by the Browns in the 20th round of the NFL Draft in 1953 out of Dayton and started at right guard and left linebacker for the team from 1953-59. Who am I?

20. I played in the Browns' defensive backfield as a safety from 1953-59. I rank fifth on the Browns in all-time interceptions with 30. Who am I?

21. I was a Browns' linebacker from 1954-62 who later became head coach of the New York Jets from 1977-82. Who am I?

Cleveland Browns Facts & Trivia

22. I began my Browns career as the team's starting middle guard in 1954 before switching to right tackle in 1955. I played for the Browns through 1962. I played in six Pro Bowls and three NFL Championship games with the Browns. I was inducted into the Hall of Fame in 1984. Who am I?

23. I was the Browns' top draft choice in 1957 out of Syracuse University and went on to lead the NFL in rushing yards in eight of my nine years in the league, all with the Browns. I finished my career with 12,312 yards rushing. I was inducted into the Pro Football Hall of Fame in 1971. Who am I?

24. I am an Ohio University product who was the Browns' starting middle linebacker from 1957-66. Who am I?

25. I was the Browns' seventh-round draft choice out of Illinois in 1958 and spent four years with the team as Jim Brown's running mate at halfback before being traded to the Washington Redskins three days prior to the 1961 season finale. I am a 1983 Hall of Fame inductee. Who am I?

26. I am a University of Mississippi product who was a key ingredient on a stalwart Browns offensive line from 1958-60 and 1962-73, mostly at right guard. Who am I?

27. I am an Ohio State University product who was the Browns' second-round choice in the 1959 NFL Draft. I was the Browns' starting left tackle from 1960-71. Who am I?

28. I led the NFL in passing in 1960 and 1961. Who am I?

29. I was a fourth-round draft choice by the Browns out of Ohio State in 1960 and played one season for them at right defensive end before being traded on August 31, 1961, to the Minnesota Vikings, where I enjoyed 19 stellar seasons. Who am I?

30. I was the Browns' third-round draft pick out of Purdue in 1960 and played in Cleveland's defensive backfield for eight years through 1967. I am tied for seventh in career interceptions for the Browns with 30. Who am I?

31. I was a quarterback whom the Browns acquired in a deal with the Los Angeles Rams on July 12, 1962, and spent seven seasons in Cleveland, ranking fourth in all-time Browns passing yards with 13,361. Who am I?

32. I gained 73 yards on a rushing play against the Detroit Lions on December 8, 1963. Who am I?

Cleveland Browns Facts & Trivia

33. I was Cleveland's No. 1 draft pick in 1964 out of Ohio State. I spent six seasons with the Browns as a speedy wide receiver with dazzling moves before being shipped to Miami on January 26, 1970, in a move that stunned the city of Cleveland. I spent five successful seasons with the Dolphins, was lured to the short-lived World Football League in 1975 before returning to the shores of Lake Erie in 1976 to close out my career, which came to an end the following year. I was a 1983 Pro Football Hall of Fame inductee. Who am I?

34. I was Cleveland's eighth-round draft pick in 1964 who enjoyed a stellar 10-year career with the Browns as a halfback. I rushed for at least 1,000 yards in three straight seasons from 1966-68, leading the league the last two. I rank second on the Browns' career rushing yardage list with 7,274 and was inducted into the Pro Football Hall of Fame in 1994. Who am I?

35. I led the Browns in highest average yards per kickoff return in 1964, 1965, and 1966. Who am I?

36. I rank fourth in all-time receptions for the Browns with 331. I scored all three Browns' touchdowns in Cleveland's 27-0 upset of the Baltimore Colts in the 1964 NFL Championship game in Cleveland. Who am I?

37. I was the Browns' starting left defensive tackle in 1964 and 1965 and was the team's head coach for one game - the 1977 season finale. Who am I?

38. I was the Browns' No. 1 draft choice out of Massachusetts in 1966 and was a tight end on the team for 10 seasons through 1975. I rank 10th in career Browns receiving yards with 4,208. Who am I?

39. I was a kicker who was drafted by the Browns out of Adams State (Colorado) in 1967, spent a year on the taxi squad, and then outdueled Lou Groza in the 1968 training camp. I remained the kicker through the 1980 season. I rank second in all-time points scored as a Brown with 1,080. Who am I?

40. I returned an interception 27 yards for a touchdown early in the third quarter that broke a 10-10 tie in the Browns' 31-20 victory over the Dallas Cowboys in the Eastern Conference Championship game on December 21, 1968, in Cleveland. Who am I?

41. I was drafted by Cleveland out of Purdue as the third overall pick in the 1970 NFL Draft the day after the Browns had acquired the pick from the Miami Dolphins in exchange for the great Paul Warfield. In my seven seasons in Cleveland, I threw 40 touchdowns passes and 81 interceptions. Who am I?

Cleveland Browns Facts & Trivia

42. I was a second-round draft pick of the Browns out of Oklahoma State in 1970 and played right defensive tackle for the team for 12 seasons through 1981, starting in all but the last two. I was named NFL Defensive Player of the Year in 1976 by the Newspaper Enterprise Association. Who am I?

43. I returned the second-half kickoff 94 yards for a touchdown that helped the Browns to a 31-21 victory over the New York Jets on September 21, 1970, in Cleveland in the first ABC *Monday Night Football* game. Who am I?

44. I was drafted by the Browns in the sixth round in 1971 out of Illinois, started some my rookie year, and went on to become the team's starting left tackle from 1972-84. Who am I?

45. I directed the Browns to a 30-24-2 (.554) record as the team's head coach from 1971-74. Who am I?

46. I was a quarterback chosen by the Browns in the 13th round of the 1972 draft. I spent two years on the taxi squad, and after backing up Mike Phipps in 1974 and 1975, became the full-time starter when Phipps went down with a separated shoulder in the 1976 season opener. I went on to become the Browns' all-time leader in passing yards with 23,713. Who am I?

47. I led the Browns in rushing yards in 1973. Who am I?

48. I was a speedy running back drafted in the second round by the Browns out of Oklahoma in 1973 who rushed for at least 1,000 yards in 1975, 1976, and 1977. I was traded to the Los Angeles Raiders on April 28, 1982. Who am I?

49. I was a former Green Bay Packers' offensive tackle who lost my first nine games as an NFL head coach in 1975 with Cleveland. I did bring the Browns back to respectability for a short time before being fired with one game remaining in the 1977 season. Who am I?

50. I am a Kent State University product who was drafted by the Browns in the ninth round of the 1975 draft. I spent three years with the Browns as a running back. Who am I?

51. I was a fourth-round draft pick of the Browns out of Oklahoma in 1975. I started at right cornerback in 1975 and 1976 and at strong safety in 1977 and 1978. Who am I?

52. I was the Browns' starting left defensive end who turned Terry Bradshaw into a pretzel in the Browns' 18-16 upset of the Steelers on

Cleveland Browns Facts & Trivia

October 10, 1976, in Cleveland Municipal Stadium. Who am I?

53. I was the Browns' top pick in the 1978 draft out of USC who spent 16 seasons as mostly the team's starting right outside linebacker. I was a fan favorite. Who am I?

54. I was the Browns' second pick in the 1978 draft out of Alabama who in 13 seasons had a team-record 662 receptions. I was inducted into the Pro Football Hall of Fame in 1999. Who am I?

55. I led not only the Browns, but the entire AFC, as a rookie in highest kickoff return yard average (26.3) in 1978. Who am I?

56. I was the Browns' starting left defensive end in 1979 and starting right defensive end in 1980 and 1981. Who am I?

57. I was the Browns' starting left inside linebacker in 1980 and 1981. Who am I?

58. I was the Browns' No. 1 draft choice out of Southern Mississippi in 1981. I started at right cornerback for nearly my entire nine-year career with Cleveland. I was selected to play in three straight Pro Bowls from 1986-88. I was greatly responsible for the birth of the famous "Dawg Pound" - i.e., the Cleveland Stadium bleachers section. My nickname was "Top Dawg." Who am I?

59. I was the Browns' top pick in the 1982 NFL Draft out of USC. I spent five prosperous seasons in Cleveland as the Browns' starting left outside linebacker. Who am I?

60. I was the Browns' starting left cornerback from 1985-92. Who am I?

61. I am a native of Boardman, Ohio, not far from Cleveland, and was granted my wish of playing for the team for which I rooted since I had been a youngster when the Browns were able to maneuver their way to snag me in the 1985 NFL supplemental draft. I spent eight-and-a-half seasons with the Browns before being released on November 8, 1993. I led the Browns to three AFC Championship games in the late 1980s. Who am I?

62. In 1985, we became only the third pair of running backs in NFL history to rush for 1,000 yards in the same season for the same team. Who are we?

63. I was Cleveland's No. 1 pick in the 1986 NFL Draft out of San Diego State who spent six years with the Browns and caught 305 passes, which ranks eighth all-time in Browns receptions. I caught a 97-yard touchdown

pass from Bernie Kosar - the second longest pass play in team history - on Monday night, October 23, 1989, against the Bears. Who am I?

64. I returned a punt 84 yards for a touchdown on September 28, 1986, against the Lions, and a week later returned a kickoff 100 yards for a score against the Steelers. Who am I?

65. I am a 1977 graduate of Canton (Ohio) McKinley High School, some 60 miles down the road from Cleveland, who was the Browns' starting strong safety in 1986 and 1987. Who am I?

66. I was Cleveland's second-round pick in the 1988 NFL Draft and spent seven seasons with the Browns, the last six as the team's starting right defensive tackle. Who am I?

67. I was the Browns' top pick in the 1990 draft out of Michigan and spent six seasons as a running back for the team. In 1991, I led the Browns, and was third in the AFC, with 11 touchdowns - nine receiving and two rushing - several in spectacular fashion. Who am I?

68. I was the Browns' No. 1 pick in the 1991 NFL Draft out of UCLA who began my career at strong safety before being switched to free safety in 1993. Who am I?

69. I was a fullback out of Stanford drafted by the Browns in the first round of the 1992 NFL Draft. I spent four seasons with the Browns. Who am I?

70. I was a Browns defensive back who returned a fumble 73 yards for a touchdown in a 24-14 victory over Houston on November 8, 1992, in the Astrodome. Who am I?

71. I was the Browns' starting tight end in 1992. Who am I?

72. I was acquired in a trade with Tampa Bay in 1993 and spent three mostly tumultuous seasons in Cleveland at the quarterback position - starting most of the time in 1994 and '95. In 1994, I did lead the Browns to their last playoff appearance. Who am I?

73. I was the Browns' starting tight end in 1993. Who am I?

74. I led the AFC in kickoff return yard average (26.9) in 1994. Who am I?

75. I am a kicker who scored 113 points for the Browns in 1995, which ranks fourth in all-time scoring in one season for the team. Who am I?

Cleveland Browns Facts & Trivia

What Position(s) Did He Play?

1. Otto Graham.
2. Tom Colella.
3. Lou Groza.
4. Tim Manoa.
5. Fair Hooker.
6. Bernie Kosar.
7. Nick Roman.
8. Anthony Pleasant.
9. Warren Lahr.
10. Gregg Rakoczy.
11. Frank Minnifield.
12. Dave Logan.
13. Lyle Alzado.
14. Jim Brown.
15. Vince Costello.
16. Dick Deschaine.
17. Al Gross.
18. Rocky Belk.
19. Larry Benz.
20. Dante Lavelli.
21. Mike Pruitt.
22. Don Shula.
23. Brian Sipe.
24. Matt Stover.
25. Mac Speedie.
26. Pat Moriarty.
27. Rob Burnett.
28. Charlie Hall.
29. Steve Holden.
30. Matt Bahr.
31. Gerald Irons.
32. Abe Gibron.
33. Eric Turner.
34. Tommy Vardell.
35. Bobby Mitchell.
36. Mike Phipps.
37. Marion Motley.
38. Reggie Rucker.
39. Dave Mays.
40. Eric Metcalf.
41. Chip Banks.
42. Don Cockroft.
43. Gene Fekete.

What Year(s) Did He Play for the Browns?

1. Bernie Kosar.
2. Dante Lavelli.
3. Curtis Dickey.
4. Anthony Blaylock.
5. Dave Logan.
6. Dale Lindsey.
7. Ozzie Newsome.
8. Paul Warfield.
9. Lou Groza.
10. Gene Fekete.
11. Dino Hall.
12. Andre Rison.
13. Earnest Byner.
14. Clay Matthews.
15. Otto Graham.
16. Horace Gillom.
17. Ken Carpenter.
18. Cleo Miller.
19. Dick Modzelewski.
20. Ed Modzelewski.
21. Felix Wright.
22. Walt Sumner.
23. Bob Kolesar.
24. Pete Perini.
25. Jerry Sherk.
26. Ray Ellis.
27. Steve Everitt.
28. Calvin Hill.
29. Harry Holt.
30. Fair Hooker.
31. Will Cureton.
32. Greg Pruitt.
33. Mike Pruitt.
34. Jim Ray Smith.
35. Frank Winters.
36. Frank Gatski.
37. Thane Gash.
38. Dub Jones.
39. James Brooks.
40. Keith Bosley.
41. Tom Flick.
42. Brian Brennan.
43. Homer Jones.

Cleveland Browns Facts & Trivia

44. Tom DeLeone.
45. Tom Cousineau.
46. Boyce Green.
47. Dub Jones.
48. Len Ford.
49. Ross Fichtner.
50. Hanford Dixon.
51. Doug Dieken.
52. Greg Pruitt.
53. Felix Wright.
54. Vinny Testaverde.
55. Leroy Kelly.
56. George Lilja.
57. Henry Bradley.
58. Jeff Gossett.
59. Brian Brennan.
60. Horace Gillom.
61. Ricky Feacher.
62. Judson Flint.
63. Bobby Jones.
64. Walt Sumner.
65. Michael Dean Perry.
66. Clarence Scott.
67. Don Rogers.
68. Reece Morrison.
69. Milt Plum.
70. Clay Matthews.
71. Ken Konz.
72. Johnny Evans.
73. Chuck Noll.
74. Paul Warfield.
75. Ozzie Newsome.

44. Mike Junkin.
45. Frank Pitts.
46. Charles White.
47. Brian Sipe.
48. Webster Slaughter.
49. Doug Dieken.
50. Cody Risien.
51. Don Greenwood.
52. Jim Kanicki.
53. Curtis Weathers.
54. Clarence Weathers.
55. Jim Shofner.
56. Ara Parseghian.
57. Reggie Rucker.
58. Joe Morris.
59. Marion Motley.
60. Vinny Testaverde.
61. Frank Minnifield.
62. Rickey Bolden.
63. Bill Cowher.
64. Thom Darden.
65. Tom Goosby.
66. Glen Young.
67. Matt Stover.
68. Chuck Noll.
69. Leroy Kelly.
70. Gene Hickerson.
71. Jim Brown.
72. Mark Harper.
73. Les Horvath.
74. Paul McDonald.
75. Don Shula.

Cleveland Browns Facts & Trivia

What Number(s) Did He Wear?

1. Leroy Kelly.
2. Brian Kinchen.
3. Don Paul.
4. Greg Pruitt.
5. Mike Pruitt.
6. Dante Lavelli.
7. Thom Darden.
8. Ozzie Newsome.
9. Milt Plum.
10. Tom DeLeone.
11. Chip Banks.
12. Michael Jackson.
13. Paul McDonald.
14. Billy Reynolds.
15. Brian Sipe.
16. Paul Warfield.
17. Jim Brown.
18. John Kissell.
19. Mike Johnson.
20. Gary Danielson.
21. Webster Slaughter.
22. Dave Logan.
23. Doug Dieken.
24. Ben Davis.
25. Lyle Alzado.
26. Steve Cox.
27. Bob Golic.
28. Clay Matthews.
29. Bill Willis.
30. Walter Beach.
31. Mike Pagel.
32. Don Cockroft.
33. Reggie Langhorne.
34. Walt Sumner.
35. George Ratterman.
36. Dino Hall.
37. Bob McKay.
38. Gene Hickerson.
39. Vinny Testaverde.
40. Cleo Miller.
41. Reece Morrison.
42. John Wooten.
43. Hanford Dixon.
44. Marion Motley.

Where Did He Play College Football?

1. Tom Cousineau.
2. David Grayson.
3. Milt Morin.
4. Dante Lavelli.
5. Stevon Moore.
6. Brian Sipe.
7. Frank Ryan.
8. Earnest Byner.
9. Bill Nelsen.
10. Chuck Noll.
11. Bernie Kosar.
12. Thom Darden.
13. Cliff Lewis.
14. Mark Miller.
15. Ozzie Newsome.
16. Larry Poole.
17. Ron Wolfley.
18. Frank Stams.
19. Michael Dean Perry.
20. Gerald McNeil.
21. Bo Scott.
22. Don Rogers.
23. Robert Lyons.
24. Chris Rockins.
25. Terry Luck.
26. Oliver Davis.
27. Harry Jagade.
28. Jim Brown.
29. Vince Costello.
30. Paul Warfield.
31. Lawyer Tillman.
32. Mike Tomczak.
33. Mac Speedie.
34. Terry Greer.
35. Jim Ninowski.
36. Don Shula.
37. Cody Risien.
38. Mike Pruitt.
39. Kevin Mack.
40. Ed King.
41. Brian Brennan.
42. Pat Moriarty.
43. Charles White.

45. Warren Lahr.
46. Matt Stover.
47. Kevin Mack.
48. Tony Jones.
49. Carl Hairston.
50. Matt Bahr.
51. Jim Houston.
52. Mike Baab.
53. Frank Parker.
54. Milt Morin.
55. Gerald McNeil.
56. Mike Phipps.
57. Rex Bumgardner.
58. Larry Benz.
59. Joe Jones.
60. Jim Copeland.
61. Willis Adams.
62. Rob Burnett.
63. Jack Gregory.
64. Mac Speedie.
65. Otto Graham.
66. Felix Wright.
67. Ed Modzelewski.
68. Michael Dean Perry.
69. George Lilja.
70. Reggie Rucker.
71. Tommy Thompson.
72. Ricky Feacher.
73. Len Ford.
74. Paul Farren.
75. Don Colo.

44. Marion Motley.
45. Jerry Sherk.
46. Frank Minnifield.
47. Bill Cowher.
48. David Brandon.
49. Steve Holden.
50. Joe DeLamielleure.
51. Sam Clancy.
52. John Garlington.
53. Bob Dahl.
54. Galen Fiss.
55. Dub Jones.
56. Clay Matthews.
57. Ken Brown.
58. John Wooten.
59. Reggie Rucker.
60. Rich Kreitling.
61. Tim Manoa.
62. Otto Graham.
63. Hanford Dixon.
64. Pepper Johnson.
65. Gerry Sullivan.
66. Gary Collins.
67. Eddie Johnson.
68. Bill Contz.
69. Bernie Parrish.
70. Bobby Mitchell.
71. Mike Junkin.
72. Mike Phipps.
73. Bill Boedeker.
74. Greg Pruitt.
75. Herman Fontenot.

Cleveland Browns Facts & Trivia

What Was/Were His Nickname(s)?

1. Joe Jones.
2. Lou Groza.
3. Jerry Sherk.
4. Otto Graham.
5. Maurice Bassett.
6. Eddie Johnson.
7. Al Baker.
8. Ozzie Newsome.
9. John Yonaker.
10. Dante Lavelli.
11. Don Cockroft.
12. Erich Barnes.
13. Frank Pitts.
14. Eric Turner.
15. Michael Jackson.
16. Frank Gatski.
17. Robert Sims.
18. William Jones.
19. Tommy Vardell.
20. Ross Fichtner.
21. Howard Cassady.
22. John Garlington.
23. Chet Hanulak.
24. Jim Ninowski.
25. Dick Ambrose.
26. Edgar Jones.
27. Herman Arvie.
28. Floyd Peters.
29. Darrell Brewster.
30. Don Phelps.
31. Forrest Grigg.
32. Ed Modzelewski.
33. Dick Modzelewski.
34. Robert Scott.
35. Mike Caldwell.
36. Charles Glass.
37. Walter Roberts.
38. Dick Schafrath.
39. Fred Morrison.
40. Dan Footman.
41. Matt Stover.
42. Marion Motley.
43. Vito Parilli.
44. Bob Kolesar.
45. Tom Wilson.
46. Ed Sutter.
47. Charley Ferguson.
48. Hanford Dixon.
49. Andre Rison.
50. Carl Hairston.
51. Homer Jones.
52. Don Greenwood.
53. Gerald McNeil.
54. John Harrington.
55. Frank Minnifield.
56. Dave Lloyd.
57. Ron Snidow.
58. Lowell Wren.
59. Johnny Brewer.
60. Greg Pruitt.
61. Mike Scarry.
62. Fred Evans.
63. Anthony Pleasant.
64. Dave Puzzuoli.
65. Doug Dieken.
66. Don Goss.
67. Johnny Davis.
68. Harry Jagade.
69. Clarence Jackson.
70. John Morrow.
71. Jim Kanicki.
72. Jim Shorter.
73. Gary Lane.
74. Tony Jones.
75. Bob Oliver.

61

Jim Brown

CLEVELAND BROWNS FULLBACK

Ht. 6'2"; Wt. 228; Born Feb. 17, 1936
College: Syracuse; Home: Cleveland, O.

After winning unanimous All-American
ratings in both football and lacrosse,
Jim was drafted No. 1 by the Browns
in 1957. He led the NFL in rushing in
each of his 5 pro years, while also
setting an all-time season rushing record with 1,527 yards in 1958 (scoring
18 TD's). Brown holds the single game
rushing mark of 237 yards, set against
Los Angeles in 1957 and against Philadelphia in 1961. He has played in the
Pro Bowl every year and
was also chosen last
year's "Player-of-the-
Game". REPRINT

ERIC TURNER

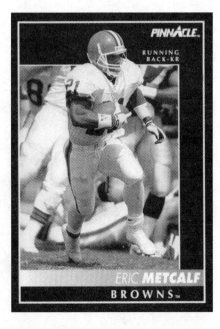

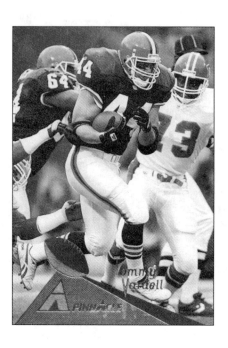

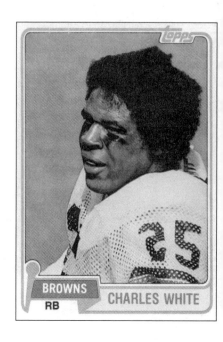

BROWNS
RB
CHARLES WHITE

KEVIN MACK
RB • Browns

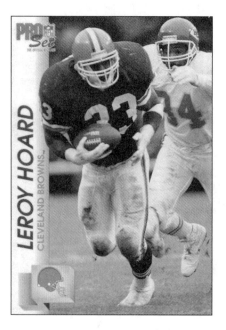

LEROY HOARD
CLEVELAND BROWNS.

PRO SET · THE OFFICIAL NFL CARD

BROWNS
RB
CALVIN HILL

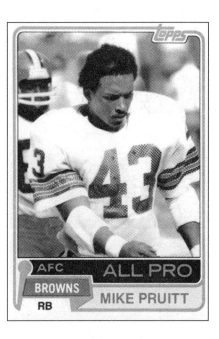

AFC ALL PRO
BROWNS
RB
MIKE PRUITT

BO SCOTT
BROWNS
RUNNING BACK

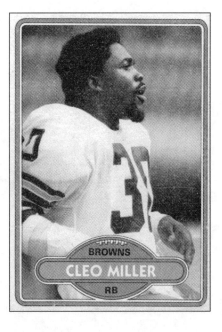

BROWNS
CLEO MILLER
RB

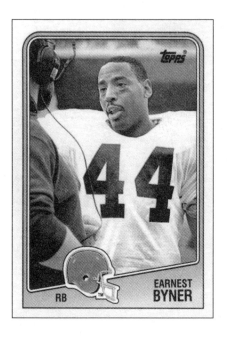

Topps

44

RB

EARNEST
BYNER

Topps

BROWNS

RB

GREG PRUITT

3

PRO ACTION

16

BILL NELSEN

NFL

FRANK RYAN

CLEVELAND BROWNS   QUARTERBACK

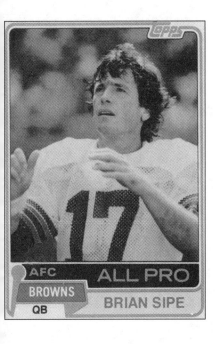

BROWNS
WR
KEITH WRIGHT

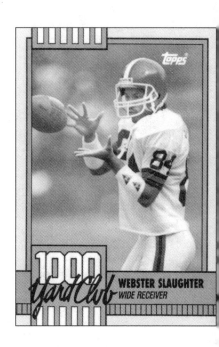

1000
Yard Club
WEBSTER SLAUGHTER
WIDE RECEIVER

BROWNS
WR
RICKY FEACHER

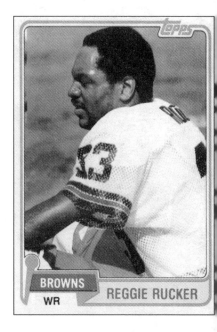

BROWNS
WR
REGGIE RUCKER

Topps

BROWNS
TE
OZZIE NEWSOME

REGGIE LANGHORNE

BROWNS™

NFL
WALTER ROBERTS
CLEVELAND BROWNS   FLANKER

PRO-LINE
Classic
LIVE

MICHAEL JACKSON
CLEVELAND BROWNS

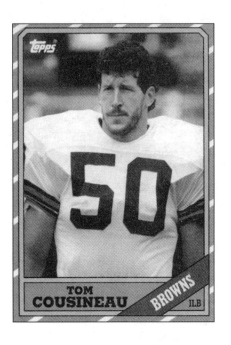

TOM COUSINEAU BROWNS ILB

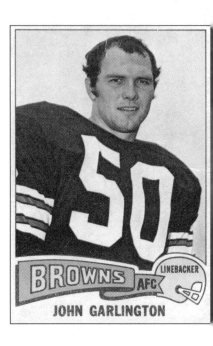

BROWNS AFC LINEBACKER

JOHN GARLINGTON

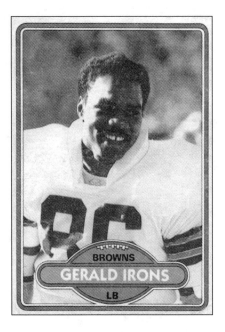

BROWNS
GERALD IRONS
LB

BROWNS
CHARLIE HALL
LB

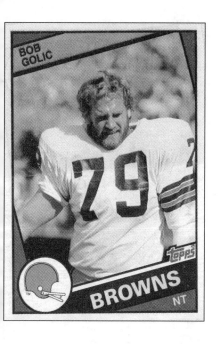

BOB GOLIC

79

BROWNS
NT

BROWNS
DE
LYLE ALZADO

71

BROWNS AFC
DEFENSIVE TACKLE

WALTER JOHNSON

92

BROWNS
P
JOHNNY EVANS

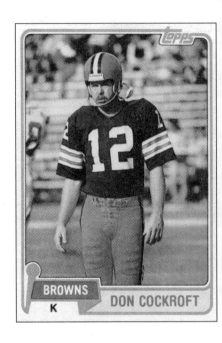

BROWNS
K
DON COCKROFT

CLEVELAND BROWNS

K
MATT STOVER

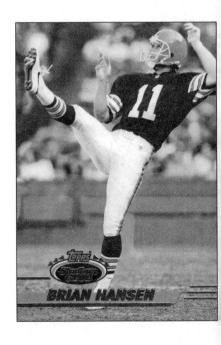

BRIAN HANSEN

THE ANSWERS

1. Players

Running Backs

1. Gene Fekete was the starting fullback, while Don Greenwood and Edgar "Special Delivery" Jones were the starting halfbacks against the Miami Seahawks on Sept. 6, 1946, in Cleveland Municipal Stadium.
2. Marion Motley gained 601 yards on the ground.
3. Don Greenwood rushed for six touchdowns.
4. Motley averaged 8.2 yards per carry.
5. Motley gained 964 yards on the ground in 1948.
6. Motley failed to lead the team in rushing yards in 1951 and '53.
7. Maurice Bassett. Bassett rushed for 444 yards.
8. Chet Hanulak.
9. Ed Modzelewski rushed for 619 yards in '55.
10. 756.
11. Jim Brown.
12. Brown rushed for 942 yards.
13. Brown scored nine touchdowns via the ground.
14. Brown was voted the NFL Rookie of the Year and Player of the Year.
15. Rookie of the Year.
16. Brown did it against Los Angeles on Nov. 24, 1957, and against Philadelphia on Nov. 19, 1961. Both games were in Cleveland.
17. Lew Carpenter.
18. 1,527.
19. Bobby Mitchell, Brown's backfield mate from '58-61, rushed for an even 500 yards.
20. In addition to rushing the ball 32 times for 178 yards, his five touchdowns on the ground set a team record for most rushing touchdowns in one game.
21. The Washington Redskins.
22. The Washington Redskins.
23. 1983.
24. 13.
25. Brown rushed for 1,863 yards in 1963.
26. He averaged 6.4 yards per carry.
27. Brown had 268 yards receiving on 24 receptions.
28. Ernie Green. The play, by the way, did not go for a touchdown.
29. Eight.
30. Brown failed to rush for at least 1,000 yards in his rookie year of 1957 and also in 1962, Paul Brown's final season as Cleveland's head coach.
31. 1962.
32. Brown gained 12,312 yards on the ground from 1957-65.
33. Four.

Cleveland Browns Facts & Trivia

34. He averaged 5.2 yards per carry.
35. Leroy Kelly
36. Three. Kelly had 1,141 yards in 1966, 1,205 in '67, and 1,239 in '68. He led the NFL in rushing yards in '67 and '68.
37. 15.
38. 11.
39. 16.
40. Bo Scott.
41. Ken Brown.
42. Zero.
43. Greg Pruitt.
44. The Kansas City Chiefs.
45. 1,000.
46. Pruitt scored on a 78-yard run in a 44-7 rout of the visiting Chiefs on Oct. 30, 1977.
47. Mike Pruitt.
48. No.
49. Larry Poole.
50. Pruitt topped the 1,000-yard mark in 1979, '80, '81, and '83.
51. He piled up 1,294 yards in 1979, which ranked second in the AFC.
52. Yes.
53. Pat Moriarty.
54. He ranks third with 6,540 yards, behind Jim Brown and Leroy Kelly.
55. Charles White.
56. Boyce Green.
57. Boyce Green.
58. Preston Carpenter did it in 1956, Ken Brown in 1973.
59. Earnest Byner.
60. Kevin Mack and Earnest Byner accomplished the feat in 1985.
61. Mack rushed for 1,104 yards.
62. Byner just made it with 1,002.
63. The Miami Dolphins.
64. Zero.
65. Zero.
66. Mack led the team in rushing yards six times - in 1985, '86, '87, '90, '91, and '92.
67. Mack rushed for 5,123 yards, which ranks fifth in club history.
68. One. He led the Browns with 576 rushing yards in 1988.
69. Byner rushed for a total of 3,364 yards in his seven-year career with Cleveland.
70. Herman Fontenot scored on a three-yard reception from Bernie Kosar.
71. 38-31, Broncos.
72. Eric Metcalf.
73. Leroy Hoard.
74. He rushed for 890 yards.
75. Zero.

Quarterbacks

1. Otto Graham.
2. Cliff Lewis.
3. 19 yards.
4. Otto Graham.
5. 25.
6. He had 25 touchdown passes and 15 interceptions.
7. Seven.
8. Graham was picked off 20 times.
9. Four.
10. He passed for a career-high 2,816.
11. Graham had a long day, completing just two of 15 passes for 20 yards and throwing two interceptions.
12. The United Press.
13. Six. He passed for three and ran for three.
14. Four games into the 1955 preseason schedule.
15. He ranks second with 23,584 yards, just 129 behind Brian Sipe.
16. Graham was enshrined in 1965.
17. Eight touchdown passes, 18 interceptions.
18. Milt Plum.
19. Plum and O'Connell were picked off four times, each twice.
20. He led the league in passing in 1960 and '61.
21. He had 21 touchdown passes and five interceptions in 1960 and 18 touchdown passes and 10 interceptions in '61.
22. Len Dawson. Dawson would go on to lead the Kansas City Chiefs to victory in Super Bowl IV.
23. Jim Ninowski.
24. Frank Ryan.
25. Jim Ninowski.
26. Ninowski was replaced by Ryan early in the second quarter of the season's seventh game, a 41-14 victory over the Steelers in Pittsburgh on Oct. 28.
27. Ninowski suffered a dislocated shoulder courtesy of Big Daddy Lipscomb.
28. Ryan passed for 25 touchdowns and was picked off 13 times.
29. The scores went for 18, 42, and 51 yards, the last a spectacular one-handed grab by Collins, who then disappeared into a sea of joyous Browns fans.
30. Ryan threw for 2,974 yards, 29 touchdowns, and 14 interceptions.
31. He threw for 367 yards against the Cardinals.
32. 75 yards.
33. 13,361.
34. Bill Nelsen.
35. The Pittsburgh Steelers. Nelsen led the Browns to a 31-24 victory over

his former team on Saturday night, Oct. 5, 1968, in Cleveland.

36. Nelsen completed an 87-yarder to tight end Milt Morin on Nov. 24, 1968, in a 47-13 victory over the Philadelphia Eagles. Ironically, the play did not go for a touchdown.

37. Paul Warfield.

38. Mike Phipps.

39. Bill Nelsen.

40. Nelsen had 13 touchdown passes and 23 interceptions (Phipps added one touchdown pass and four interceptions, meaning the division champion Browns' quarterback position remarkably accounted for 14 touchdown passes and 27 interceptions).

41. He passed for 13 touchdowns and 16 interceptions.

42. Fair Hooker (the Dolphins rebounded and won the game, 20-14, and went on to win the first of two straight Super Bowl titles).

43. Five.

44. Nine touchdown passes, 20 interceptions.

45. Nine touchdown passes, 17 interceptions.

46. Four touchdown passes, 19 interceptions.

47. 40 touchdown passes, 81 interceptions.

48. The Chicago Bears.

49. Brian Sipe.

50. The Pittsburgh Steelers.

51. Dave Mays.

52. Sipe completed 337 of 554 passes for team records of 4,132 yards and 30 touchdown, and threw just 14 interceptions. He led the NFL with a 91.4 passer rating.

53. Strong safety Mike Davis made the interception, which sealed the Raiders' 14-12 victory in the AFC Divisional Playoff in frozen Cleveland Stadium.

54. Sipe was named NFL Player of the Year by the Associated Press, Most Valuable Player by the Pro Football Writers Association of America and *The Sporting News*, Offensive Player of the Year by *Pro Football Weekly*, and AFC Most Valuable Player by United Press International.

55. Sipe passed for a club-record 23,713 yards.

56. Lefty Paul McDonald, who directed the Browns to a 10-9 win.

57. Ricky Feacher (the Browns went on to lose, 27-10).

58. McDonald completed 271 of 493 passes for 3,472 yards, 14 touchdowns, and 23 interceptions.

59. Tom Flick.

60. Bernie Kosar.

61. Gary Danielson.

62. He fumbled.

63. 66.

64. Kosar threw for 3,854 yards in '86.

65. He passed for an eye-popping 489 yards.

66. Arrowhead Stadium in Kansas City.

67. Don Strock.
68. Mike Pagel (the Browns lost, 42-0).
69. Todd Philcox, who stepped in for the injured Bernie Kosar. The Browns defeated the Raiders in Los Angeles, 28-16 (Metcalf scored all four Browns touchdowns as he also had a six-yard run for a score).
70. Mike Tomczak.
71. The Browns released Bernie Kosar.
72. Vinny Testaverde.
73. Mark Rypien.
74. Rookie Eric Zeier.
75. He completed 26 of 46 passes for 310 yards with one touchdown and an interception.

Wide Receivers/Tight Ends

1. Dante Lavelli. Lavelli had 40 receptions for 843 yards in '46.
2. Dante Lavelli with eight.
3. Mac Speedie with 67 catches for 1,146 yards.
4. Dante Lavelli. Lavelli caught nine touchdown passes.
5. 209.
6. 228, a team record.
7. He caught 62 balls for 1,028 yards and seven touchdowns.
8. Speedie caught an NFL-high 62 balls for 911 yards and five touchdowns.
9. Lavelli caught 47 balls for 802 yards and seven touchdowns.
10. Ray Renfro.
11. Darrell Brewster.
12. Lavelli caught three balls for a team-best 95 yards. Included was a 50-yard touchdown reception from Otto Graham with 39 seconds left in the opening half that gave the Browns a 17-7 lead.
13. Lavelli was inducted into the Hall in 1975.
14. Six.
15. Six.
16. Gern Nagler.
17. Rich Kreitling had 659 yards receiving on 44 receptions.
18. Gary Collins.
19. Collins had 35 catches for 544 yards and eight touchdown receptions.
20. Paul Warfield.
21. Warfield hauled in 52 catches, accumulated 920 receiving yards, and had eight touchdown receptions.
22. Collins scored on receptions of 18, 42, and 51 yards, courtesy of quarterback Frank Ryan.
23. Gary Collins.
24. Warfield, sidelined for most of the year with a shoulder injury, caught a total of three passes for 30 yards.

25. The two combined for five catches for 71 yards (Collins 3-41, Warfield 2-30).

26. Milt Morin.

27. The big tight end caught 23 passes for 333 yards and three touchdowns.

28. No.

29. Warfield became the first Browns' player to accumulate 1,000 yards receiving in a season (1,067) since Speedie rang up 1,146 21 years earlier.

30. 82 yards. Warfield scored on an 82-yard pass play from Bill Nelsen in a 27-21 victory over the St. Louis Cardinals on Dec. 14, 1969, in St. Louis.

31. 21. Collins had 11, Warfield 10.

32. Collins ranks fourth with 331 catches.

33. The Miami Dolphins.

34. Fair Hooker. The man with the "name" hauled in 45 catches for 649 yards.

35. Frank Pitts, acquired in a trade with Kansas City on Sept. 8, 1971.

36. He had 36 receptions, 620 receiving yards, and eight touchdown catches.

37. Fair Hooker. The Dolphins recovered, though, and won the game, 20-14, and went on to win their first of two straight Super Bowls.

38. Steve Holden, from Arizona State, led the Browns with 452 yards receiving on 30 receptions.

39. Reggie Rucker.

40. Rucker caught 60 balls for 770 yards.

41. Oscar Roan.

42. Warfield caught 38 passes for 613 yards and six touchdowns.

43. He averaged 19.2 yards per catch.

44. Warfield was inducted in 1983.

45. Gary Parris.

46. Ozzie Newsome.

47. Reggie Rucker. No. 33 caught 43 balls for 893 yards and eight touchdowns.

48. Willis Adams.

49. Dave Logan.

50. Ricky Feacher, who caught 35- and 34-yard scoring strikes from Brian Sipe.

51. Reggie Rucker.

52. Newsome caught 69 passes - a team record until the great tight end broke his own mark by hauling in 89 passes in 1983, and again in '84.

53. He had 1,002 receiving yards and six touchdown catches.

54. Ricky Feacher and Ozzie Newsome. They each had three.

55. Rucker caught 310 passes for 4,953 yards and 32 touchdowns from 1975-81.

56. Bobby Jones, who spent just one season in Cleveland. Jones caught 36 balls for 507 yards and four touchdowns in '83.

57. The Cincinnati Bengals.

58. Rocky Belk.
59. Duriel Harris.
60. Ron Brown.
61. The Denver Broncos.
62. 191.
63. 1,001.
64. Clarence Weathers.
65. Brian Brennan. The third-year receiver had 55 catches, 838 yards receiving, and six touchdown catches.
66. Webster Slaughter.
67. 39.
68. Brian Brennan, who completely faked out Broncos strong safety Dennis Smith.
69. Webster Slaughter. Slaughter had 806 receiving yards and seven touchdown catches. He had 47 receptions.
70. Lawyer Tillman.
71. Michael Jackson.
72. Derrick Alexander.
73. Michael Jackson.
74. The Browns signed Andre Rison, who started slowly and wound up with 47 catches for 701 yards and three touchdowns in '95.
75. Keenan McCardell.

Offensive Linemen

1. Lou Groza.
2. Groza retired prior to the 1960 season but returned the following year.
3. Groza was on the receiving end of a 23-yard lob pass from Otto Graham on a tackle-eligible play in the late stages of a 45-21 rout of the Washington Redskins on Dec. 10, 1950, in the nation's capitol.
4. 1974.
5. Frank Gatski.
6. 1985.
7. Gibron was a guard.
8. Sandusky played for Cleveland from 1950-55.
9. Chuck Noll.
10. Mike McCormack.
11. Jim Ray Smith. Smith had requested the trade due to business interests.
12. Gene Hickerson.
13. John Wooten.
14. Dick Schafrath.
15. John Morrow.
16. Fred Hoaglin.
17. Bob McKay.

Cleveland Browns Facts & Trivia

18. John DeMarie.
19. Henry Sheppard.
20. Left tackle Doug Dieken, center Tom DeLeone, and right guard Joe DeLamielleure.
21. Doug Dieken.
22. Cody Risien.
23. Paul Farren.
24. Baab played center for the New England Patriots.
25. Gregg Rakoczy.
26. Lilja played in four games in '84.
27. Bolden played for Cleveland from 1984-89, mostly at left tackle.
28. Dan Fike.
29. Larry Williams, who started at the same position for part of 1986.
30. Keith Bosley.
31. Tony Jones.
32. Ed King.
33. Jay Hilgenberg. Hilgenberg spent one season with the Browns.
34. Steve Everitt.
35. Herman Arvie.

Defensive Backs

1. Tom Colella (it is a team record that still stands today but was equaled 32 years later).
2. Ray Terrell.
3. The team's starting quarterback, Otto Graham.
4. Cliff Lewis.
5. Tommy James with nine.
6. Cornerback Warren Lahr.
7. Lahr picked off 44 passes in his career.
8. Don Shula. The future coach of the Baltimore Colts and Miami Dolphins was a member of the Browns' defensive backfield in 1951 and '52.
9. Ken Konz.
10. Cornerback Don Paul. Paul's picks were returned for 190 yards.
11. Ken Konz and Don Paul.
12. 30.
13. Bernie Parrish.
14. Bobby Franklin.
15. The Chicago Bears.
16. Bernie Parrish with seven.
17. Ross Fichtner with seven.
18. He had seven, which tied him with Vince Costello for the team lead.
19. Parrish had 29 thefts from 1959-66.
20. Fichtner picked off 27 passes from 1960-67.
21. Mike Howell.

Cleveland Browns Facts & Trivia

22. 162.
23. Barnes was a Brown from 1965-71.
24. Barnes led the Browns with five picks in 1970.
25. Walt Sumner.
26. 1970.
27. Clarence Scott.
28. Two.
29. 39.
30. Free safety Thom Darden with 45.
31. Darden led the Browns seven times - from 1972-74, '76-78, and in 1979 (he shared the team lead in '73 with Ben Davis).
32. Thom Darden.
33. The Dallas Cowboys.
34. Ron Bolton.
35. Hanford Dixon.
36. Right.
37. Strong safety Al Gross.
38. It came against the New York Giants in the Meadowlands.
39. Frank Minnifield. Minnifield was Dixon's sidekick through 1989 and continued on with the Browns through 1992.
40. Ray Ellis.
41. Don Rogers.
42. Felix Wright.
43. The Los Angeles Rams. Wright's first pick was returned 68 yards, the second 40 yards and a score.
44. He returned an interception 48 yards for a touchdown.
45. Nine.
46. Eric Turner.
47. Mustafaa went a team-record 97 yards for a touchdown.
48. The Arizona Cardinals.
49. Antonio Langham.
50. Stevon Moore. The strong safety had five.

Linebackers

1. Lou Saban.
2. Tommy Thompson.
3. Walt Michaels.
4. Hal Herring.
5. Noll was Cleveland's starting left linebacker from 1955-57.
6. Tom Catlin.
7. Fiss played for the Browns from 1956-66, both at left and right linebacker.
8. Vince Costello.
9. The New York Giants.

10. Costello stole 18 passes.
11. He was shipped to the New York Giants in exchange for a draft pick.
12. Dale Lindsey.
13. The Dallas Cowboys.
14. Three.
15. Right linebacker Johnny Brewer.
16. Fran Tarkenton.
17. Bob Matheson.
18. John Garlington.
19. Billy Andrews.
20. It came against the New York Jets in the first ABC *Monday Night Football* game.
21. Charlie Hall.
22. The Philadelphia Eagles.
23. Bob Babich.
24. Dick Ambrose.
25. Gerald Irons.
26. Clay Matthews.
27. Matthews played 16 seasons with Cleveland from 1978-93.
28. In this battle for the AFC Central title, Matthews recovered a snap late in the fourth quarter that sailed over quarterback Warren Moon's head deep in the Oilers' backfield - and then tried to lateral the ball to mammoth defensive tackle Chris Pike. The attempted toss bounced free, and the ball was retrieved by wide receiver Ernest Givins at the Houston 28 with 4:51 to play. The Oilers scored on the next play, a 72-yard touchdown pass from Moon to Drew Hill. The Browns came back, however, and won the game in the final minute, 24-20 - much to Matthews's appreciation.
29. 34-30.
30. The Atlanta Falcons.
31. 1980.
32. Don Goode.
33. Chip Banks from USC.
34. It happened on Nov. 20, 1983, in a key late-season contest in Foxboro, Mass. Banks picked off a Steve Grogan pass and sprinted 65 yards for a score to give the Browns a 10-0 second-quarter lead over the Patriots on the way to a 30-0 rout.
35. 11.
36. Tom Cousineau.
37. The Montreal Alouettes of the CFL.
38. He stole four passes that year.
39. They were Chip Banks on the left outside, Eddie Johnson on the left inside, Tom Cousineau on the right inside, and Clay Matthews on the right outside.
40. "The Assassin" was a starter in five of those years - at left inside linebacker from 1984-87 and right inside linebacker for part of the 1988 season.

41. Scott Nicholas.
42. Mike Johnson.
43. Mike Junkin.
44. David Grayson.
45. Clifford Charlton.
46. Van Waiters.
47. David Brandon did it against his former team.
48. Frank Stams.
49. Carl Banks.
50. Pepper Johnson.

Defensive Linemen

1. George Young and John Yonaker.
2. Bill Willis.
3. George Young.
4. Chet Adams.
5. Len Ford.
6. John Kissell.
7. Gain played for Cleveland in 1952 and from 1954-64.
8. Carlton Massey.
9. Don Colo.
10. Paul Wiggin.
11. Jim Houston.
12. Jim Marshall. Marshall went on to enjoy great success with the Vikings as a member of the famed "Purple People Eaters" defensive line.
13. Bill Glass.
14. Glass spent seven seasons in Cleveland from 1962-68.
15. Dick Modzelewski.
16. Jim Kanicki.
17. Walter Johnson.
18. Marvin Upshaw.
19. Jerry Sherk.
20. Jack Gregory.
21. Nick Roman.
22. Mack Mitchell.
23. Joe "Turkey" Jones.
24. St. Clair started at right defensive end for parts of the 1976 and '77 seasons, then switched to left defensive end for the 1978 season (he wasn't a regular starter in 1979).
25. Lyle Alzado.
26. Alzado spent three years on the shores of Lake Erie. He was left defensive end in 1979 and right defensive end in 1980 and '81.
27. Bob Golic.
28. Reggie Camp.

29. Carl Hairston.
30. Sam Clancy.
31. Michael Dean Perry.
32. Rob Burnett.
33. Anthony Pleasant.
34. James Jones.
35. Anthony Pleasant.

Punters

1. Tom Colella.
2. Horace Gillom.
3. Horace Gillom.
4. 80 yards (the longest in the NFL that season).
5. Don Cockroft. Cockroft had 3,321 punting yards 22 years later in 1973.
6. Don Cockroft.
7. Gillom averaged 45.5 yards per punt in 1951 and 45.7 yards per attempt in 1952.
8. Fred Morrison, Horace Gillom, Ken Konz, Dick Deschaine, Junior Wren, Jim Shofner, and Sam Baker.
9. Gary Collins.
10. 1965. Collins averaged 46.7 yards per punt that year.
11. Collins ranks third with 13,764.
12. Don Cockroft.
13. Cockroft was the team's No. 1 punter for nine years from 1968-76.
14. Houston (1970) and Kansas City (1973).
15. 1971, '73, '74, and '75
16. He holds the Nos. 2, 4, 7, and 9 spots.
17. 82.
18. 90.
19. 3,643.
20. 26,362.
21. Greg Coleman.
22. Johnny Evans.
23. Evans averaged 41.2 yards per punt in '79.
24. Evans had 8,463 yards punting.
25. Steve Cox.
26. Jeff Gossett.
27. 1,935.
28. In the midst of punting the ball 97 times for a team-record 3,817 yards, Wagner led the league in punts inside the 20-yard line with 32.
29. Wagner was the league leader in punts blocked with four.
30. Brian Hansen.
31. Hansen's average in '93 was the highest since 1965 when Gary Collins led the league with a 46.7-yard average.

Cleveland Browns Facts & Trivia

32. Third.
33. The 73-yarder came at home against the Denver Broncos, and the 72-yarder occurred on the road against the Cincinnati Bengals.
34. Tom Tupa.
35. 43.6.

Kickers

1. Lou Groza, who also played left tackle for the first part of his career. He totaled 1,608 points.
2. Groza accounted for 83 points.
3. Groza retired for the 1960 season but returned in 1961 - but for kicking duties only.
4. Sam Baker
5. The Brooklyn Dodgers.
6. 16 yards.
7. The Pittsburgh Steelers.
8. Groza scored 115 points in the Browns' last NFL Championship season of 1964. He was successful on 49 of 50 extra point attempts and 22 of 33 field goal tries.
9. Groza connected on 810 out of 832 PATs (point after touchdowns) for a success rate of 97.4 percent.
10. Groza made good on 264 of 481 field goal attempts for a 54.9 percent success rate.
11. Don Cockroft, a third-round draft selection out of Adams State (Colo.) the year before.
12. Cockroft was Cleveland's kicker from 1968-80.
13. Cockroft was perfect in 1969, '71, and '73. He was 45 for 45 in '69, 34 of 34 in '71, and 24 of 24 in '73.
14. 1970.
15. 26 yards.
16. Before he connected on a pair of 30-yard field goals in the third quarter, Cockroft had misfired on two treys and an extra point in the first half.
17. Cockroft connected on a 57-yarder in a 27-20 victory over the Broncos in Denver on Oct. 29, 1972.
18. 1,080.
19. Dave Jacobs.
20. Jacobs was released after just five games of the 1981 season, the day after another poor showing in a loss to the Los Angeles Rams. Jacobs had connected on only four of 12 field goal attempts on the season.
21. The Browns obtained Matt Bahr for a future draft choice.
22. The Super Bowl bound San Francisco 49ers, the team from which he was traded less than a month-and-a-half earlier.
23. The Pittsburgh Steelers. The Browns won in sudden death, 37-31.

24. Bahr was a Brown from 1981-89.
25. Bahr ranks fourth with 677 points.
26. Bahr connected on a 52-yarder on Oct. 26, 1986, against the Vikings in the Metrodome.
27. Mark Moseley, whom the Browns signed in late November when Matt Bahr went down with a season-ending injury.
28. Steve Cox nailed a 60-yarder on Oct. 21, 1984, in a 12-9 loss to the Bengals in Cincinnati.
29. Jeff Jaeger.
30. Jerry Kauric.
31. Matt Stover.
32. Both treys came against the Houston Oilers in the Astrodome - a 55-yarder on Nov. 17, 1991, and a 53-yarder on December 12, 1993.
33. Four.
34. Stover totaled 113 points in 1995 and 110 in '94.
35. Jacksonville

Punt Returners

1. Otto Graham.
2. Tom Colella, who was also the Browns' main punter that year, averaged 21.5 yards on eight returns.
3. Tom Colella.
4. Cliff Lewis.
5. He ranks fifth with 710 yards.
6. Don Phelps.
7. Ken Carpenter.
8. Billy Reynolds.
9. Konz had 13 returns for 187 yards, an NFL-high 14.4-yard average. Included was a 65-yard return for a touchdown against Washington on Nov. 25.
10. 78 yards. Mitchell's gem was the Browns' lone score in a 48-7 pummeling by the New York Giants on Dec. 6, 1959, in Yankee Stadium.
11. 11.2.
12. Mitchell ranks seventh with 607 yards.
13. Howard "Hopalong" Cassady, the former Ohio State Heisman Trophy winner.
14. Jim Shorter with 134 return yards and a 19.1-yard average.
15. Jim Shofner.
16. Leroy Kelly.
17. The New York Giants.
18. Walter "The Flea" Roberts.
19. Leroy Kelly.
20. Kelly returned a 67-yarder against the Cowboys in Dallas on Nov. 21

and a 56-yarder against the Steelers in Pittsburgh a week later on Nov. 28.
21. The Pittsburgh Steelers.
22. Walt Sumner.
23. Reece Morrison.
24. Leroy Kelly with 30 returns for 292 yards, a 9.7-yard average.
25. He ranks third with 990 yards.
26. Greg Pruitt.
27. 349.
28. The Denver Broncos.
29. Steve Holden.
30. Rolly Woolsey.
31. Keith Wright.
32. Dino Hall. Hall's 1979 total of 295 ranks ninth all-time in Browns history.
33. He averaged 10.2 yards per return in '79.
34. Fourth with 901 yards.
35. Ninth with 467 yards.
36. Dwight Walker.
37. Brian Brennan.
38. Gerald "The Ice Cube" McNeil.
39. 84 yards, the longest in the NFL that season.
40. 496.
41. 1,545.
42. Webster Slaughter's.
43. Eric Metcalf.
44. The Chicago Bears.
45. Metcalf will never forget that day, and evening, for two reasons. First, he returned a pair of punts for touchdowns (which led the NFL in most punt returns for touchdowns for the entire *season*) for 91 (longest in the league in '93) and 75 yards - the second with 2:05 remaining - in the Browns' thrilling 28-23 victory over the visiting Pittsburgh Steelers. Second, Metcalf became the only player in league annals to score on punt returns of at least 75 yards in the same game.
46. Second.
47. 12.9.
48. The Cincinnati Bengals.
49. He ranks second with 1,341.
50. Derrick Alexander.

Kick Returners

1. Edgar "Special Delivery" Jones. Jones had 12 returns for 307 yards, a 25.6-yard average. He also "special delivered" a touchdown off a 96-yard return in a season-ending 66-14 victory at Brooklyn on Dec. 8.
2. Marion Motley. Motley returned 13 kickoffs for 322 yards, a 24.8-yard

Cleveland Browns Facts & Trivia

average, in 1947. He followed that up with 14 returns for 337 yards, a 24.1-yard average, in 1948.

3. Dub Jones.
4. Marion Motley with 12.
5. Dub Jones with 204.
6. Bill Boedeker.
7. Don Phelps. Phelps returned 12 balls for 325 yards, a 27.1-yard average.
8. Ken Carpenter.
9. Billy Reynolds. Reynolds had 413 yards on 14 returns.
10. Carl Ward returned a kickoff 104 yards for a - surprise! - touchdown on Nov. 26, 1967, in a 42-37 victory at home against Washington.
11. Leroy Bolden.
12. A team-high 236 yards.
13. Mitchell scored on a 90-yarder at home against Dallas on Oct. 16, 1960.
14. He averaged 26.8 yards per return.
15. 1,550.
16. Tom Wilson.
17. Walter "The Flea" Roberts and Leroy Kelly.
18. Leroy Kelly.
19. Roberts averaged 27.4 yards per return.
20. 454.
21. Ben Davis.
22. Charlie Leigh.
23. Bo Scott.
24. Homer Jones.
25. 238.
26. Ken Brown. Brown had 20 returns for 473 yards, a 23.7-yard average.
27. Greg Pruitt. "Do It" Pruitt averaged 27.5 yards per return on 16 returns for 453 yards.
28. It came against the New England Patriots in Foxboro, Mass.
29. Billy Lefear. The return did not go for a touchdown, however.
30. Ricky Feacher.
31. Keith Wright. Wright had 30 returns for 789 yards in '78.
32. Wright ranks sixth with 1,767 yards.
33. Dino Hall.
34. Hall accumulated 3,185 kickoff return yards in his five-year career with the Browns.
35. Glen Young with a 25.7-yard average.
36. He ranks third with 2,079 yards.
37. Gerald McNeil.
38. 997.
39. Herman Fontenot. He had a 19.5-yard average.
40. Eric Metcalf.
41. He led the league in kickoff returns (52), kickoff return yards (1,052),

longest kickoff return (101 yards), and kickoff returns for touchdowns (two).
42. The Buffalo Bills.
43. Metcalf ranks second with 2,806 yards.
44. Randy Baldwin.
45. Baldwin had 30 returns for 675 yards, a 22.5-yard average.
46. Leroy Hoard.
47. Randy Baldwin.
48. 26.9.
49. He had 1,872, which ranks fourth.
50. Earnest Hunter.

2. Head Coaches

Paul Brown

1. Brown was born on Sept. 7, 1908, in Norwalk, Ohio, located in the northern part of the state.
2. He was brought up in Massillon, Ohio.
3. Massillon (Ohio) Washington High School.
4. Quarterback.
5. Brown transferred to Miami University his sophomore year when he realized he was too light (135 pounds) for Big Ten football; he graduated in 1930. Brown played quarterback on the football team and was the center fielder on the Redskins' baseball team his junior year.
6. Severn Prep in Maryland. Severn was a prep school for the Naval Academy. Brown's record in his two years as head coach there was 16-1-1 (.917).
7. He attended law school for a year-and-a-half.
8. Massillon (Ohio) Washington High School.
9. The Tigers were 6-3 in 1932.
10. 58-1-1, a .975 winning percentage.
11. Brown went 80-8-2 for a winning percentage of .900, and won six Ohio state titles (via popular acclaim) from 1935-40 (his '37 team was also honored as state champs by the Dickson Rating System). Brown's 1935, '36, '39, and '40 clubs were honored as United States Scholastic Champions.
12. Ohio State University.
13. Ohio State University.
14. Francis Schmidt.
15. 6-1-1 (.813).
16. The Buckeyes were 9-1. They captured the Big Ten title and a share of the national championship.

Cleveland Browns Facts & Trivia

17. 3-6.
18. He was the head coach and athletic officer for two years, 1944 and '45, at the Great Lakes Naval Training Center, outside of Chicago.
19. The team was 15-5-2 (.727) - 9-2-1 (.792) in 1944 and 6-3-1 (.650) in '45.
20. The Cleveland entry in the new eight-team All-America Football Conference (AAFC).
21. Arthur "Mickey" McBride, the team owner.
22. Otto Graham.
23. The Browns were named after Paul Brown himself, the only man in NFL annals after whom a team has been named. In a public name-the-team contest, it was agreed the epithet most frequently appearing in the entries would be the choice. "Panthers" was the winner - until Brown learned that Cleveland had fielded a semi-pro team in the 1920s with the same name, which folded. Brown wanted no part of a shoddy tradition and rejected the "Panthers" name. The second choice was "Browns," due most likely, it was said, to Brown's popularity throughout the state of Ohio. Although Brown was somewhat hesitant on his name being affixed to the team, he eventually gave in and agreed to it.
24. The Browns competed in the AAFC's Western Division from 1946-48.
25. They didn't compete in a division. The AAFC, down to seven teams by then, had no divisions that year, just one seven-team conference.
26. The New York Yankees. The Browns defeated the Yankees, 14-9, on Dec. 22, 1946, at Cleveland, and 14-3 on Dec. 14, 1947, in Yankee Stadium.
27. They were 52-4-3 (.903), winning all four conference titles.
28. The Philadelphia Eagles. On Saturday night, Sept. 16, 1950, Brown's Cleveland team destroyed the heavily-favored, defending NFL Champion Eagles, 35-10, in Philadelphia's Municipal Stadium.
29. The Browns defeated the Los Angeles Rams, 30-28, on a field goal by Lou Groza with 28 seconds left on Dec. 24 in Cleveland.
30. The Browns won the title in 1954 by blasting the Lions, 56-10, on Dec. 26 in Cleveland, and repeated in 1955 by hammering the Rams, 38-14, in front of nearly 88,000 fans in the Los Angeles Memorial Coliseum.
31. It occurred on Dec. 21, 1958, in Yankee Stadium. The Browns lost to the Giants, 10-0, in an Eastern Conference Playoff, a rematch of the regular-season finale that the Giants won the week before in the same venue.
32. Art Modell, who purchased majority ownership of the Cleveland franchise on Mar. 21, 1961, fired Brown following the 1962 season due to a personality conflict between the two.
33. 158-48-8 (.753).
34. 9-5 (.643).
35. Brown passed away on Aug. 5, 1991, due to complications from pneumonia.

Other Head Coaches

1. Blanton Collier.
2. No.
3. Collier was the offensive backfield coach.
4. Collier began his coaching career in 1928 at Paris (Ky.) High School. In addition to coaching the football team, he coached the basketball, baseball, and track teams. He was also the school's athletic director.
5. Georgetown (Ky.) College.
6. Collier met Brown while enlisted in the Navy at the Great Lakes Naval Training Center, outside of Chicago. Brown, the head coach there, gave Collier a job and eventually brought him with him when he took the head coaching job with the Cleveland team in the AAFC.
7. 10-4 (.714).
8. They won the NFL Championship, shocking the Baltimore Colts, 27-0, on Dec. 27 in the title game in Cleveland.
9. Four. They beat Baltimore in 1964, then lost to Green Bay in 1965, Baltimore in 1968, and Minnesota in 1969.
10. Mile High Stadium in Denver. The Browns defeated the Broncos, 27-0, on Dec. 20, 1970.
11. 76-34-2 (.688).
12. 3-4 (.429).
13. Nick Skorich, who had been the Browns' offensive line coach and in charge of overall offense from 1964-70 and was hired to replace Blanton Collier in Jan. 1971, piloted the Philadelphia Eagles from 1961-63.
14. None.
15. 15-24-3 (.393).
16. Bellaire.
17. The University of Cincinnati.
18. The Pittsburgh Steelers.
19. The Pittsburgh Steelers, Green Bay Packers, and Philadelphia Eagles.
20. The Browns shut out the Houston Oilers, 31-0, on Sept. 19, 1971, in Cleveland Municipal Stadium.
21. The Browns finished 9-5 and won the weak AFC Central Division, then were beaten rather easily by the Baltimore Colts at home in the AFC Divisional Playoffs.
22. 20-14.
23. Skorich was fired on Dec. 12, 1974, with the Browns in last place in the AFC Central Division at 4-9. He did, however, coach the final game of the season, a loss in Houston, three days later.
24. Forrest Gregg.
25. Southern Methodist University.
26. In addition to his playing duties, he was an assistant coach.
27. The San Diego Chargers.
28. The Cleveland Browns.

29. Nine.
30. 8-1.
31. Gregg was 17-9 from Nov. 23, 1975-Oct. 30, 1977.
32. The Houston Oilers.
33. Former Browns defensive tackle Dick Modzelewski coached the team to a 20-19 loss on Dec. 18, 1977.
34. Sam Rutigliano.
35. The University of Tennessee. The Volunteers won the national title in 1951.
36. Tulsa University.
37. Columbia.
38. The University of Connecticut and the University of Maryland.
39. Lou Saban.
40. New England Patriots, New York Jets, New Orleans Saints.
41. O.J. Simpson.
42. Rutigliano was voted AFC Coach of the Year by United Press International. The Browns - a.k.a., the "Kardiac Kids" those seasons - were 9-7 in 1979 and 11-5 and AFC Central Division Champions in 1980.
43. Red Right 88. With the Browns on the Raiders' 13-yard line, 49 seconds to go, and trailing by only two on the frozen field of Cleveland Stadium, Rutigliano called for a pass play. Brian Sipe was intercepted by strong safety Mike Davis.
44. He was fired on Oct. 22, 1984, the day after the Browns lost on a last-second field goal in Cincinnati to drop to 1-7 on the year. The loss to the rival Bengals, 1-6 entering the game, was one of many close defeats that the Browns could very well have won that season.
45. Defensive coordinator Marty Schottenheimer.
46. He played for the Buffalo Bills from 1965-68 and the Boston Patriots in 1969 and '70.
47. The University of Pittsburgh.
48. Morten Andersen of the New Orleans Saints.
49. They won four and lost four.
50. Three. They won the division in 1985 with an 8-8 record, 1986 with a 12-4 record, and 1987 with a 10-5 mark.
51. 44-27 (.620).
52. 2-4.
53. Schottenheimer, who had run the offense himself in 1988, apparently did not want the team to hire an offensive coordinator. Team majority owner and president Art Modell, on the other hand, evidently felt the offensive coordinator duties were too much for Schottenheimer to handle along with the head coaching chores. The two agreed to part ways following the '88 season, and Schottenheimer went on to become head coach of the Kansas City Chiefs.
54. Bud Carson.
55. The famed "Steel Curtain" defense of the Pittsburgh Steelers.
56. The New York Jets.

57. The Pittsburgh Steelers. The Browns creamed Carson's former team, 51-0, on Sept. 10, 1989, in Three Rivers Stadium.
58. The New York Jets. The Browns defeated Carson's former team, 38-24, on Sept. 17, 1989, in Cleveland Stadium.
59. The Browns finished 9-6-1 (.594) and won the AFC Central Division title in 1989. It was an up-and-down year for the team as they started 3-1, fell to 3-3, improved to 7-3, then dropped to 7-6-1 before winning their last two games in thrilling fashion.
60. The Browns defeated the Buffalo Bills in a 34-30 nailbiter.
61. The Broncos led by only three, 24-21.
62. The Buffalo Bills. The Browns absorbed their worst shutout loss - and worst home defeat - ever in a 42-0 whitwashing.
63. Assistant coach Jim Shofner. The Browns won just a single game under Shofner, a 13-10 triumph over the Falcons on Dec. 16 at home.
64. New York Giants defensive coordinator Bill Belichick.
65. Safety Eric Turner out of UCLA.
66. The Dallas Cowboys.
67. 0-6.
68. Bernie Kosar.
69. With the Browns *leading* the Vikings, 13-3, in the third quarter, Belichick inexplicably replaced quarterback Mike Tomczak with a guy named Todd Philcox. The Browns lost, 17-13.
70. 204.
71. The New England Patriots.
72. The Pittsburgh Steelers.
73. With the Browns trailing, 31-10, with seconds to go in the game and his team on the Chargers' 23-yard line, Belichick called on kicker Matt Stover to attempt a 40-yard field goal. Stover connected as time expired, prompting one member of the Cleveland media to remark that was the first time he had ever seen a *losing* coach run up the score.
74. 3-1.
75. 36-44 (.450).

3. Browns vs. ...

Browns vs. Giants

1. The Giants dealt the Browns their first-ever shutout, 6-0, on Oct. 1, 1950, in Cleveland Municipal Stadium. The Browns would not be shut out again for 21 years.
2. 8-3.
3. Because Philadelphia was upset by Washington the same day, leaving the Eagles tied for second with the Giants at 7-5.

Cleveland Browns Facts & Trivia

4. George Ratterman.
5. Ray Krouse.
6. 17 yards.
7. Pat Summerall.
8. 24.
9. Thousands of fans swarmed the field. Several attacked Cleveland coach Paul Brown; one of the goal posts was torn down. The game was halted for almost 20 minutes. The mess nearly resulted in a forfeit victory for the Browns.
10. No. The Giants won, 37-21.
11. 52-20.
12. They pummeled the Giants, 45-10.
13. 12-10.
14. Dave Mays.
15. Eric Schubert.
16. 21. The last time the Giants had played in Cleveland was on Sept. 30, 1973, a 12-10 Browns' victory.
17. The Browns shut them out, 10-0, on Nov. 18, 1951, and 7-0 on Oct. 25, 1953, both in New York.
18. Once. New York administered the first-ever shutout on Cleveland by the score of 6-0 on Oct. 1, 1950, in Cleveland.
19. The Browns took the season series 11 times - seven when the teams played twice a year (1951, '53, '54, '57, and from '64-66) and four when they played just one game in a season (1968, '73, '77, and '85).
20. The Giants swept the Browns six times - four when the teams played twice a year (1950, '52, '58, and '59) and twice when they played just one game in a season (1991 and '94).
21. The Browns began the streak with a 42-20 victory on Oct. 25, 1964, and the skein lasted through a 49-40 triumph on Dec. 4, 1966.
22. The Giants began the streak with a 21-17 victory on Nov. 2, 1958, and the streak lasted through a 17-13 win on Nov. 6, 1960.
23. Six. The Browns defeated the Giants, 6-3, in the 1957 season opener on Sept. 29 in Cleveland.
24. Six. The Giants beat the Browns, 6-0, on Oct. 1, 1950, in Cleveland.
25. 34. It happened twice - in a 37-34 loss on Dec. 14, 1952, and a 38-34 defeat on Oct. 29, 1967, both games in New York.
26. 40. The Giants lost to the Browns in a 49-40 track meet on Dec. 4, 1966, in Cleveland.
27. 48 points. The Browns annihilated the Giants, 62-14, on Dec. 6, 1953, in Cleveland.
28. 41 points. The Giants crushed the Browns, 48-7, on Dec. 6, 1959, in Yankee Stadium.
29. 89 points. The Browns outscored the Giants by a 49-40 count on Dec. 4, 1966, in Cleveland.
30. Six points. The Giants defeated the Brown, 6-0, on Oct. 1, 1950, in Cleveland.

Cleveland Browns Facts & Trivia

31. Twice. The teams tied, 35-35, on Nov. 27, 1955, in the Polo Grounds and 7-7 on Dec. 17, 1961, in Yankee Stadium.
32. Twice. The Browns won the first meeting by a score of 8-3 in a 1950 American Conference Playoff game in Cleveland on Dec. 17. The Giants took the second meeting, 10-0, in a 1958 Eastern Conference Playoff in New York on Dec. 21.
33. 25-17-2 (.591).
34. 13-9 (.591).
35. The Browns have scored exactly 1,000 points against New York and surrendered 808.

Browns vs. Steelers

1. The Browns won, 30-17, on Oct. 7, 1950, in Forbes Field in Pittsburgh.
2. The first came on Oct. 17, 1954, in Pittsburgh, a 55-27 drubbing, the second on Oct. 28, 1956, in Cleveland, a 24-16 loss.
3. Bobby Layne.
4. Len Dawson.
5. John Henry Johnson.
6. The "Three Rivers Jinx."
7. Cockroft's winning kick came from 26 yards out.
8. 14-0, Browns (the Steelers came back to win, 31-14).
9. Joe "Turkey" Jones.
10. Larry Anderson.
11. Sipe was picked off six times.
12. Because the Browns experimented with orange numbers on their brown jerseys that night.
13. 27-24.
14. Eric Metcalf, who became the only player in NFL history to return two punts for touchdowns of at least 75 yards in the same game.
15. Twice. The Browns won, 17-7, on Sept. 16, 1985, in Cleveland; the Steelers won, 20-3, on Nov. 13, 1995, in Pittsburgh, the Browns' last Monday night appearance.
16. Once. The Browns beat the Steelers, 19-13, on Dec. 26, 1987, in Three Rivers Stadium, clinching the AFC Central title.
17. The Browns shut out the Steelers, 17-0, and 28-0, respectively, in 1951; 24-0 in 1957; and 51-0 in 1989. The first and third games were in Cleveland, the second and fourth in Pittsburgh.
18. Twice. Pittsburgh bageled the Browns, 30-0, on Dec. 3, 1972, and 35-0, on Dec. 23, 1990, both games coming in Three Rivers Stadium.
19. The Browns have swept the Steelers 15 times. They did it from 1950-53, in 1955, '57, '58, '62, '65, and from '67-69 and '86-88.
20. The Steelers have swept the Browns nine times. They did it in 1959, '74, '75, from '77-79, in '81, '94, and '95.

21. The streak began with a 30-17 victory on Oct. 7, 1950, in Pittsburgh, the first-ever meeting between the teams, and lasted through a 20-16 triumph on Nov. 22, 1953, also in Pittsburgh.

22. Pittsburgh began the streak with a 28-14 victory on Oct. 2, 1977, in Cleveland; the last win in the streak came on Nov. 25, 1979, a 33-30 sudden-death thriller in Three Rivers.

23. 10. The Browns nipped the Steelers, 10-9, on Dec. 19, 1982, in a mudfest in Cleveland.

24. Nine. Pittsburgh beat the Browns, 9-7, on Nov. 10, 1963, in Pitt Stadium on the University of Pittsburgh campus. It marked the only time in the rivalry that the winning team has scored fewer than 10 points.

25. 35. The Browns fell to the Steelers, 51-35, on Oct. 7, 1979, in Cleveland Stadium. The Browns trailed, 27-0, at one point.

26. 31. The Steelers lost to the Browns, 42-31, on Oct. 18, 1969, and 37-31 in overtime on Nov. 23, 1986. Both games were in Cleveland.

27. 51 points. The Browns recorded nine turnovers in a 51-0 season-opening thrashing of the Steelers in Three Rivers Stadium on Sept. 10, 1989.

28. 36 points. Pittsburgh crushed the Browns, 42-6, on Oct. 5, 1975, in Cleveland.

29. 86 points. Pittsburgh outscored Cleveland, 51-35, on Nov. 7, 1979, in Cleveland.

30. 16 points. It happened twice - a 9-7 Steelers victory on Nov. 10, 1963, in Pittsburgh, and a 13-3 Browns triumph on Sept. 9, 1990, in Cleveland.

31. Zero.

32. The Browns and Steelers have met once in postseason play, a 29-9 Steelers victory on Jan. 7, 1995, in Pittsburgh.

33. 52-40 (.565).

34. 33-13 (.717).

35. The Browns have outscored the Steelers, 1,989-1,756.

Browns vs. Bengals

1. Ohio Stadium on the Ohio State University campus in Columbus, Ohio.

2. The Browns won, 30-27, on Oct. 11, 1970, in front of 83,520 spectators in Cleveland Municipal Stadium.

3. The Bengals were 8-1, the Browns 0-9.

4. It came by a resounding score of 45-24 on Oct. 3, 1976.

5. Pete Johnson.

6. Ricky Feacher.

7. Ricky Feacher.

8. Steve Cox.

9. Sam Rutigliano.

10. It was the Browns' only pass of the entire second half.

11. Beginning with a 66-yard bomb from Bernie Kosar to Reggie Langhorne

Cleveland Browns Facts & Trivia

on the first play from scrimmage, the Browns dominated the Bengals and waltzed their way to a 34-3 AFC Central Division-clinching victory.

12. Right defensive end Carl "Big Daddy" Hairston - or was that Carl Lewis? - was on the receiving end of a lateral from Clay Matthews at the Browns' 40-yard line. Matthews had intercepted Boomer Esiason at the Cleveland four. Matthews then ran 36 yards down the sideline before flipping the ball to the 6-foot-3, 260-pound Hairston, who rumbled 40 yards to the Bengals' 20.

13. Eric Thomas.

14. Because he not only returned a 92-yard punt for a touchdown in the Browns' 28-20 season-opening victory in the Queen City, but six games later did it again, this time a 73-yard punt return for a score in Cleveland's 37-13 triumph in Cleveland Stadium.

15. It occurred on Dec. 9, 1972, in Cincinnati. The Browns won the crucial contest, 27-24, when linebacker Billy Andrews intercepted Bengals quarterback Virgil Carter in the end zone with little time left.

16. The first one was on Sept. 15, 1983, in Cleveland in front of 79,700 fans; the Browns won, 17-7, in a game highlighted by Ozzie Newsome's sensational, diving 19-yard touchdown reception from Brian Sipe that gave the Browns a 7-0 first-quarter lead. Three years later, almost to the day, on Sept. 18, 1986, again in Cleveland, the Bengals easily won what was hyped as the "Bernie (Kosar) vs. Boomer (Esiason) Show," 30-13, in front of 78,779 spectators.

17. 1987. The Browns blanked the Bengals, 34-0, in Riverfront Stadium on Oct. 18 in a game dominated by the Browns due largely to the fact that a number of regular players returned to the Cleveland lineup, unlike Bengals players, for the players' strike-marred game.

18. Once. Cincinnati handed the Browns a 21-0 defeat in Cleveland Stadium on Dec. 3, 1989.

19. Seven. The Browns swept their archrivals from the south in 1971, '72, '80, '87, and from '93-95.

20. Six. The Bengals swept the Browns in 1974, '81, '82, '84, '89, and '90 (the Bengals won the only meeting in '82).

21. The Browns won seven straight games from the Bengals beginning with a 37-21 victory on Dec. 6, 1992, in Cleveland, through a 26-10 triumph on Dec. 17, 1995, also in Cleveland (and the last home game for the Browns).

22. The streaks lasted from Dec. 9, 1973-Sept. 21, 1975; Oct. 23, 1983-Nov. 10, 1985; and Sept. 25, 1989-Dec. 30, 1990.

23. 13. The Browns defeated the Bengals, 13-3, on Sept. 18, 1977, in Cincinnati and 13-10 in overtime on Sept. 10, 1978, in Cleveland.

24. 10. The Bengals beat the Browns, 10-7, on Nov. 6, 1977, in Cleveland.

25. 24. The Browns twice scored 24 points while losing to the Bengals - 34-24 on Oct. 13, 1974, and 45-24 on Oct. 3, 1976, both in Cleveland.

26. 27. It happened three times - a 30-27 loss on Oct. 11, 1970, a 31-27 defeat on Dec. 5, 1971, and a 28-27 loss on Oct. 21, 1979. All three games were in Cleveland.

27. 34 points. The Browns routed the Bengals, 34-0, in a game the Browns won largely due to the fact that several regular Browns returned to action for the strike-marred contest, unlike Bengals players.
28. 32 points. Cincinnati routed the Browns, 48-16, in the 1978 season finale on Dec. 17 in Riverfront Stadium, a game the Browns trailed just 24-16 in the third quarter.
29. 69 points. The Bengals dominated the Browns, 45-24, on Oct. 3, 1976, in Cleveland.
30. 16 points. In the 1977 season opener in Cincinnati on Sept. 18, the Browns surprised the Bengals, 13-3.
31. Zero.
32. Zero.
33. 27-24 (.529).
34. 17-8 (.680).
35. The Browns have scored 1,052 points against the Bengals and surrendered 1,053.

Browns vs. AAFC/Rest of NFL

1. The Browns won, 44-0.
2. The Brooklyn Dodgers. The Browns routed the Dodgers, 66-14, in the 1946 season finale on Dec. 8 in Ebbets Field as nine different Browns scored touchdowns.
3. The New York Yankees. The Browns beat the New Yorkers, 14-9, on Dec. 22, 1946, in Cleveland and 14-3 on Dec. 14, 1947, in New York.
4. Mac Speedie.
5. 8-0.
6. The Browns were a perfect 6-0 against the Colts from 1947-49.
7. The Buffalo Bills.
8. The Browns defeated the San Francisco 49ers, 21-7, in front of just 22,550 fans in Cleveland Municipal Stadium.
9. The Los Angeles Dons and San Francisco 49ers.
10. The Brooklyn-New York Yankees. Speedie achieved his feat by way of 11 receptions in a 31-0 triumph in Yankee Stadium.
11. The Philadelphia Eagles. The Browns stunned the two-time defending champions, 35-10, on Sept. 16, 1950, in Philadelphia.
12. 369.
13. The Browns defeated the Los Angeles Rams, 30-28, on Dec. 24, 1950, in front of only 29,751 fans in Cleveland Municipal Stadium.
14. Dub Jones.
15. The Detroit Lions.
16. The Philadelphia Eagles.
17. It occurred on Nov. 4, 1956. The Browns won, 24-7.
18. The Chicago Cardinals.
19. A team-record 237 (which he would duplicate four years later against

Cleveland Browns Facts & Trivia

the Philadelphia Eagles).
20. The Detroit Lions. The Lions blasted the Browns, 59-14, on Dec. 29 in Briggs Stadium.
21. Jim Brown.
22. The Chicago Bears.
23. The St. Louis Cardinals.
24. The Baltimore Colts.
25. The Packers beat the Browns, 23-12, in Lambeau Field.
26. The Dallas Cowboys. Dallas blew the Browns out, 52-14, on Christmas Eve 1967 in the Cotton Bowl, but the Browns won the last two - 31-20 on Dec. 21, 1968, in Cleveland and 38-14 on Dec. 28, 1969, in Dallas.
27. 34-0.
28. The Minnesota Vikings. Both games were in Metropolitan Stadium in Bloomington, Minn.
29. The New York Jets. The Browns won, 31-21.
30. The Washington Redskins.
31. Frank Pitts.
32. Fair Hooker.
33. 7-3.
34. Greg Pruitt.
35. Brian Sipe.
36. The New England Patriots.
37. The Seattle Seahawks. The Browns lost, 20-19, despite 259 rushing yards, most of which came from Greg Pruitt (127) and Cleo Miller (98).
38. Dan Pastorini.
39. The New York Jets. The game was in Shea Stadium.
40. It broke a string of 154 passes without an interception by Staubach.
41. Ahmad Rashad.
42. Mike Davis.
43. The San Diego Chargers.
44. San Francisco. The Browns entered the game 4-6, the 49ers 8-2.
45. Yes.
46. Harry Holt.
47. 3-12 (.200).
48. It was the team's second straight shutout, the first time the Browns posted consecutive bagels in 32 seasons (they had disposed of Tampa Bay, 20-0, the week before).
49. Morten Andersen of the Saints.
50. 8-7 (.533).
51. Ron Davenport.
52. The Chicago Bears.
53. 10 points. The Browns were down, 20-10, with 4:14 to go in the game when the Miracle on West Third Street occurred.
54. He took a "drive" from Northeast Ohio to Southern California.
55. The Atlanta Falcons.
56. The Buffalo Bills.

57. Jeremiah Castille.
58. Lloyd Burruss.
59. The Houston Oilers and the Houston Oilers.
60. The Buffalo Bills.
61. The Buffalo Bills.
62. The Atlanta Falcons. The Browns barely won, 13-10, on Dec. 16 at home.
63. 30-21 (.588).
64. 32-30.
65. Eric Metcalf did the honors. He had three rushing touchdowns and one touchdown reception.
66. 4-6 (.400).
67. Michael Jackson.
68. The Browns are 9-3 (.750) against the Saints.
69. 1-3 (.250).
70. 32-9-1 (.774).
71. Mark Rypien.
72. Jay Novacek.
73. 6-8 (.429).
74. 5-0.
75. 0-2.

4. Individual Records

Service

1. Lou Groza holds the record with 21 seasons of service (1946-59, '61-67).
2. Clay Matthews played 16 straight seasons from 1978-93.
3. Lou Groza played in 268 games from 1946-59 and '61-67.
4. Dieken played in 203 straight games from his rookie year of 1971 through his final season of 1984.
5. Doug Dieken started 194 consecutive games from 1971-84.

Scoring

1. Lou Groza scored 1,608 points from 1946-59 and '61-67.
2. Jim Brown with 126 points in 1965.
3. 36 points. Dub Jones did it by scoring six touchdowns on Nov. 25, 1951, against the Chicago Bears in Cleveland.
4. Lou Groza holds the record with 84 points scored in 1946.
5. Lou Groza scored in 107 straight games from 1950-59.
6. He scored 126 from 1957-65.

7. Jim Brown scored 21 in 1965.

8. Dub Jones scored six touchdowns (four rushing, two receiving) in the Browns' 42-21 rout of the Chicago Bears on Nov. 25, 1951, in Cleveland Municipal Stadium.

9. Jim Brown (1957), Kevin Mack (1985), and Eric Metcalf (1989) each had 10.

10. Jim Brown did it three times - he scored 108 in 1958 and '62 and 126 in '65.

11. Jim Brown scored at least one touchdown in 10 consecutive games in 1965.

12. Lou Groza with 834 from 1946-59 and '61-67.

13. Lou Groza attempted 52 extra points in both 1948 and '66.

14. Lou Groza with eight on Dec. 6, 1953, against the New York Giants.

15. 810. Lou Groza totaled that amount from 1946-59 and '61-67.

16. Lou Groza made good on 51 PAT's in 1948 and '66.

17. The New York Giants. The Browns routed the New Yorkers, 62-14, in Cleveland.

18. Lou Groza connected on 138 straight extra point attempts from 1963-66.

19. Lou Groza with 264 from 1946-59 and '61-67.

20. Matt Stover had 29 field goals in 1995.

21. Don Cockroft had five field goals on Oct. 19, 1975, in a 16-15 loss at Denver, and Matt Stover connected on five treys in a 29-26 overtime win in Cincinnati on Oct. 29, 1995.

22. Lou Groza attempted 481 field goals in his career from 1946-59 and '61-67.

23. Lou Groza attempted 33 field goals in 1952 and '64; Matt Stover had 33 field goal tries in 1995.

24. Don Cockroft and Matt Stover. Cockroft attempted seven field goals on Oct. 19, 1975, at Denver, and Stover attempted seven on Oct. 25, 1992, at New England.

25. Steve Cox nailed a 60-yarder on Oct. 21, 1984, in a 12-9 loss to the Bengals in Cincinnati.

26. Lou Groza went 14 games with at least one field goal from 1950-51.

27. Matt Stover connected on 23 straight treys from 1994-95.

28. 80.6 on 108 field goals out of 134 attempts.

29. Matt Stover was successful 92.9 percent of the time in 1994 when he connected on 26 of 28 field goal tries.

30. Walter Johnson had two safeties from 1965-76.

31. Seventeen times a player recorded one safety in a game.

Rushing

1. Jim Brown holds the record with 2,359 attempts from 1957-65.

2. Jim Brown with 305 in 1961.

Cleveland Browns Facts & Trivia

3. Jim Brown carried the ball 37 times on Oct. 4, 1959, against the Chicago Cardinals.

4. 12,312.

5. 1963.

6. Jim Brown gained 237 yards twice - on Nov. 24, 1957, against the Los Angeles Rams and on Nov. 19, 1961, against the Philadelphia Eagles. Both games were in Cleveland.

7. Jim Brown with seven. He topped the 1,000-yard mark from 1958-61 and '63-65.

8. Bobby Mitchell had a 90-yarder for a score in a 31-17 victory over the Washington Redskins on Nov. 15, 1959, in the nation's capitol.

9. 58.

10. Nine.

11. Jim Brown. He did it in six straight games in 1958. He began the streak with a 171-yard game on Sept. 28 in a season-opening victory over the Rams in Los Angeles; the streak lasted through a 113-yard performance in a Week 6 loss at home to the Giants. The streak came to an end on Nov. 9 when Brown gained 83 yards in a 30-10 home loss to the Lions.

12. Jim Brown with 106 from 1957-65.

13. Jim Brown did it twice - in 1958 and '65.

14. He did it in a 38-31 victory over the Colts in Baltimore on Nov. 1, 1959.

15. Leroy Kelly. Kelly rushed for at least one touchdown nine straight games in 1968.

16. Marion Motley averaged 5.6 yards per rush from 1946-53.

17. Jim Brown averaged 6.4 yards per rush in 1963 on 291 carries for 1,863 yards.

18. Marion Motley averaged 17.1 yards per rush on 11 carries for 188 yards in the Browns' 45-7 rout of the Steelers in Cleveland on Oct. 29, 1950.

Passing

1. Brian Sipe had 3,439 pass attempts from 1974-83.

2. 1981.

3. Brian Sipe had 57 pass attempts in the Browns' 44-14 loss to the San Diego Chargers in the opening Monday night game of the 1981 season.

4. Brian Sipe completed 1,944 passes from 1974-83.

5. Brian Sipe with 337 in 1980.

6. Sipe did it at home against the San Diego Chargers on Dec. 5, 1982. The Browns lost, though, 30-13.

7. Bernie Kosar completed 15 straight passes from Oct. 29, 1989, against Houston at home through Nov. 5, 1989, at Tampa Bay.

8. Otto Graham completed a screen pass to Mac Speedie that went for a 99-yard touchdown in a 28-7 Browns win at Buffalo on Nov. 2, 1947.

9. Brian Sipe threw for 23,713 yards from 1974-83.

10. Brian Sipe with 4,132 yards in 1980.

Cleveland Browns Facts & Trivia

11. Brian Sipe with 444 yards in a 42-28 home win over Baltimore on Oct. 25, 1981.

12. Otto Graham with 174 from 1946-55.

13. Brian Sipe. He did it in 1980.

14. Otto Graham had six touchdown passes in a 61-14 rout of the Los Angeles Dons on Oct. 14, 1949.

15. Frank Ryan passed for at least one touchdown in 23 consecutive games from the final game of the 1965 season through the eighth game of the '67 season.

16. Brian Sipe was intercepted 149 times from 1974-83.

17. Brian Sipe was picked off 26 times in 1979.

18. The Pittsburgh Steelers - in a 32-10 loss on Nov. 22, 1981, in Cleveland and a 44-17 defeat on Oct. 16, 1983, in Pittsburgh.

19. Bernie Kosar attempted 308 straight passes without an interception from 1990-91.

20. Bernie Kosar had a 2.6 interception rate (81 interceptions in 3,150 pass attempts) from 1985-93.

21. 1991. He threw just nine interceptions in 494 pass attempts.

22. Bernie Kosar. Kosar completed 58.8 percent of his passes (1,853 completions out of 3,150 attempts) from 1985-93.

23. 1992. Kosar completed 103 out of 155 pass attempts.

24. Vinny Testaverde. The former University of Miami Heisman Trophy winner completed a remarkable 21 of 23 pass attempts in a 42-14 rout of the Rams in Los Angeles on Dec. 26, 1993. Remarkably, both of Testaverde's incompletions were *intentional*.

Receiving

1. Ozzie Newsome caught 662 passes from 1978-90.

2. 1983 and '84.

3. Newsome caught 14 balls for 191 yards at home against the New York Jets on Oct. 14, 1984. The Browns lost, by the way, 24-20.

4. Eric Metcalf caught 54 passes in 1989.

5. Ozzie Newsome had at least one reception in 150 straight games from 1979-89.

6. Ozzie Newsome with 7,980 from 1978-90.

7. Webster Slaughter. The San Diego State product had 1,236 receiving yards in 1989.

8. Mac Speedie with 228 on Nov. 20, 1949, in a 31-0 victory over Brooklyn-New York.

9. Ozzie Newsome with six (1979-81, '83-85).

10. Mac Speedie turned a screen pass from Otto Graham into a 99-yard scoring play on Nov. 2, 1947, against Buffalo.

11. Gary Collins totaled 70 touchdown receptions from 1962-71.

12. Gary Collins with 13 in 1963.

13. Dante Lavelli was on the receiving end of four touchdown passes in the Browns' 61-14 rout of the Los Angeles Dons on Oct. 14, 1949, in Los Angeles.
14. Gary Collins caught a touchdown pass in seven straight games from Week 13 in 1963 to Week 5 in 1964.
15. Ray Renfro averaged 19.6 yards per catch for his 281 receptions from 1952-63.
16. Clarence Weathers averaged 28.1 yards per catch in 1985 on 16 receptions for 449 yards.
17. Rich Kreitling averaged 52.3 yards per catch on Oct. 2, 1960, against Pittsburgh on three catches for 157 yards.
18. Ray Renfro (1952-63) and Webster Slaughter (1986-91) with 14.
19. Gary Collins (1965), Milt Morin (1968), and Webster Slaughter (1989).
20. Paul Warfield in 1964 and Derrick Alexander in 1994.

Interceptions

1. Thom Darden intercepted 45 passes from 1972-74 and '76-81.
2. Tom Colella and Thom Darden with 10. Colella did it in 1946, Darden in 1978.
3. Tommy James. He did it on Nov. 15, 1950, against the Chicago Cardinals and on Nov. 1, 1953, against Washington.
4. Thom Darden with 820 from 1972-74 and '76-81.
5. Bernie Parrish had 238 in 1960.
6. Bernie Parrish had 115 interception return yards off two picks on Dec. 11, 1960, against the Bears.
7. Najee Mustafaa returned one 97 yards for a touchdown on Oct. 10, 1993, at home against Miami.
8. Warren Lahr with five from 1950-59 (note: Lahr did play in 1949 but had no touchdowns off interceptions).
9. Warren Lahr. He did it in 1950 and '51.
10. Bobby Franklin with two against the Chicago Bears on Dec. 11, 1960.
11. Oliver Davis averaged 21.7 yards per return off 11 interceptions from 1977-80.
12. Bernie Parrish averaged 39.7 yards per return off six interceptions in 1960.
13. Bernie Parrish averaged 57.5 yards per return off two interceptions on Dec. 11, 1960, against the Bears.
14. Ben Davis intercepted at least one pass in seven consecutive games in 1968.

Punting

1. Don Cockroft with 651 from 1968-80.
2. Bryan Wagner with 97 in 1989.
3. Horace Gillom punted a dozen times on Dec. 3, 1950, against the Eagles and Bryan Wagner did it on Nov. 19, 1989, against the Chiefs.
4. Horace Gillom averaged 43.1 yards per punt on 492 attempts from 1947-56.
5. Gary Collins averaged 46.7 yards per punt on 65 attempts in 1965.
6. Horace Gillom. Gillom averaged 55.4 yards per punt on seven attempts in the Browns' 28-0 home win over Baltimore on Sept. 21, 1947.
7. 80 yards.
8. Brian Hansen with 63 from 1991-93.
9. Bryan Wagner placed 32 punts inside the opponents' 20-yard line in 1989.

Punt Returns

1. Gerald McNeil with 161 from 1986-89.
2. Gerald McNeil with 49 in 1989.
3. Seven. It has been done six times.
4. Gerald McNeil had 1,545 punt return yards from 1986-89.
5. Gerald McNeil had 496 punt return yards in 1989.
6. Eric Metcalf had 166 punt return yards against the Pittsburgh Steelers on Oct. 24, 1993.
7. Eric Metcalf. Metcalf returned a punt 92 yards for a touchdown on Sept. 4, 1994, against the Bengals in Cincinnati.
8. Greg Pruitt averaged 11.8 yards per punt return on 56 attempts from 1973-81.
9. Tom Colella averaged 21.5 yards per return on eight attempts in 1946.
10. Eric Metcalf averaged 28.8 yards per punt return off four attempts on Sept. 4, 1994, at Cincinnati.
11. Eric Metcalf returned five punts for touchdowns from 1989-94.
12. Metcalf. He did it in 1993 and '94. Kelly did it in 1965.
13. 91 and 75 yards respectively - both for touchdowns. The second was the game-winner with 2:05 left.

Kickoff Returns

1. Dino Hall returned 151 kickoffs from 1979-83.
2. Eric Metcalf with 52 in 1990.
3. Dino Hall with nine against Pittsburgh on Oct. 7, 1979.
4. Dino Hall with 3,185 from 1979-83.

5. Eric Metcalf with 1,052 in 1990.

6. Dino Hall had 172 kickoff return yards on Oct. 7, 1979.

7. Carl Ward returned a kickoff 104 yards for a touchdown on Nov. 26, 1967, in a 42-37 home win over Washington.

8. Greg Pruitt averaged 26.3 yards per return from 1973-81.

9. Billy Reynolds averaged 29.5 yards per return in 1954.

10. Gerald McNeil averaged 48.3 yards per return off three attempts on Oct. 5, 1986, at Pittsburgh, including a 100-yarder for a score late in the first half.

11. Bobby Mitchell returned three kickoffs for touchdowns from 1958-61.

12. 1990.

13. One. It has been done 11 times.

Combined Net Yards

1. Jim Brown with 2,650 from 1957-65.

2. Jim Brown with 353 in 1961.

3. Jim Brown and Mike Pruitt each had 39 attempts - Brown on Oct. 4, 1959, at the Chicago Cardinals and Pruitt on Dec. 3, 1981, at Houston.

4. Jim Brown had 15,459 combined net yards from 1957-65.

5. Jim Brown gained 2,131 all-purpose yards in 1963.

6. Jim Brown had 313 combined net yards on Nov. 19, 1961, against the Eagles.

7. Ozzie Newsome averaged 11.9 yards per gain on 8,147 combined net yards off 682 attempts from 1978-90.

8. Eric Metcalf averaged 9.27 yards per gain on 1,752 all-purpose yards off 189 attempts in 1990.

9. Ken Carpenter averaged 15.9 yards per gain on 239 combined net yards off 15 attempts on Nov. 30, 1952, in a 48-24 rout of the Redskins in Washington.

Fumbles

1. Brian Sipe fumbled the ball 62 times from 1974-83.

2. Paul McDonald had 16 fumbles in 1984.

3. Otto Graham did it on Oct. 25, 1953, against the Giants, Ken Brown on Oct. 8, 1972, against the Chiefs, and Paul McDonald on Dec. 20, 1981, against the Seahawks.

4. Len Ford recovered 19 opponents' fumbles from 1950-57.

5. Len Ford and Mike Johnson. Ford did it in 1954, Johnson in 1992.

6. Two (it has been done 22 times).

7. Vince Costello (1957-66), Walter Johnson (1965-76), David Grayson (1987-90), and Stevon Moore (1992-95) each did it twice.

8. Don Paul returned a fumble 89 yards for a touchdown in a 24-0 Browns victory over Pittsburgh on Nov. 10, 1957, in Cleveland.

Quarterback Sacks

1. Clay Matthews with 76.5 from 1978-93.
2. Bill Glass with 14.5 in 1965.
3. Jerry Sherk on Nov. 14, 1976, at home against Philadelphia and Mack Mitchell on Nov. 20, 1977, in New York against the Giants.
4. Bill Glass had at least one sack in seven straight games in 1966.
5. Clay Matthews with 568 from 1978-93.
6. Reggie Camp with 125.5 in 1984.
7. Reggie Camp had 39 sack yards on Nov. 25, 1984, against the Falcons in Atlanta.
8. Mack Mitchell with eight in 1975.
9. Chip Banks had three quarterback sacks in the opening game of the 1982 season on Sept. 12 in Seattle, a 21-7 Browns win.

5. Individual Records (Postseason)

Scoring

1. Lou Groza with 83 from 1946-59 and '61-67.
2. 18. Marion Motley did it on Dec. 19, 1948, at home against Buffalo in the AAFC Championship game, Otto Graham did it on Dec. 26, 1954, at home against Detroit in the NFL Championship game, and Gary Collins did it on Dec. 27, 1964, at home against Baltimore in the NFL title game.
3. Lou Groza scored in 13 straight games from the AAFC Championship game on Dec. 22, 1946, against the New York Yankees through the NFL Championship game on Dec. 29, 1957, against the Detroit Lions.
4. Otto Graham and Earnest Byner with six apiece.
5. Three. Marion Motley did it in the 1948 AAFC Championship game against Buffalo, Otto Graham did it in the 1954 NFL Championship game against Detroit, and Gary Collins did it in the 1964 NFL title game against Baltimore.
6. Bo Scott holds the record with two. Scott scored a pair of two-yard runs in the Browns' 38-14 destruction of the Cowboys in the Eastern Conference title game on Dec. 28, 1969, in the Cotton Bowl.
7. Edgar "Special Delivery" Jones scored in four consecutive games from

the 1947 AAFC title game against New York through the 1949 AAFC title contest against San Francisco.

8. Lou Groza attempted 44 extra points from 1946-59 and '61-67.

9. Eight by Lou Groza in the Browns' 56-10 rout of the Lions in the NFL Championship game on Dec. 26, 1954, in Cleveland Municipal Stadium.

10. 44 by Lou Groza from 1946-59 and '61-67.

11. Lou Groza connected on eight points after touchdown in the 1954 NFL title game against Detroit.

12. Lou Groza made good on 44 straight extra point tries from Dec. 22, 1946, through Dec. 24, 1967 (Groza retired for the 1959 season before returning in 1960).

13. Lou Groza was successful on 13 field goal tries from 1946-59 and '61-67.

14. Three. Lou Groza did it in the Browns' 17-16 loss to the Lions in the NFL Championship game on Dec. 27, 1953, in Detroit, Mark Moseley did it in the Browns' 23-20 double overtime win over the New York Jets in an AFC Divisional Playoff game on Jan. 3, 1987, in Cleveland, and Matt Bahr did it in the Browns' 24-23 defeat to Houston in the AFC Wild Card game on Dec. 24, 1988, in Cleveland.

15. Lou Groza attempted a total of 17 field goals from 1946-59 and '61-67 (note: does not include portion of game against New York Giants on Dec. 17, 1950).

16. Mark Moseley attempted six field goals in the Browns' 23-20 double overtime triumph over the Jets in the AFC Divisional Playoffs on Jan. 3, 1987, in Cleveland Stadium (note: does not include portion of game against New York Giants on Dec. 17, 1950).

17. 52 yards, by two players Lou Groza and Matt Bahr. Coincidentally, both treys occurred in the Los Angeles Memorial Coliseum - but against two different teams. Groza's kick came on Dec. 23, 1951, in the Browns' 24-17 loss to the Rams in the NFL Championship game; Bahr equaled "The Toe's" feat 31 year later, on Jan. 8, 1983, in the Browns' 27-10 loss to the Raiders in an AFC First-Round Playoff game.

18. Matt Bahr made at least one field goal in four straight games from Jan. 9, 1988, against Indianapolis through Jan. 6, 1990, against Buffalo.

19. Lou Groza connected on nine straight field goals from Dec. 23, 1951, against the Rams in Los Angeles in the NFL title game through Jan. 2, 1966, against the Packers in Green Bay in the NFL title contest.

20. Matt Bahr made eight of 10 field goal tries.

21. The Browns have scored on two safeties in their postseason history. The first occurred on Dec. 17, 1950, in Cleveland Municipal Stadium when Bill Willis tackled Giants quarterback Charlie Conerly in the end zone. The second one was a team safety, which occurred on Jan. 17, 1988, in Mile High Stadium in Denver when Broncos punter Mike Horan gave up an intentional two-pointer late in the game by stepping out of the end zone.

Rushing

1. Kevin Mack had 107 rushing attempts from 1985-93.

2. Jim Brown with 27 in the Browns' 27-0 victory over the Baltimore Colts in the 1964 NFL Championship game (note: does not include game against Buffalo on Dec. 4, 1949).

3. Marion Motley with 512 (note: does not include games against Buffalo on Dec. 4, 1949, New York Giants on Dec. 17, 1950, and Los Angeles on Dec. 24, 1950).

4. Earnest Byner rushed for 161 yards in the Browns' 24-21 loss to the Miami Dolphins in an AFC Divisional Playoff on Jan. 4, 1986, in the Orange Bowl.

5. Marion Motley, Harry Jagade, and Earnest Byner. Motley gained 109 yards on 13 carries against the Yankees in the AAFC Championship game on Dec. 14, 1947, in New York, and accumulated 133 yards on 14 carries against the Bills in the AAFC title game a year later in Cleveland. Jagade accomplished his marks against the Detroit Lions both times - in the 1952 NFL title game in Cleveland and in the 1953 NFL title game in Detroit. Amazingly, Jagade gained 104 yards on 15 carries in both games! Byner's feats both occurred in the AFC Divisional Playoffs. His first was a 161-yard performance (on 16 rushes) against the Miami Dolphins on Jan. 4, 1986, in the Orange Bowl. Two years later, on Jan. 9, 1988, he racked up 122 yards against the Indianapolis Colts in Cleveland (note: does not include game against Los Angeles on Dec. 24, 1950).

6. Marion Motley and Harry Jagade. Motley did it against New York (109 yards) in the 1947 AAFC Championship game and against Buffalo (133) in the 1948 AAFC title contest. Both of Jagade's gems were against the Lions in NFL Championship games - the first in the 1952 game and the second in the 1953 affair. Eerily, Jagade's stats for each game read: 15 rushes, 104 rushing yards.

7. Otto Graham scored six rushing postseason touchdowns from 1946-55.

8. Three. Marion Motley scored on runs of 29, 31, and five yards against Buffalo in the 1948 AAFC Championship game, and Otto Graham had two one-yard scores and a five-yard touchdown against Detroit in the 1954 NFL Championship game.

9. Edgar Jones scored one rushing touchdown in four straight postseason games from the AAFC title game on Dec. 14, 1947, in New York, through the AAFC title contest on Dec. 11, 1949, at home against the 49ers.

10. Marion Motley averaged an incredible 8.7 yards per carry on 512 yards via 59 carries from 1946-53 (note: does not include games against Buffalo on Dec. 4, 1949, New York Giants on Dec. 17, 1950, and Los Angeles on Dec. 24, 1950).

11. Earnest Byner averaged 10.1 yards per carry (16 carries, 161 yards) in the Browns' 24-21 defeat to the Miami Dolphins in an AFC Divisional Playoff game on Jan. 4, 1986, in the Orange Bowl.

Passing

1. Otto Graham with 301 from 1946-55.
2. Bernie Kosar with 64 against the New York Jets in the AFC Divisional Playoffs on Jan. 3, 1987, in Cleveland.
3. Otto Graham completed 159 passes from 1946-55.
4. Bernie Kosar completed 33 in 64 attempts in Cleveland's 23-20 double overtime win over the Jets in an AFC Divisional Playoff game on Jan. 3, 1987, in Cleveland.
5. Otto Graham with 2,001 from 1946-55.
6. Bernie Kosar passed for 489 yards in an AFC Divisional Playoff against the Jets on Jan. 3, 1987, in Cleveland.
7. Bernie Kosar threw 15 touchdown passes from 1985-93.
8. Otto Graham tossed four touchdown passes in the Browns' 30-28 victory over the Los Angeles Rams in the 1950 NFL Championship game in Cleveland Municipal Stadium.
9. Bernie Kosar passed for at least one touchdown in five straight postseason games from an AFC Divisional Playoff against Miami on Jan. 4, 1986, through the AFC Championship game against Denver on Jan. 17, 1988.
10. Otto Graham was intercepted 17 times from 1946-55.
11. Mike Phipps was picked off five times during the Browns' 20-14 loss to the Dolphins in an AFC Divisional Playoff on Dec. 24, 1972, in the Orange Bowl.
12. Paul McDonald with a zero interception rate (he threw no interceptions in 37 pass attempts in an AFC First-Round Playoff game against the Raiders in Los Angeles on Jan. 8, 1983).
13. Bernie Kosar with a 56.2 completion percentage on 146 completions in 260 pass attempts from 1985-93.
14. Bernie Kosar completed 69 percent of his passes on 20 completions in 29 attempts in the Browns' 34-30 triumph over Buffalo in an AFC Divisional Playoff on Jan. 6, 1990, in Cleveland.

Receiving

1. Dante Lavelli with 30 from 1946-56 (note: does not include game against New York Giants on Dec. 17, 1950, and portion of games against Buffalo on Dec. 4, 1949, and Los Angeles on Dec. 24, 1950).
2. Paul Warfield had eight receptions in the Browns' 38-14 victory over the Dallas Cowboys in the Eastern Conference title game on Dec. 28, 1969, in the Cotton Bowl in Dallas (note: does not include game against Los Angeles on Dec. 24, 1950).
3. Dante Lavelli, Mac Speedie, and Webster Slaughter. Lavelli and Speedie did it in the AAFC Championship game against the New York Yankees on Dec. 22, 1946; Slaughter did it in an AFC Divisional Playoff

against the New York Jets on Jan. 3, 1987 (note: does not include game against Los Angeles on Dec. 24, 1950).

4. Dante Lavelli with 526 from 1946-56 (note: does not include game against New York Giants on Dec. 17, 1950, and portion of games against Buffalo on Dec. 4, 1949, and Los Angeles on Dec. 24, 1950).

5. Gary Collins with 130 yards in the 1964 NFL Championship game against Baltimore on Dec. 27, 1964, in Cleveland Municipal Stadium (note: does not include games against Buffalo on Dec. 4, 1949, and Los Angeles on Dec. 24, 1950).

6. Dante Lavelli, Gary Collins, and Webster Slaughter.

7. Gary Collins with three in the Browns' 27-0 upset of the Colts in the 1964 NFL Championship game in Cleveland.

8. Webster Slaughter with three from the AFC title game in Denver on Jan. 17, 1988, through an AFC Divisional Playoff at home against Buffalo on Jan. 6, 1990.

9. Darrel Brewster averaged 20.3 yards per reception on 11 catches for 223 yards from 1952-58 (note: does not include game against New York Giants on Dec. 17, 1950, and portion of games against Buffalo on Dec. 4, 1949, and Los Angeles on Dec. 24, 1950).

10. Paul Warfield averaged 33 yards per reception on three catches for 99 yards in the Browns' 52-14 loss to the Dallas Cowboys in the Eastern Conference title game on Dec. 24, 1967, in Dallas (note: does not include games against Buffalo on Dec. 4, 1949, and Los Angeles on Dec. 24, 1950).

11. Mac Speedie, Gary Collins, Ricky Feacher, Ozzie Newsome, Earnest Byner, Webster Slaughter, and Michael Jackson.

Punting

1. Horace Gillom totaled 47 punts from 1947-56.

2. Horace Gillom had nine punts during the Browns' 8-3 victory over the New York Giants in an American Conference Playoff on Dec. 17, 1950, in Cleveland Municipal Stadium.

3. Horace Gillom had 1,943 punting yards from 1947-56.

4. Gary Collins averaged 42.5 yards per punt on 14 punts for 595 yards from 1962-71.

5. Steve Cox averaged 48.5 yards per punt (six punts, 291 yards) in Cleveland's 27-10 loss to the Los Angeles Raiders in an AFC First-Round Playoff game on Jan. 8, 1983, in the Memorial Coliseum in Los Angeles.

6. Team Records

Games Won

1. They won 12 games in 1986 (they went 12-4 for a .750 winning percentage).
2. The Browns won 16 straight games from Nov. 27, 1947-Dec. 5, 1948.
3. The Browns won all 14 of their games in 1948.
4. They won 15 straight home games from Oct. 19, 1947-Nov. 6, 1949.
5. The Browns won nine straight road games from Nov. 27, 1947-Dec. 5, 1948.

Games Lost

1. The 1990 team lost 13 games, winning just three, a .188 winning percentage.
2. The Browns lost 11 straight games from Dec. 7, 1974-Nov. 16, 1975.
3. The Browns began the 1975 season with nine straight losses.
4. The Browns lost their final five games of the 1981 season.
5. They lost six straight in 1990, from Sept. 23-Dec. 2.
6. The Browns lost 11 consecutive road affairs from Dec. 7, 1974-Sept. 26, 1976.

Scoring

1. The 1946 Browns scored 423 points.
2. The Browns blasted the Brooklyn Dodgers, 66-14, on Dec. 8, 1946, in Brooklyn.
3. The 1990 Browns gave up 462 points.
4. The Browns were trashed, 58-14, by the Oilers in Houston on Dec. 9, 1990.
5. 140 points. The 1982 Browns did it.
6. The 1946 team yielded just 144 points.
7. 89 points. The Browns defeated the Giants, 49-40, on Oct. 1, 1950.
8. Six. The Browns lost to the Giants, 6-0, on Oct. 1, 1950, and defeated Philadelphia by the same score on Nov. 21, 1954.
9. The 1966 Browns scored 54 touchdowns.
10. Nine. They did it twice - on Oct. 14, 1949, in a 61-14 rout of the Los Angeles Dons and on Dec. 8, 1946, in a 66-14 blowout of the Brooklyn Dodgers. Both were away games.
11. The 1990 Browns had 59 touchdowns scored on them.
12. Eight. It happened twice - in a 55-27 loss at Pittsburgh on Oct. 17,

Cleveland Browns Facts & Trivia

1954, and a 58-14 loss at Houston on Dec. 9, 1990.

13. 1982.

14. They yielded 19 touchdowns in 1950.

15. The Browns went 14 quarters in 1992 without allowing a touchdown.

16. They had 27 rushing touchdowns in 1946.

17. The Browns rushed for six touchdowns on Nov. 24, 1957, against the Rams.

18. The Browns allowed 21 rushing touchdowns in both 1975 and '90.

19. The Browns allowed six rushing touchdowns in a 49-17 home loss to Green Bay on Oct. 15, 1961.

20. The 1982 and '92 Browns scored seven rushing touchdowns.

21. The Browns allowed just four rushing touchdowns in 1954.

22. The Browns and Rams combined for eight rushing touchdowns - the Browns six, the Rams two - on Nov. 24, 1957.

23. The Browns rushed for at least one touchdown in 13 straight games from 1968-69.

24. The 1966 Browns had 33 touchdown passes.

25. The Browns had six touchdown passes against the Los Angeles Dons on Oct. 14, 1949, the New York Giants on Dec. 12, 1964, and the Atlanta Falcons on Oct. 30, 1966.

26. The Browns had seven touchdown passes in 1975.

27. Opponents totaled 32 touchdown passes on the Browns in 1990.

28. The St. Louis Cardinals had six touchdown passes in a 49-13 rout of the Browns on Sept. 26, 1965, in Cleveland.

29. Seven in 1956.

30. The 1946 and '66 Browns connected on 52 extra points.

31. Eight on Dec. 6, 1953, against the Giants and on Nov. 7, 1954, against the Redskins.

32. 17 in 1982.

33. Opponents connected on 56 extra points in 1990.

34. Seven. It has been done four times - on Oct. 17, 1954, against Pittsburgh, Oct. 15, 1961, and Nov. 12, 1967, against Green Bay, and Dec. 9, 1990, against Houston.

35. 17 in 1946.

36. 166. They did it from Oct. 5, 1957-Nov. 2, 1969.

37. The 1986 and '94 Browns were successful on 26 field goals apiece.

38. Five. They did it on Oct. 19, 1975, in a 16-15 loss in Denver and Oct. 29, 1995, in a 29-26 overtime win in Cincinnati.

39. The Browns made two field goals in nine attempts in 1949.

40. Opponents connected on 31 treys in 1993.

41. Four. It has been done 17 times.

42. 1953.

43. Three in 1970.

44. One. It has been done 17 times.

45. Three - in 1974 and '87.

46. Two. The New Orleans Saints did it in a 28-21 victory over the Browns

275

on Sept. 13, 1987, in the Superdome.

47. Four in 1993.

48. Two by the Browns and Seahawks on Nov. 14, 1993, in the Kingdome, a 22-5 Browns loss.

49. Four in 1994.

50. One. It has been done five times - on Sept. 4, 1994, against the Bengals; Sept. 18, 1994, against the Cardinals; Oct. 13, 1994, against the Oilers; Oct. 30, 1994, against the Broncos; and Dec. 9, 1995, against the Vikings.

51. One - in 1994.

52. One - by the Oilers on Oct. 13, 1994, in the Astrodome, an 11-8 Browns triumph.

53. The Browns scored 21 first-quarter points en route to a 38-17 victory over the Dallas Cowboys in the Cotton Bowl on Dec. 3, 1961.

54. 28. They have done it on three occasions - in a 38-24 victory over Cincinnati on Dec. 13, 1987, a 42-31 triumph over Tampa Bay on Nov. 5, 1989, and a 31-0 rout of Indianapolis on Dec. 1, 1991.

55. The Browns tallied 24 third-quarter points in a 62-14 rout of the New York Giants on Dec. 6, 1953.

56. 28 points in a 42-20 victory over the New York Giants on Oct. 25, 1964.

57. 35. The Browns did this in a 42-31 victory in Tampa on Nov. 5, 1989.

58. The Browns have totaled 35 second-half points three times - in a 62-3 trashing of Washington on Nov. 7, 1954, a 42-20 rout of the New York Giants on Oct. 25, 1964, and a 42-21 victory over the Pittsburgh Steelers on Nov. 28, 1965.

59. The Browns scored in 274 straight games from Oct. 7, 1950-Oct. 17, 1971.

60. 20. The Browns rallied for a 49-40 victory over the New York Giants on Dec. 4, 1966, in Cleveland after trailing, 34-14.

61. 23 points. The Browns let a 23-0 lead slip away and lost to the Eagles, 32-30, on Nov. 10, 1991, in Cleveland.

62. 59 points. The Browns wasted the Redskins, 62-3, on Nov. 7, 1954, in Cleveland.

63. 48 points - twice. The Browns were trounced, 55-7, in Green Bay on Nov. 12, 1967, and lost to the tune of 51-3 in Minnesota on Nov. 9, 1969.

First Downs

1. The Browns had 364 first downs in 1981.

2. The Browns totaled 35 first downs in a 37-31 sudden-death victory at home over Pittsburgh on Nov. 23, 1986.

3. 146 in 1946.

4. Cleveland had just one first down on Dec. 3, 1950, at home in a rainstorm against Philadelphia. The Browns won, though, 13-7.

Cleveland Browns Facts & Trivia

5. Opponents tallied 342 first downs against the 1995 Browns.
6. The Steelers piled up 36 first downs in a 33-30 overtime win on Nov. 25, 1979, in Three Rivers Stadium.
7. 147 in 1954.
8. Four. It happened twice - in a 62-3 win over Washington on Nov. 7, 1954, and a 42-13 victory over Houston on Oct. 21, 1973. Both games were at home.
9. The Browns and Steelers totaled 58 first downs on Nov. 25, 1979, in Pittsburgh, a 33-30 Browns overtime loss.
10. The 1963 team rushed for 135 first downs.
11. The Browns rushed for 21 first downs in a 28-21 victory over the Philadelphia Eagles on Dec. 13, 1959, in Philadelphia.
12. The Browns had 62 first downs rushing in 1949.
13. Zero. The Browns had no first downs rushing in a 24-21 victory over the Dallas Cowboys on Dec. 4, 1988, in Cleveland.
14. Browns opponents had 138 first downs rushing in 1983.
15. The Pittsburgh Steelers gained 20 first downs rushing in a 23-7 victory over the Browns on Oct. 10, 1964, in Cleveland.
16. The 1954 Browns gave up only 56 first downs rushing.
17. The Chicago Cardinals had zero first downs rushing on Dec. 7, 1952, and the Houston Oilers had none on Sept. 22, 1974.
18. The 1980 Browns gained 207 first downs through the air.
19. A loss. The Browns were drilled at home, 44-14, by the San Diego Chargers in the opening Monday night game of the 1981 season.
20. The 1946 team had 60.
21. Zero. This occurred on Dec. 3, 1950, against Philadelphia.
22. The 1995 Browns.
23. The Miami Dolphins had 26 first downs passing in a 38-31 Monday night victory on Dec. 12, 1988, in Miami.
24. The 1946 team yielded just 56.
25. Zero by the Buffalo Bills on Nov. 24, 1974 (the Bills still won, though, 15-10).
26. 37 in 1981.
27. Seven. It was done twice - on Oct. 23, 1977, against the Bills and on Sept. 27, 1981, against the Falcons.
28. Four in 1952.
29. 38. It happened twice - in 1978 and '80.
30. Nine by the Chicago Bears on Nov. 25, 1951, in Cleveland.
31. 10 in 1961.

Rushing

1. The Browns rushed for 2,639 yards in 1963.
2. The Browns rushed for 338 yards on Oct. 29, 1950, in a 45-7 rout of the Pittsburgh Steelers.
3. The 1982 Browns had 873.
4. The Browns were held to minus-five yards rushing in a season-opening 21-14 home loss to the Cowboys on Sept. 17, 1967.
5. 2,604 in 1979.
6. The Pittsburgh Steelers racked up 361 yards on the ground as they outscored the Browns by a score of 51-35 on Oct. 7, 1979, in Cleveland.
7. Browns opponents totaled 1,050 yards rushing in 1954.
8. The New York Giants had just four yards rushing on Nov. 28, 1954.
9. Browns opponents averaged 87.5 yards per carry in 1954.
10. The 1978 Browns ran the ball 559 times.
11. The Browns ran the ball 60 times on Oct. 2, 1955, in a 38-3 victory over the 49ers in San Francisco.
12. The 1982 Browns rushed the ball 256 times.
13. 10 on Nov. 9, 1969, in Minnesota, a 51-3 Browns loss.
14. 577 in 1979.
15. 64 by the Steelers on Oct. 10, 1964, in a 23-7 victory over the Browns in Cleveland.
16. Opponents rushed 306 times in 1982.
17. 14. It happened twice - both times by the Bengals, both times in Cincinnati, and both times Browns victories - 20-17 on Sept. 20, 1981, and 28-17 on Oct. 17, 1993.
18. The 1963 Browns averaged 5.7 yards per rush on 460 rushes for 2,639 yards.
19. The 1971 Browns averaged 3.4 yards per rush on 461 carries for 1,558 yards.

Passing

1. The 1981 Browns had 4,331 yards through the air.
2. The Browns passed for 444 yards in a 42-28 triumph over the Baltimore Colts on Oct. 25, 1981, in Cleveland Stadium.
3. The 1947 Browns averaged 10.1 yards per pass attempt (296 passes for 2,990 yards).
4. The 1956 team threw for only 1,175 yards.
5. Zero. The Browns had no passing yards at home against Philadelphia on Dec. 3, 1950, albeit a 13-7 Browns win.
6. The 1980 Browns yielded 4,089 passing yards.
7. The Minnesota Vikings passed for 456 yards on Dec. 14, 1980, in Minnesota, the last 46 of which were gained on the final play, a Hail Mary toss from Tommy Kramer (to Thom Darden) to Ahmad Rashad for a

Cleveland Browns Facts & Trivia

miraculous 28-23 Vikings victory.

8. Browns opponents passed for 1,103 yards in 1956.
9. The Browns held the Philadelphia Eagles to just three yards passing in a 16-0 triumph on Nov. 18, 1956, in Philadelphia.
10. The 1981 Browns had 624 pass attempts.
11. The Browns threw the ball 57 times in a 44-14 loss to the San Diego Chargers on Monday night, Sept. 7, 1981, in Cleveland.
12. The Browns had just 195 pass attempts in 1957.
13. Zero. The Browns had no pass attempts in a 13-7 home win over the Philadelphia Eagles on Dec. 3, 1950.
14. 573 in 1995.
15. The Los Angeles Raiders attempted 59 passes in a 28-16 loss to the Browns on Sept. 20, 1992, in Los Angeles.
16. Opponents attempted 226 passes in 1956.
17. Seven by the Buffalo Bills on Nov. 24, 1974, in Cleveland (the Bills won, however, 15-10).
18. The 1981 Browns had 348 completions.
19. The Browns completed 33 passes in a 30-13 home loss to San Diego on Dec. 5, 1982.
20. The 1956 Browns completed just 105 passes.
21. The Browns completed no passes on Dec. 3, 1950, against the Eagles.
22. The 1995 Browns allowed 360 passes to be completed.
23. The Minnesota Vikings completed 38 passes on Dec. 14, 1980, in Minnesota.
24. The 1957 Browns allowed just 105 pass completions.
25. The Buffalo Bills completed only one pass on Nov. 24, 1974, in Cleveland.
26. The Browns completed 63 percent of their passes in 1953.
27. The Browns completed just 46.9 percent of their passes in 1972.

Interceptions

1. The 1946 team picked off 41 passes.
2. The Browns picked off eight passes on Dec. 3, 1946, in a 34-0 victory over the Miami Seahawks in South Florida.
3. The 1975 Browns intercepted only 10 passes.
4. Browns opponents intercepted 31 passes in 1977.
5. Six. Opponents have done it three times - the Steelers on Oct. 17, 1954, and Nov. 22, 1981, and the Cardinals on Sept. 26, 1965.
6. 1.8 in 1960.
7. Five in 1960.
8. Six in 1990.
9. The 1960 Browns had 624 yards in interception returns.
10. 213 on Dec. 11, 1960, against the Chicago Bears.

11. 102 in 1982.
12. In 1984, Browns opponents had 518 return yards off interceptions.
13. The Pittsburgh Steelers had 147 interception return yards in a 55-27 rout of the Browns on Oct. 17, 1954, in Pittsburgh.
14. In 1960, Browns opponents had only 58 interception return yards.
15. The 1960 Browns scored six touchdowns off interceptions.
16. The Chicago Bears on Dec. 11, 1960. The Browns won the game by a score of 42-0 in Cleveland.
17. Opponents scored four touchdowns off interception returns in 1970.
18. Two. It occurred twice - by the Steelers on Oct. 17, 1954, and the Lions on Oct. 18, 1970.

Punting

1. The 1989 Browns had 97 punts.
2. The Browns have had 12 punts in a game twice - on Dec. 3, 1950, against the Eagles and Nov. 19, 1989, against the Chiefs.
3. In 1994, Browns opponents punted the ball 97 times.
4. 11. It has been done five times - by the Giants on Nov. 18, 1951, the Steelers on Oct. 4, 1952, the Raiders on Nov. 18, 1973, the Chiefs on Nov. 19, 1989, and the Vikings on Dec. 17, 1989.
5. In 1989, the Browns and their opponents totaled 191 punts.
6. The Browns and Chiefs combined for 23 punts on Nov. 19, 1989, in Cleveland. The game ended in a 10-10 tie.
7. The Browns punted the ball 45 times in 1982.
8. In 1982, Browns opponents punted the ball 40 times.
9. The Browns and Cowboys combined for one punt on Dec. 3, 1961, in Dallas, a 38-17 Browns victory.
10. 45.7 in both 1962 and '65.
11. The Browns averaged 54.8 yards per punt in a 16-7 victory over the New York Giants on Nov. 28, 1954, in New York.
12. Browns opponents averaged 45.5 yards per punt in 1960.
13. Pittsburgh averaged 57.5 yards per punt on Nov. 20, 1960.

Punt Returns

1. The Browns returned 61 punts in 1954.
2. The Browns have had eight punt returns in a game three times - on Nov. 7, 1954, against the Redskins, Nov. 28, 1954, against the Giants, and Nov. 18, 1956, against the Eagles.
3. The Browns returned just 20 punts twice - in 1962 and '64.
4. Browns opponents returned 68 punts in 1974.
5. 12 by the Philadelphia Eagles on Dec. 3, 1950.

Cleveland Browns Facts & Trivia

6. In 1982, Browns opponents returned 15 punts.
7. The 1993 Browns had 563 yards in punt returns.
8. The Browns had 166 punt return yards in a 28-23 victory over the Pittsburgh Steelers on Oct. 24, 1993.
9. The 1968 team had 96.
10. Opponents totaled 704 yards in punt returns in 1974.
11. The Houston Oilers rung up 149 on Sept. 22, 1974, in Cleveland, a 20-7 Browns win nonetheless.
12. 39 in 1959.
13. 15.7 in 1947.
14. The Browns averaged only four yards per punt return in 1968.
15. Browns opponents averaged 18 yards per punt return in 1977.
16. Browns opponents averaged just 1.2 yards per punt return in 1959.
17. The 1993 team scored three touchdowns off punt returns.
18. Two. The Browns - thanks to Eric Metcalf - returned two punts for scores in a thrilling 28-23 victory over Pittsburgh on Oct. 24, 1993, in Cleveland.
19. Three in 1977.
20. Two by the Denver Broncos on Sept. 26, 1976, in Denver, a 44-13 Broncos rout.

Kickoff Returns

1. The Browns returned 75 kickoffs in 1979.
2. Nine - on Oct. 17, 1974, and Oct. 7, 1979, both in defeats to the Steelers.
3. The Browns returned 27 kickoffs in 1951.
4. In 1986, opponents returned 78 kicks.
5. Washington returned nine kickoffs on Nov. 7, 1954, as the Browns overwhelmed the Redskins to the tune of 62-3.
6. In 1982, Browns opponents returned 23 kickoffs.
7. The 1978 Browns had 1,697 yards in kickoff returns.
8. The Browns totaled 256 yards in kickoff returns in a 38-34 victory over the visiting Eagles on Nov. 7, 1965.
9. The Browns had 496 kickoff return yards in 1951.
10. 1,517 in 1964.
11. Browns opponents had 236 yards in kick returns twice - the Redskins on Dec. 15, 1963, and the Giants on Dec. 4, 1966.
12. Browns opponents in 1982 totaled 424 yards in kick returns.
13. The 1967 Browns averaged 25.4 yards per kickoff return.
14. The Browns averaged 16.1 yards per kickoff return in 1991.
15. The 1975 Browns allowed 26.6 yards per kickoff return.
16. The 1980 Browns allowed 14.3 yards per return.
17. The 1958 and '90 teams.

18. One. They have done it 13 times.
19. The 1966 and '67 Browns.
20. The Green Bay Packers did it on Nov. 12, 1967, in a 55-7 trouncing of the Browns in Milwaukee.

Total Net Yards

1. The 1981 Browns racked up 5,915 total net yards.
2. The Browns accumulated 607 total net yards in a 61-14 rout of the Los Angeles Dons on Oct. 14, 1949.
3. The 1982 Browns had 2,718 total net yards.
4. The Browns gained just 60 total net yards in a 27-0 home loss to the Broncos on Oct. 24, 1971.
5. The 1979 Browns yielded 5,650 total net yards.
6. The Browns gave up 606 total net yards in a 33-30 overtime loss in Pittsburgh on Nov. 25, 1979.
7. The 1954 Browns allowed 2,658 net yards.
8. The Browns allowed just 53 net yards in a 51-0 obliteration of the Steelers in Three Rivers Stadium on Sept. 10, 1989.
9. Four. The Browns gained at least 400 total net yards from Oct. 19-Nov. 9, 1980.
10. 19. The Browns gained at least 300 total net yards from Nov. 19, 1978-Dec. 2, 1979.

Fumbles

1. The 1978 Browns fumbled the ball 50 times.
2. Nine. It happened twice - in a 42-21 loss in Seattle on Dec. 20, 1981, and a in a 30-0 defeat in Pittsburgh on Dec. 23, 1990.
3. The 1959 Browns fumbled just eight times.
4. Browns opponents had 39 fumbles in 1972.
5. Eight - by the 49ers in a 34-14 loss to Cleveland on Nov. 12, 1950, and by the Pittsburgh Steelers in a 45-12 loss to the Browns on Oct. 5, 1958.
6. Browns opponents fumbled just 11 times in 1956.
7. The Browns and Seahawks combined for 13 fumbles on Dec. 20, 1981, in the Kingdome (the Browns had nine of them).
8. The 1978 Browns lost 29 fumbles.
9. Eight on Dec. 23, 1990, against the Steelers in Pittsburgh.
10. The Browns lost only five fumbles in 1959.
11. The Browns recovered 28 opponents' fumbles in 1951.
12. The Browns recovered six 49ers fumbles on Nov. 12, 1950.
13. Seven in 1995.

Quarterback Sacks

1. The Browns allowed 55 quarterback sacks in 1984.
2. The Browns twice allowed 11 quarterback sacks - on Sept. 30, 1984, in Kansas City and Sept. 6, 1992, in Indianapolis.
3. 14 in 1994.
4. The Browns sacked opposing quarterbacks 48 times twice - in 1992 and '93.
5. The Browns sacked the opposing quarterback 11 times in a 23-7 victory over the Falcons in Atlanta on Nov. 18, 1984.
6. 22 in 1982.
7. The Browns went 20 games from 1972-73 with at least one sack.
8. 359 in 1989.
9. 95 by the Atlanta Falcons on Nov. 18, 1984.
10. The Browns and Chiefs allowed a total of 13 sacks on Sept. 30, 1984, in Arrowhead Stadium (the Browns permitted 11).
11. Zero. It has been done four times - on Nov. 17, 1968, in a game between the Browns and Steelers; on Oct. 3, 1976, in a game between the Bengals and Browns; on Dec. 3, 1989, also in a game between the Bengals and Browns; and on Oct. 8, 1990, in a game between the Browns and Broncos.

7. Team Records (Postseason)

Scoring

1. 56. The Browns hammered the Detroit Lions, 56-10, in the NFL Championship game on Dec. 26, 1954, in Cleveland.
2. 59. The Detroit Lions blasted the Browns, 59-14, in the NFL Championship game on Dec. 29, 1957, in Detroit.
3. 73. Detroit defeated the Browns, 59-14, in the NFL title game on Dec. 29, 1957, in Detroit.
4. 10. The Giants shut out the Browns, 10-0, in an Eastern Conference Playoff on Dec. 21, 1958, in New York.
5. The Browns tallied eight touchdowns in a 56-10 rout of the Lions in the NFL Championship game on Dec. 26, 1954, in Cleveland.

Cleveland Browns Facts & Trivia

6. Eight. Detroit did this in a 59-14 destruction of the Browns in the NFL title game on Dec. 29, 1957, in the Motor City.

7. Seven. It happened twice - from the fourth quarter of the Browns' 14-9 victory over New York in the 1946 AAFC Championship game through the second quarter of their 49-7 rout of Buffalo in the 1948 AAFC title game.

8. The Browns scored five rushing touchdowns in their 56-10 triumph over the Detroit Lions in the 1954 NFL Championship game in Cleveland.

9. The Browns twice yielded four touchdowns via the ground. Dallas did it in a 52-14 victory over Cleveland in the Eastern Conference Championship game on Dec. 24, 1967, in Dallas. A year later, Baltimore did the honors in a 34-0 defeat of the Browns in the NFL Championship game on Dec. 29, 1968, in Cleveland.

10. The Lions and Browns combined for six rushing touchdowns in the Browns' 56-10 victory in the 1954 NFL title game in Cleveland Municipal Stadium. The Browns had five of them.

11. The Browns rushed for at least one touchdown in six straight postseason games from their NFL Championship game loss in Los Angeles on Dec. 23, 1951, through their NFL Championship game defeat in Detroit on Dec. 29, 1957.

12. Four. The Browns passed for four touchdowns in their 30-28 victory over the Los Angeles Rams in the 1950 NFL Championship game.

13. Five. The Lions did it in a 59-14 demolition of the Browns in the 1957 NFL Championship game in the Motor City.

14. Eight in the 1954 NFL Championship game at home against Detroit (the Browns won, 56-10).

15. Eight by the Lions in the 1957 NFL Championship game in Detroit (the Lions won, 59-14).

16. The Browns tallied at least one touchdown in 13 consecutive games from an AFC Divisional Playoff loss in Miami on Dec. 24, 1972, through an AFC Divisional Playoff loss in Pittsburgh on Jan. 7, 1995.

17. Three. They did it against Detroit in the NFL Championship game on Dec. 27, 1953, in Detroit, the New York Jets in an AFC Divisional Playoff on Jan. 3, 1987, in Cleveland, and the Houston Oilers in the AFC Wild Card game on Dec. 24, 1988, in Cleveland.

18. Three. Green Bay did it in the NFL Championship game on Jan. 2, 1966, and Denver did it twice in the AFC Championship game - on Jan. 11, 1987, and on Jan. 14, 1990.

19. One. The Browns did it twice - against the Giants in an American Conference Playoff on Dec. 17, 1950, and against Denver in the AFC Championship game on Jan. 17, 1988.

20. One. Pittsburgh is the only team to do it - in a 29-9 rout of the Browns in an AFC Divisional Playoff on Jan. 7, 1995, in Pittsburgh.

21. One. The Giants and Browns combined for one on Dec. 17, 1950, in an American Conference Playoff (the Browns had it), the Browns and Broncos combined for one on Jan. 17, 1988, in the AFC Championship game (the Browns had it), and the Browns and Steelers combined for one on Jan. 7,

Cleveland Browns Facts & Trivia

1995, in an AFC Divisional Playoff (the Steelers had it).
22. 14. They did it in a 56-10 victory over the Lions in the NFL Championship game on Dec. 26, 1954, in Cleveland Municipal Stadium.
23. 21. They did it in their 56-10 triumph over Detroit in the 1954 NFL title game in Cleveland.
24. 21. The Browns did it twice, and both came in Denver in the AFC Championship game. The first time was on Jan. 17, 1988, a 38-33 Broncos victory. The second time occurred on Jan. 14, 1990, a 37-21 Broncos win.
25. 21. The Browns did this on Dec. 19, 1948, in a 49-7 rout of the Buffalo Bills in the AAFC title game.
26. The Browns rung up 35 points in the opening half of their 56-10 victory over the Lions in the 1954 NFL Championship game in Cleveland.
27. The Browns scored 35 points in the second half of their 49-7 conquest of the Buffalo Bills in the 1948 AAFC Championship game in Cleveland Municipal Stadium.
28. The Browns went 16 straight postseason games without being blanked from a 38-14 win over Dallas in the Eastern Conference title game on Dec. 28, 1969, in Dallas through a 29-9 loss to Pittsburgh in an AFC Divisional Playoff on Jan. 7, 1995, in Pittsburgh.
29. 10. The Browns overcame a 20-10 deficit late in the fourth quarter of an AFC Divisional Playoff at home against the New York Jets on Jan. 3, 1987, and eventually won, 23-20, in double overtime. 30. 18. The Browns blew a 21-3 third-quarter lead in Miami on Jan. 4, 1986, in an AFC Divisional Playoff. The Dolphins won, 24-21.
31. 46 points. The Browns routed Detroit, 56-10, in the 1954 NFL title game in Cleveland.
32. 45 points. Detroit manhandled the Browns, 59-14, in the 1957 NFL title game in Detroit.

Rushing

1. The Browns racked up 251 yards on the ground in a 24-21 AFC Divisional Playoff loss to the Dolphins on Jan. 4, 1986, in Miami.
2. The Browns gained just 24 yards rushing in a 10-0 loss to the New York Giants in an Eastern Conference Playoff on Dec. 21, 1958, in Yankee Stadium.
3. The Browns yielded 238 yards on the ground in a 29-9 loss to the Pittsburgh Steelers in an AFC Divisional Playoff game on Jan. 7, 1995, in Pittsburgh.
4. The Browns held Buffalo to just 49 yards rushing in a 34-30 triumph over the Bills in an AFC Divisional Playoff on Jan. 6, 1990, in Cleveland Stadium.
5. The Browns ran the ball 47 times in a 38-14 victory over the Los Angeles

Rams in the NFL title game on Dec. 26, 1955, in the Los Angeles Memorial Coliseum.

6. The Browns ran the ball just 13 times in a 10-0 loss to the Giants in an Eastern Conference Playoff game in New York on Dec. 21, 1958.

7. The New York Giants rushed the ball 53 times in their 10-0 victory over the Browns in an Eastern Conference Playoff game on Dec. 21, 1958, in Yankee Stadium.

8. New England had only 16 rushing attempts in their 20-13 loss to the Browns in an AFC Wild Card game on Jan. 1, 1995, in Cleveland.

Passing

1. The Browns totaled 494 passing yards in their 23-20 double overtime victory over the Jets in an AFC Divisional Playoff on Jan. 3, 1987, in Cleveland.

2. The Browns had only 38 passing yards in their 17-16 loss to the Lions in the 1953 NFL title game in Detroit.

3. Buffalo scorched the Browns' defense for 405 yards through the air in an AFC Divisional Playoff game in Cleveland on Jan. 6, 1990. The Browns were fortunate to escape with a 34-30 victory.

4. The New York Giants had just 48 passing yards in an 8-3 loss to the Browns in a 1950 American Conference Playoff game in Cleveland.

5. The Browns attempted 65 passes in a 23-20 double overtime victory over the New York Jets in an AFC Divisional Playoff game on Jan. 3, 1987, in Cleveland Stadium.

6. Nine in an 8-3 win over the Giants in an American Conference Playoff game on Dec. 17, 1950, in Cleveland.

7. The Buffalo Bills attempted 54 passes in their 34-30 loss to the Browns in the AFC Divisional Playoffs on Jan. 6, 1990, in Cleveland.

8. Detroit threw just 10 passes in their 17-7 triumph over the Browns in the 1952 NFL Championship game in Cleveland.

9. The Browns completed 34 passes in their 23-20 double overtime win over the New York Jets in the AFC Divisional Playoffs on Jan. 3, 1987, in Cleveland.

10. The Browns twice completed only three passes in a postseason game - in a victory over the Giants in an American Conference Playoff on Dec. 17, 1950, and in a loss to the Lions in the NFL title game on Dec. 27, 1953, in Detroit.

11. Buffalo completed 28 passes in a 34-30 loss to the Browns in an AFC Divisional Playoff on Jan. 6, 1990, in Cleveland.

12. The Giants completed just three passes in an American Conference Playoff loss in Cleveland on Dec. 17, 1950.

Cleveland Browns Facts & Trivia

Interceptions

1. The Browns intercepted seven passes in a 38-14 victory over the Los Angeles Rams in the 1955 NFL Championship game.
2. Miami picked off five Cleveland passes in a 20-14 win over the Browns in an AFC Divisional Playoff game on Dec. 24, 1972, in the Orange Bowl in Miami.
3. One. It happened eight times - against San Francisco on Dec. 11, 1949, Detroit on Dec. 28, 1952 and Dec. 29, 1957, Minnesota on Jan. 4, 1970, Miami on Dec. 24, 1972, the New York Jets on Jan. 3, 1987, Denver on Jan. 14, 1990, and Pittsburgh on Jan. 7, 1995.
4. 123 against Dallas in the 1969 Eastern Conference title game in the Cotton Bowl, a 38-14 Browns victory.
5. Baltimore had 79 yards off interception returns in a 20-3 win over the Browns in an AFC Divisional Playoff on Dec. 26, 1971, in Cleveland Municipal Stadium.
6. The Browns accomplished the feat against the Buffalo Bills on Dec. 19, 1948, and Dec. 4, 1949, and against the Dallas Cowboys on Dec. 21, 1968, and Dec. 28, 1969.
7. Dallas. The Cowboys did it in the Eastern Conference title game on Dec. 24, 1967, in Dallas.

Punting

1. Nine on Dec. 17, 1950, in an 8-3 victory over the Giants in an American Conference Playoff in Cleveland.
2. The Jets punted 14 times in their 23-20 double overtime loss to the Browns in an AFC Divisional Playoff on Jan. 3, 1987, in Cleveland.
3. The Browns and Jets combined for 22 punts (the Jets 14, the Browns eight) in a double overtime AFC Divisional Playoff game on Jan. 3, 1987, in Cleveland.
4. Five. The Browns and Colts did it in an AFC Divisional Playoff on Jan. 9, 1988, and the Browns and Broncos did it eight days later in the AFC Championship game.
5. The Browns averaged 48.5 yards per punt on six attempts in their 27-10 AFC First-Round Playoff loss to the Raiders in Los Angeles on Jan. 8, 1983.
6. Los Angeles averaged 50.8 yards per punt on four attempts in the 1950 NFL title game in Cleveland on Dec. 24, 1950. The Browns won, 30-28.

Punt Returns

1. Seven. They did it twice - in a 14-12 AFC Divisional Playoff loss to Oakland on Jan. 4, 1981, and in a 23-20 double overtime victory over the New York Jets on Jan. 3, 1987. Both games were in Cleveland.
2. Five. The Giants did it in an American Conference Playoff on Dec. 17, 1950, and in an Eastern Conference Playoff on Dec. 21, 1958, in New York, and the Raiders did it in an AFC First-Round Playoff on Jan. 8, 1983, in Los Angeles.
3. The Browns had 81 punt return yards against the Oakland Raiders in an AFC Divisional Playoff on Jan. 4, 1981, in Cleveland.
4. The Dallas Cowboys had 155 yards in punt returns in their 52-14 rout of the Browns in the Eastern Conference Championship game on Dec. 24, 1967, in the Cotton Bowl.

Kickoff Returns

1. The Browns returned seven kickoffs each in their 1957 NFL Championship game loss in Detroit and in their 1967 Eastern Conference Title game defeat in Dallas.
2. Seven. The Rams did it in their 38-14 NFL title game loss to the Browns on Dec. 26, 1955, in Los Angeles, and the Colts did it in their 38-21 loss to the Browns in an AFC Divisional Playoff on Jan. 9, 1988, in Cleveland.
3. The Browns had 180 kickoff return yards in a 34-30 AFC Divisional Playoff win at home over Buffalo on Jan. 6, 1990.
4. Los Angeles totaled 215 kickoff return yards in the NFL Championship game on Dec. 26, 1955, in Los Angeles. The Rams lost to the Browns, 38-14.
5. Buffalo. The Browns returned one 90 yards for a touchdown in the third quarter of the their 34- 30 triumph in an AFC Divisional Playoff game in Cleveland.

Total Net Yards

1. The Browns had 558 total net yards in a 23-20 double overtime victory over the Jets on Jan. 3, 1987, in Cleveland.
2. The Browns were held to just 86 total net yards in a 10-0 loss to the Giants in an Eastern Conference Playoff on Dec. 21, 1958, in New York.
3. The Los Angeles Raiders piled up 510 in a 27-10 victory over the Browns in an AFC First-Round Playoff game on Jan. 8, 1983, in the Los Angeles Memorial Coliseum.
4. The Browns allowed the New York Yankees just 146 total net yards in the 1946 AAFC title game in Cleveland.
5. Two. They did it against the Colts (404) in an AFC Divisional Playoff on

Cleveland Browns Facts & Trivia

Jan. 9, 1988, and against the Broncos (464) in the AFC Championship game on Jan. 17, 1988.

6. The Browns did it in five straight games from their 313-yard performance in a 24-21 AFC Divisional Playoff loss in Miami on Jan. 4, 1986, through a 464-yard output in a 38-33 defeat in Denver in the AFC Championship game on Jan. 17, 1988.

Fumbles

1. The Browns fumbled the ball six times in three different postseason games - against Buffalo in the AAFC title game on Dec. 19, 1948, against Baltimore in the AFC Divisional Playoffs on Dec. 26, 1971, and against Oakland in an AFC Divisional Playoff on Jan. 4, 1981.
2. The New York Giants fumbled the ball six times in a 1958 Eastern Conference Playoff but beat the Browns, 10-0, in Yankee Stadium.
3. Nine. The Bills and Browns combined for nine fumbles in the 1948 AAFC Championship game in Cleveland Municipal Stadium. The Browns had six, the Bills three.
4. The Browns lost three fumbles on three different occasions - against Buffalo in the 1948 AAFC Championship game, against Los Angeles in the 1950 NFL title game, and against Denver in the AFC Championship game on Jan. 17, 1988.
5. The Browns recovered three fumbles each by the Buffalo Bills in the 1948 AAFC title game and the Detroit Lions in the 1954 NFL title contest.

Quarterback Sacks

1. The Browns allowed six quarterback sacks each on Dec. 21, 1958, against the Giants in an Eastern Conference Playoff game, and on Jan. 8, 1983, against the Raiders in an AFC First-Round Playoff game.
2. The Browns had nine sacks against the New York Jets in an AFC Divisional Playoff game on Jan. 3, 1987, in Cleveland Stadium. The Browns won, 23-20, in double overtime.
3. The Browns had at least one sack in eight straight games from their 23-20 double overtime victory over the Jets in an AFC Divisional Playoff game on Jan. 3, 1987, through their 20-13 AFC Wild Card win over the Patriots on Jan. 1, 1995.
4. The Jets lost 54 yards on pass attempts against the Browns in an AFC Divisional Playoff on Jan. 3, 1987, in Cleveland.
5. The Browns and Jets combined for 13 sacks in an AFC Divisional Playoff game on Jan. 3, 1987, in Cleveland won, 23-20, by the Browns. The Browns had nine sacks, the Jets four.
6. The Browns and Giants combined to produce no quarterback sacks in their American Conference Playoff game on Dec. 17, 1950, in Cleveland. The Browns won, 8-3.

8. Miscellaneous

Firsts

1. Arthur "Mickey" McBride.
2. Paul Brown.
3. Bowling Green State University in Bowling Green, Ohio, some two hours west of Cleveland.
4. Otto Graham.
5. Dick Hoerner in 1947.
6. The Brooklyn Dodgers. The Browns won, 35-20, on Aug. 30, 1946, in the Rubber Bowl in Akron, Ohio.
7. The Miami Seahawks. The Browns won the game, 44-0, on Sept. 6, 1946, in Cleveland Municipal Stadium.
8. Cliff Lewis.
9. Mac Speedie. Speedie caught a 19-yard touchdown pass from Cliff Lewis in the early stages of the opening quarter of the Browns' 44-0 rout of the Miami Seahawks on Sept. 6, 1946, in Cleveland.
10. Lou Groza.
11. The Chicago Rockets. The Browns won the game, 20-6, on the evening of Sept. 13, 1946.
12. The San Francisco 49ers defeated the Browns, 34-20, on Oct. 27, 1946, in Cleveland.
13. The Browns defeated the New York Yankees, 14-9, in the AAFC Championship game on Dec. 22, 1946, in Cleveland.
14. The Browns beat the New York Yankees, 14-3, on Dec. 14, 1947.
15. Ken Carpenter.
16. They beat the Green Bay Packers, 38-7, on Aug. 12, 1950, in Toledo, Ohio.
17. The Browns surprised the football world by destroying the two-time defending champion Philadelphia Eagles, 35-10, on Sept. 16, 1950, in Philadelphia.
18. Dub Jones scored them on a long touchdown pass from Otto Graham.
19. Lou Groza.
20. The New York Giants. The Browns lost, 6-0, on Oct. 1, 1950.
21. The Browns defeated the New York Giants, 8-3, in an Eastern Conference Playoff game on Dec. 17, 1950, in Cleveland.
22. The Los Angeles Rams. The Browns were defeated by the Rams, 24-17, in the NFL Championship game on Dec. 23, 1951.
23. The New York Jets. The Browns defeated the Jets, 31-21, on Sept. 21, 1970, in Cleveland Municipal Stadium in what was also the first-ever *Monday Night Football* game.
24. The Houston Oilers. The Browns defeated the Oilers, 21-10, on Dec. 7, 1970, in the Astrodome.

25. The Browns edged the New England Patriots, 30-27, on Monday night, Sept. 26, 1977, in Cleveland.
26. The Pittsburgh Steelers. The Browns lost a heartbreaker, 15-9, on Sept. 24, 1978, in Three Rivers Stadium.
27. 1956.
28. 1956 when they went 5-7 (.417).
29. Jim Brown with 1,527 in 1958.
30. Brian Sipe threw for 3,793 yards in 1979.
31. Mac Speedie had 1,146 receiving yards in 1947.
32. The following men were selected to play in the 1950 Pro Bowl: Tony Adamle, Otto Graham, Lou Groza, Weldon Humble, Marion Motley, Mac Speedie, and Bill Willis.
33. Jim Brown was voted NFL Rookie of the Year in 1957 by both the Associated Press and United Press.
34. Paul Brown. Brown copped AAFC Coach of the Year honors in 1947 from *Pro Football Illustrated*.
35. Otto Graham was named by the AAFC as its MVP in 1947 (he was enshrined into the Hall of Fame in 1965).

The Last Time ...

1. ... Dec. 17, 1995, when Earnest Byner rushed for 121 yards in a 26-10 victory over the Bengals in Cleveland Stadium.
2. ... Dec. 3, 1995, when San Diego's Aaron Hayden gained 127 yards on the ground in the Chargers' 31-13 victory over the Browns in Jack Murphy Stadium.
3. ... Nov. 23, 1986, when Bernie Kosar passed for 414 yards in a 37-31 sudden death victory over the Pittsburgh Steelers in Cleveland Stadium.

4. ... Dec. 23, 1989, when Houston's Warren Moon passed for 414 yards in the Oilers' 24-20 loss to the Browns in the Astrodome in a season-ending battle for the AFC Central Division title.
5. ... Sept. 14, 1992, when Matt Stover missed an extra point try in the Browns' 27-23 defeat to the Dolphins in Cleveland.
6. ... Oct. 22, 1995, when Jacksonville's Mike Hollis failed on an extra point try late in the first quarter of the Jaguars' 23-15 victory over the Browns in Cleveland Stadium.
7. ... Dec. 17, 1995, when Rob Burnett blocked a 22-yard attempt by Cincinnati's Doug Pelfrey late in the second quarter of the Browns' 26-10 victory over the Bengals in Cleveland Stadium.
8. ... Nov. 3, 1991, when Cincinnati's Eric Thomas blocked Matt Stover's 34-yard try that would have won the game as time expired (the Bengals won, 23-21).
9. ... Sept. 24, 1995, when Mike Caldwell returned an interception of Kansas City's Steve Bono 24 yards late in the Browns' 35-17 triumph over

the Chiefs in Cleveland.

10. ... Nov. 5, 1995, when Houston's Blaine Bishop returned an Eric Zeier pass 62 yards early in the fourth quarter of the Oilers' 37-10 rout of the Browns in Cleveland Stadium.

11. ... Sept. 5, 1993, when Stevon Moore returned a fumble by Cincinnati's David Klingler 22 yards early in the fourth quarter of the Browns' 27-14 opening-day victory over the Bengals in Cleveland Stadium.

12. ... Nov. 14, 1993, when Seattle's Robert Blackmon returned a Todd Philcox fumble five yards on the opening play from scrimmage of the Seahawks' 22-5 win over the Browns in the Kingdome.

13. ... Oct. 23, 1994, when Gerald Dixon blocked a punt by Cincinnati's Lee Johnson deep in Bengals territory that was recovered in the end zone by Cleveland's Travis Hill for a touchdown late in the third quarter of the Browns' 37-13 triumph.

14. ... Nov. 21, 1993, when Houston's Bubba McDowell blocked a Brian Hansen punt early in the fourth quarter of the Oilers' 27-17 triumph over the Browns in Cleveland.

15. ... Oct. 2, 1995, when Derrick Alexander returned one 69 yards in the first quarter of the Browns' 22-19 loss to the Bills in Cleveland.

16. ... Sept. 19, 1988, when Indianapolis's Clarence Verdin returned one 73 yards in the Colts' 23-17 loss to the Browns in Cleveland Stadium.

17. ... Sept. 4, 1994, when Randy Baldwin returned a second-quarter kickoff 85 yards for a touchdown in the Browns' 28-20 opening-day victory over the Bengals in Cincinnati.

18. ... Sept. 7, 1986, when Chicago's Dennis Gentry returned one 91 yards for a score in the Bears' 41-31 opening-day victory over the Browns in Soldier Field.

19. ... Nov. 14, 1993, when Anthony Pleasant sacked Seattle rookie quarterback Rick Mirer in the end zone in first-quarter action of the Browns' 22-5 loss to the Seahawks in the Kingdome.

20. ... Nov. 14, 1993, when Seattle's Antonio Edwards sacked Todd Philcox in the end zone in the late stages of the Seahawks' 22-5 victory over the Browns in the Kingdome.

21. ... Nov. 23, 1986, when they gained 536 total net yards in a 37-31 sudden death victory over the Steelers in Cleveland.

22. ... Jan. 2, 1983, when Pittsburgh totaled 521 net yards in a 37-21 rout of the Browns in Three Rivers Stadium.

23. ... Sept. 18, 1994, when they whipped Arizona, 32-0, in Cleveland Stadium.

24. ... Sept. 27, 1992, when Denver bageled the Browns, 12-0, in Cleveland.

Cleveland Browns Facts & Trivia

Who Am I?

1. Cliff Lewis.
2. Marion Motley.
3. Lou Groza.
4. Paul Brown.
5. Dante Lavelli.
6. Bill Willis.
7. Otto Graham.
8. Frank Gatski.
9. Mac Speedie.
10. Jeff Durkota.
11. Warren Lahr.
12. Lou Saban.
13. Edgar Jones.
14. Len Ford.
15. Dub Jones.
16. Bert Rechichar.
17. Bob Gain.
18. Ray Renfro.
19. Chuck Noll.
20. Ken Konz.
21. Walt Michaels.
22. Mike McCormack.
23. Jim Brown.
24. Vince Costello.
25. Bobby Mitchell.
26. Gene Hickerson.
27. Dick Schafrath.
28. Milt Plum.
29. Jim Marshall.
30. Ross Fichtner.
31. Frank Ryan.
32. Ernie Green.
33. Paul Warfield.
34. Leroy Kelly.
35. Walter Roberts.
36. Gary Collins.
37. Dick Modzelewski.
38. Milt Morin.
39. Don Cockroft.
40. Dale Lindsey.
41. Mike Phipps.
42. Jerry Sherk.
43. Homer Jones.
44. Doug Dieken.

What Position(s) Did He Play?

1. Quarterback.
2. Punter, defensive back.
3. Kicker, offensive lineman.
4. Running back.
5. Wide receiver.
6. Quarterback.
7. Defensive end.
8. Defensive end.
9. Defensive back.
10. Offensive lineman.
11. Defensive back.
12. Wide receiver.
13. Defensive end.
14. Running back.
15. Linebacker.
16. Defensive lineman.
17. Safety.
18. Wide receiver.
19. Safety.
20. Wide receiver.
21. Running back.
22. Running back, Defense back.
23. Quarterback.
24. Kicker.
25. Wide receiver.
26. Running back.
27. Defensive end.
28. Linebacker.
29. Wide receiver.
30. Kicker.
31. Linebacker.
32. Offensive lineman.
33. Safety.
34. Running back.
35. Running back.
36. Quarterback.
37. Running back.
38. Wide receiver.
39. Quarterback.
40. Running back.
41. Linebacker.
42. Kicker, punter.
43. Running back.
44. Offensive lineman.

45. Nick Skorich.
46. Brian Sipe.
47. Ken Brown.
48. Greg Pruitt.
49. Forrest Gregg.
50. Larry Poole.
51. Tony Peters.
52. Joe Jones.
53. Clay Matthews.
54. Ozzie Newsome.
55. Keith Wright.
56. Lyle Alzado.
57. Robert L. Jackson.
58. Hanford Dixon.
59. Chip Banks.
60. Frank Minnifield.
61. Bernie Kosar.
62. Kevin Mack, Earnest Byner.
63. Webster Slaughter.
64. Gerald McNeil.
65. Ray Ellis.
66. Michael Dean Perry.
67. Leroy Hoard.
68. Eric Turner.
69. Tommy Vardell.
70. Stevon Moore.
71. Mark Bavaro.
72. Vinny Testaverde.
73. Brian Kinchen.
74. Randy Baldwin.
75. Matt Stover.

45. Linebacker.
46. Running back.
47. Wide receiver, running back.
48. Defensive lineman.
49. Safety.
50. Defensive back.
51. Offensive lineman.
52. Running back.
53. Safety.
54. Quarterback.
55. Running back.
56. Offensive lineman.
57. Defensive lineman.
58. Punter.
59. Wide receiver.
60. Punter, wide receiver.
61. Wide receiver.
62. Defensive back.
63. Wide receiver.
64. Defensive back.
65. Defensive lineman.
66. Defensive back.
67. Defensive back.
68. Running back.
69. Quarterback.
70. Linebacker.
71. Defensive back.
72. Punter, quarterback.
73. Linebacker, offense lineman.
74. Wide receiver.
75. Tight end.

Cleveland Browns Facts & Trivia

What Year(s) Did He Play for the Browns?

1. 1985-93.
2. 1946-56.
3. 1985-86.
4. 1988-91.
5. 1976-83.
6. 1965-72.
7. 1978-90.
8. 1964-69, '76-77.
9. 1946-59, '61-67.
10. 1946.
11. 1979-83.
12. 1995.
13. 1984-88, '94-95.
14. 1978-93.
15. 1946-55.
16. 1947-56.
17. 1950-53.
18. 1975-82.
19. 1964-66.
20. 1955-59.
21. 1985-90.
22. 1969-74.
23. 1946.
24. 1955.
25. 1970-81.
26. 1986-87.
27. 1993-95.
28. 1978-81.
29. 1983-86.
30. 1969-74.
31. 1975.
32. 1973-81.
33. 1976-84.
34. 1956-62.
35. 1987-88.
36. 1946-56.
37. 1988-90.
38. 1948-55.
39. 1992.
40. 1987.
41. 1984.
42. 1984-91.
43. 1970.

What Number(s) Did He Wear?

1. 44.
2. 88.
3. 20.
4. 34.
5. 43.
6. 56, 86.
7. 27.
8. 82.
9. 16.
10. 54.
11. 56.
12. 1, 81.
13. 16.
14. 46.
15. 17.
16. 42.
17. 32.
18. 45, 72.
19. 59.
20. 18.
21. 84.
22. 85.
23. 73.
24. 28.
25. 77.
26. 15.
27. 79.
28. 57.
29. 30, 60.
30. 49.
31. 10.
32. 12.
33. 88.
34. 29.
35. 16.
36. 26.
37. 78.
38. 66.
39. 12.
40. 30.
41. 26.
42. 60.
43. 29.

Cleveland Browns Facts & Trivia

44. 1987-88.
45. 1971-73.
46. 1980-82, '84.
47. 1974-83.
48. 1986-91.
49. 1971-84.
50. 1979-83, '85-89.
51. 1946-47.
52. 1963-69.
53. 1979-85.
54. 1985-88.
55. 1958-63.
56. 1948-49.
57. 1975-81.
58. 1991.
59. 1946-53.
60. 1993-95.
61. 1984-92.
62. 1984-89.
63. 1980-82.
64. 1972-74, '76-81.
65. 1963.
66. 1984-85, '87-88.
67. 1991-95.
68. 1953-59.
69. 1964-73.
70. 1958-60, '62-73.
71. 1957-65.
72. 1986-90.
73. 1949.
74. 1980-85.
75. 1951-52.

44. 76, 36.
45. 80, 24.
46. 3.
47. 34.
48. 66.
49. 78.
50. 9.
51. 82.
52. 61.
53. 78.
54. 89.
55. 89.
56. 15.
57. 90, 22.
58. 23.
59. 80, 64.
60. 64.
61. 80.
62. 90.
63. 81.
64. 58, 88.
65. 60, 14.
66. 22.
67. 36.
68. 92.
69. 62.
70. 33.
71. 82, 42.
72. 83.
73. 53, 80.
74. 74.
75. 70.

Cleveland Browns Facts & Trivia

Where Did He Play College Football?

1. Ohio State.
2. Fresno State.
3. Massachusetts.
4. Ohio State.
5. Mississippi.
6. San Diego State.
7. Rice.
8. East Carolina.
9. USC.
10. Dayton.
11. Miami (Fla.).
12. Michigan.
13. Duke.
14. Bowling Green.
15. Alabama.
16. Kent State.
17. West Virginia.
18. Notre Dame.
19. Clemson.
20. Baylor.
21. Ohio State.
22. UCLA.
23. Akron.
24. Oklahoma State.
25. Nebraska.
26. Tennessee State.
27. Indiana.
28. Syracuse.
29. Ohio.
30. Ohio State.
31. Auburn.
32. Ohio State.
33. Utah.
34. Alabama State.
35. Michigan State.
36. John Carroll (Ohio).
37. Texas A&M.
38. Purdue.
39. Clemson.
40. Auburn.
41. Boston College.
42. Georgia Tech.
43. USC.

What Was/Were His Nickname(s)?

1. "Turkey."
2. "The Toe."
3. "The Sheik."
4. "Automatic."
5. "Mo."
6. "The Assassin."
7. "Bubba."
8. "The Wizard of Oz."
9. "Jumbo."
10. "Glue Fingers."
11. "Donny O."
12. "E", "The Old Man."
13. "Riddler."
14. "E-rock."
15. "Thriller."
16. "Gunner."
17. "Mickey."
18. "Dub."
19. "Touchdown."
20. "Rocky."
21. "Hopalong."
22. "Junior."
23. "The Jet."
24. "Nino."
25. "Bam."
26. "Special Delivery."
27. "Big V."
28. "Pete."
29. "Pete."
30. "Dopey."
31. "Chubby."
32. "Big Mo."
33. "Little Mo."
34. "Bo."
35. "Zeke."
36. "Chip."
37. "The Flea," "Mr. Rodgers."
38. "Shaf."
39. "Curley."
40. "Big Foot."
41. "Stove Top."
42. "The Train."
43. "Babe."

Cleveland Browns Facts & Trivia

44. Nevada.
45. Oklahoma State.
46. Louisville.
47. North Carolina State.
48. Memphis State.
49. Arizona State.
50. Michigan State.
51. Pittsburgh.
52. Louisiana State.
53. Notre Dame.
54. Kansas.
55. Tulane.
56. USC.
57. No college.
58. Colorado.
59. Boston.
60. Illinois.
61. Penn State.
62. Northwestern.
63. Southern Mississippi.
64. Ohio State.
65. Illinois.
66. Maryland.
67. Louisville.
68. Penn State.
69. Florida.
70. Illinois.
71. Duke.
72. Purdue.
73. No college.
74. Oklahoma.
75. Louisiana State.

44. "Doc."
45. "Touchdown Tommy."
46. "Scud."
47. "High Pockets," "Hooks."
48. "Top Dawg."
49. "Full Moon."
50. "Big Daddy."
51. "Rhino."
52. "Slooie."
53. "The Ice Cube."
54. "Pinky."
55. "Minnie."
56. "Stoney."
57. "Snides."
58. "Junior."
59. "Tonto."
60. "Do It."
61. "Mo."
62. "Dippy."
63. "A.P."
64. "Puz."
65. "Diek."
66. "Tiny."
67. "B-1."
68. "Chick."
69. "Jazz."
70. "Mandrake."
71. "Smokey."
72. "Shortman."
73. "Tack."
74. "T-Bone."
75. "Wild Man."

About the Author

This is Roger's second book. His first is entitled *Cincinnati Bengals Facts & Trivia*. Now that he has professional football in the state of Ohio covered, what's next for Roger? He's not sure but would like his next work to be either another *Facts & Trivia* book or perhaps a biography on a former athlete. Anything else about football would also be considered.

Roger, who is 32 and resides in Jackson Township, just outside of Canton, Ohio, the home of the Pro Football Hall of Fame, works in sales and is a freelance writer. He earned a Bachelor of Arts Degree in Communications from the University of Akron (Ohio) in 1992. He is a 1985 graduate of football-tradition rich Canton McKinley High School. He continues to be a student of football history and an ardent Browns Fan.

It's been rough these past three years,
Now we can wipe away the tears,
because football is coming back to town,
in the form of the new Cleveland Browns.
                                    - Roger Gordon